D1570447

Closing the Frontier

Closing the Frontier
Radical Response in Oklahoma, 1889-1923

By John Thompson

University of Oklahoma Press : Norman and London

Library of Congress Cataloging-in-Publication Data

Thompson, John, 1953–
  Closing the frontier.

  Bibliography: p. 249
  Includes index.
  1. Frontier and pioneer life—Oklahoma.
  2. Radicalism—Oklahoma—History.   3. Oklahoma—
  History.   I. Title.
  F699.T49   1986   976.6   86–1609
  ISBN 0–8061–1996–9

Publication of this work has been made possible in part by a grant from the Andrew W. Mellon Foundation.

The paper in this book meets the guidelines for permanence and durability of the Committee on Production Guidelines for Book Longevity of the Council on Library Resources, Inc.

Contents

Preface   xi

Chapter 1   Introduction   3

            Part One. The Oklahoma Frontier,
            1889–1907   17

        2   The Frontier in the South and East   19

        3   The Frontier in the West   48

        4   Frontier Populism   70

            Part Two. The Closing of the Oklahoma
            Frontier, 1907–1916   97

        5   Southern and Eastern Oklahoma   99

        6   Northern and Western Oklahoma   116

        7   Socialism: The Ideology of the Shrinking
            Frontier   127

            Part Three. Postfrontier Oklahoma,
            1916–1923   165

        8   Prosperity and Poverty   167

        9   Class Conflict   180

       10   Neopopulism: The Radical Postfrontier
            Ideology   194

       11   Conclusion   216

Notes   227
Bibliography   249
Index   259

Illustrations

An unpaved road in eastern Oklahoma, 1915   25
A mine cave-in in McAlester, 1929   37
The R. E. Richardson home in Hollis, 1904   43
A Boomer poster promoting western Oklahoma   50
A dugout home in western Oklahoma   52
A family of homesteaders in western Oklahoma   64
An attorney's office, Guthrie, 1889   85
Students chopping wood at Euchee Mission, Sapulpa 102
Eugene V. Debs at a Socialist encampment at
    Snyder, ca. 1900   137
Oscar Ameringer   154

Maps

Distribution of farm tenancy, 1924   9
Cotton farming, acres harvested, 1929   26
Wheat farming, acres harvested, 1929   56
Oil and gas fields, 1926   69
Mineral-bearing regions of Oklahoma   123

Preface

THIS BOOK grew out of my need to understand contradictory elements in the culture of my native state.[1] I was introduced to the subject indirectly as a child, when I listened to arguments between my father and my maternal grandmother. My father's family were business leaders, Episcopalians, and Republicans from the urban central area of Oklahoma, while my grandmother's family were Methodists and populist Democrats with Indian blood from Pushmataha and Choctaw counties, deep inside "Little Dixie." In the typical discussion my father contrasted the lazy, corrupt, and backward life of southeastern Oklahomans with the increasing prosperity of residents of Oklahoma City. My grandmother would counter that great crimes had been committed in the process. Although my father was more logical, better informed, and less hyperbolic, I developed the suspicion that my grandmother was closer to the truth. For instance, Grandma frequently described her experiences in the Tulsa race riot of 1921. My father would deny that a riot of that magnitude was possible. If it had actually happened, he would have read about it in his Oklahoma history courses.

Of course, the riot occurred, but it was omitted from some of the early history books. My father, however, could not have known how brazenly the censorship of the state's history had been accomplished. The list of crucial though embarrassing aspects of Oklahoma history that were misrepresented included the theft of the Indians' lands, the disenfranchisement of blacks, the suppression of Socialists, the dispersion of tenants, and the true causes of the dust bowl and the "Okie" migration. Neither have professional historians been blameless. The preoccupation of Oklahoma historians with conventional political narratives prevented them from correcting these misconceptions.

I subsequently learned that debates like the continuing one between my father and my grandmother were not uncommon and that many Oklahomans had memories that did not coincide with the history textbooks. Wherever I raised the subject, I found a substantial minority of Oklahomans who were troubled that their past had been misrepresented, even if they were reluctant to volunteer information. One of the more vivid instances occurred when I asked my great-aunt, who lives in Frogville (ten miles southeast of Hugo), whether she remembered the Socialists. Although my aunt initially denied that she knew any, she later exclaimed: "Eugene V. Debs! I'll never forget that name. Did you know that you have kin named after Eugene V. Debs? Even now there are a lot of folks down here named Gene!" My aunt eventually explained that she had not talked about the Socialists for years because she had several Socialist neighbors who were good, honest, family people who had been sent to prison by Ku Klux Klan "thugs."

As a result of these influences this manuscript is heavily anecdotal. Many historians look askance at such a methodology. Those who do may be outraged to learn that not only the evidence but many of the theoretical underpinnings of the work are based on recollections of coworkers, relatives, neighbors, and passing acquaintances. Nearly every point in the arguments presented in this book has been stated almost literally by a thoughtful Oklahoman who had no idea that it would be of interest to academicians. In fact, I originally outlined this piece during work breaks inside an oil rig "doghouse." My coworkers gave me a hard time for being studious, but they also gave me several valuable pieces of advice. Then, as I was finishing this work, I was a guest on a late-night call-in radio program. I did not receive calls from the large numbers of right-wingers that I expected. Instead, the show was dominated by articulate elderly persons explaining why Oklahoma was once radical and how the Ku Klux Klan and the chambers of commerce disrupted the Socialists and their allies. A few even got in touch with me after the program to offer help in my research.

I do not mean to suggest that Oklahoma is not one of the most conservative states in the country or that large numbers of leftists are hiding in the hills. I simply want to describe how during my research I found dozens of Oklahomans, most of whom had never been to college and often had not even finished high school, who heavily influenced this book. Now that it is completed, I cannot remember whether it was I who first thought of a given point or whether it was a casual laborer I met while loading trucks or a fisherman I met in the Ouachita Mountains or an old man I met in a laundromat. The chances are that these differing kinds of Oklahomans and I worked out the idea together as we discussed our state's history. They were wonderful colleagues, and I thank them.

I also thank my wife, Jocelyn Lupkin, and my family. I must also express my appreciation to Paul Clemens, James Reed, and Lloyd Gardner, of Rutgers University, and James Green, whose *Grass-Roots Socialism* provided both academic guidance and inspiration.

Above all, I thank Freda Ameringer. At this writing, at age ninety-three she is recovering from a stroke and a broken collarbone. Owing to her disciplined rehabilitation efforts she has been able to vote using her injured arm, and soon she will be back working for the ERA and grass-roots organizing in the Willard Neighborhood Center.

Oklahoma City   JOHN THOMPSON

Closing the Frontier

What we lack, O God, is not of Thy doing but of man's. In man's greed for gold, he has destroyed the fruitfulness of the earth. In his lust for power and dominion he has brought misery upon us all. The land cries out against those who waste it. Thy children cry out against those who abuse and oppress them.

—*Ceremony of the Land*, composed by the Reverend Howard Kester and Evelyn Smith (Munro); first performed at the Second Annual Convention of the Southern Tenant Farmers' Union, January, 1936, Little Rock, Arkansas

1

Introduction

THE HISTORY of Oklahoma—a state noted for its eccentricities—
can be enhanced by a unique concept, the Great Frontier. The
Great Frontier, according to Walter Prescott Webb, was not
merely a huge frontier area. He saw it as an entire phase in the
world's development. It was the stage in history when Western
society broke loose from a static world-view and began a period of
unrestrained expansion. The Great Frontier was both an economic and a cultural development sparked by the discovery of
the New World, which was crucial to the growth of capitalism
and industrialization. It was an outlook which transformed the
medieval conception of human beings as powerless members of
an atemporal natural order and replaced it with a vision of human beings as agents with the power to manipulate nature.[1]

The Great Frontier and corporate capitalism were inextricably
bound together. They represented the economic and ideological
forces that undermined both the medieval conception of man as
merely a participant in the "Great Chain of Being" and its economic corollary that there is only a finite amount of wealth to be
accumulated, enjoyed, and preserved.[2] Although it was factors
such as disease cycles and the discovery of the resources of the
New World, and not the business acumen of individuals, which
allowed the economic boom of the Great Frontier, human beings
claimed a good deal of the credit for the increased wealth.[3]

Although they did not use the term, Fernand Braudel and
Immanuel Wallerstein described the dynamics of the phenomenon
that Webb called the Great Frontier. Braudel and Wallerstein did
this by discovering the patterns followed by corporate capitalism

3

as it came to dominate the West. They showed how this social and economic process drew on the resources and markets of the fringes of a region. An economic region developed where the natural resources and the population of underdeveloped fringe areas were appropriated for the benefit of a rising core. The center of the region enjoyed great prosperity, and sometimes the colony also gained short-term benefits, as long as the economy expanded. The cheapest labor and materials, however, were soon expended, and, rather than conserving these resources, capitalism shifted to an untouched area with less expensive supplies. Usually the affluent of a declining region invested their gains and remained wealthy after their economy stagnated, but the masses had no such opportunity. The poor of both the core and the colonies were left within a ravished and overpopulated shell.[4]

Frederick Jackson Turner, Ray Allen Billington, Paul Gates, and Allan Bogue have helped show how this process worked on the American frontier. A pattern developed in which for a generation or two great numbers of people rushed into an area of the wilderness. Then for another generation or two the area established an equilibrium. Migration subsided, and the world market supplied adequate capital in return for cheap raw goods. Towns, roads, and institutions were established, and it appeared that the frontier had been successfully subdued. Then a population crisis invariably developed, and a process of out-migration began.[5]

According to the original myth of the frontier, the process was arduous but healthy. The migration into an area supposedly acted as a safety valve which kept wages high. Moreover, these pioneers were so successful that they reared families that were large enough that some of the sons could stay on the farm and benefit from a revolution in agriculture while the others could find careers in the cities.[6]

The popular myth of the American frontier, however, is no longer tenable. Migration did not provide an adequate safety valve for the overpopulated core. Even when a demographic crisis did not occur naturally, capitalist entrepreneurs were not averse to creating one by recruiting immigrants. Also, the subsequent exodus from the farm to the city was not the result of Horatio Alger success stories. On the contrary, the system's requirements for cheap resources and a release for population pressure encouraged devastatingly rapid settlements. The terrible haste in which these fragile environments were settled crippled the land and the people of many frontier areas. The sharp outmigration that followed a brief pioneering period often occurred because natural resources had been so abused that former pioneers were forced to abandon their homes and either participate in another wasteful frontier settlement or return to the crowded cities.[7]

Although this method of expansion produced amazing short-term gains, the human cost was enormous. The rewards that were to be derived from rapid settlement spurred a short-sighted competitiveness that further crippled the land. Moreover, this prompted the participants in the race to take the path of least resistance so that problems such as overpopulation and the depletion of resources were ignored until they had grown too large to be sidestepped.[8]

The best example is the building of the railroad. The American West could not have been settled in a matter of decades if it had not been for the railroads. Unfortunately, though, uncontrolled competition led to the building of unnecessary and impractical lines which were destined to be a drain on local economies. The ruthless battles between different railroad companies caused lines to be built on Indian lands and resulted in war. Competition between railroaders prompted bribery and fraud and helped corrupt the political and judicial institutions of new societies. Moreover, conflicts between the railroads and the people caused struggles which had elements of class conflict but were often unproductive attempts by each side to get something for nothing. Then, when the railroads were finally built, the need to make a profit by completely filling railroad cars often encouraged settlements immediately to extract minerals from the area without regard for the next generation.[9]

As the capitalist expansion of the Great Frontier accelerated, the system not only consumed natural resources at a faster rate but also left progressively larger surpluses of population. Throughout American history hundreds of thousands of pioneers had continually spilled over from one frontier to another.[10] By 1889, however, when Oklahoma was settled, there were few new places for the dispossessed to go. Consequently, Oklahoma became a resting place for an inordinately large number of people who "ain't got no place in this world anymore." By 1910 the state held 1,657,155 people (by way of comparison, barely 2 million people lived in the state in 1960). Its impoverished population included a mixture of homeless Indians, recently disenfranchised blacks, mortgaged small farmers, underemployed construction workers, coal miners, oil-field workers and propertyless farmers.[11]

Oklahoma's first settlers, the Five Civilized Tribes, had been promised the land "as long as grass shall grow and waters run." The five tribes were joined by twenty-three tribes of Plains Indians, who settled in the western part of the territory. The land could have supported both groups of Indians had they been left alone. The Indian Nations even welcomed a few whites, as long as their visitors did not attempt to own land or violate the Indians' codes. Several thousand white tenant farmers peacefully lived in Indian Territory. They were soon joined, however, by hundreds of white businessmen, who cooperated with dishonest tribesmen and established poaching, smuggling, bootlegging, and cattle-rustling networks.[12]

The Indian Nations thus became a mecca for both fraudulent businessmen and common criminals. As the wild West came to a close in cowtowns like Dodge City and Reno City, eastern Oklahoma became the last refuge of cattle thieves, gunfighters, and train and bank robbers. This junglelike environment was aggravated by the local legal system, which kept the Indians from prosecuting whites in their courts. "Hanging Judge Parker," the federal judge who presided over the region from 1875 to 1895, attempted to restore order by hanging eighty-nine convicted felons. Oklahoma, however, being the last frontier, seemed to be destined to remain the most lawless area in the United States.[13]

In the western half of the territory the Indians were finally displaced by a second group of illegal aliens, the Boomers. The United States government and the Indian governments combined to try to keep these squatters out of Oklahoma. They would spend "one night breathing state air and then return." The Boomers, who were neither as noble nor as desperate as they have been portrayed in popular myth persisted, and by 1889 the prairie was opened. The result of their efforts was a land run which symbolized the way in which the American frontier was settled, a frantic rush for economic opportunity. Within another decade white immigration had completely displaced the Indians.[14]

Under ordinary circumstances the homesteaders of the Oklahoma prairie would not have been considered horribly impoverished. Most of them were poor. Many had lost their land in Kansas or Texas, and some were blacklisted miners or unemployed laborers, but they were not on the verge of starvation when they came to the territory. These homesteaders were facing a frighteningly difficult task when they attempted to settle a semiarid prairie, but success would have been obtainable had it not been for two obstacles, undercapitalization and overpopulation. They could endure natural disasters like tornadoes or the drought of 1910, but when the bankers withdrew credit, as they did in the depression of 1907, there was little that the farmers could do. The second problem, which seems to have been inherent in almost every frontier situation, was overpopulation. The initial process of breaking the sod and building homes, roads, and towns required more people than could be supported, in the long run, by the dry prairie.[15]

Consequently, a growing number of Oklahomans joined thousands of dispossessed Kansans and Texans. These migrants steadily slipped into the eastern territory until the 1890s, when the various Indian Nations were dissolved. By 1890 the population of the former Indian Nations had increased from 70,000 in 1889 to a crowded 258,657.[16]

Early in the twentieth century it appeared that the Great Frontier had given Oklahomans a cross that was too heavy. The western part of the state was impoverished by drought. Any pioneering society must expect weather to be an obstacle, but at the same time western farmers had to cope with a depression. In the east the number of tenant farmers had doubled to 64 percent of all farmers. Then, in the cities, Oklahoma City and Tulsa, the boom in construction that had built the towns in the first place and had drawn large numbers of laborers, had collapsed, leaving a mixture of transient nonagricultural workers. Moreover, the rapid settlement had worn out the soil, and the state's most valuable resources, lumber and coal, were firmly in the hands of large companies.[17]

The close of the last frontier of the Great Frontier also produced a phenomenon which can be described as the antithesis of the Great Frontier. The poverty which accompanied the frontier's settlement, as well as cultural conflicts produced by the process, created a variety of radical political ideologies. Although the development of the wilderness brought wealth to the established core, the persons who occupied the new land lived in an impoverished environment which produced an intense hatred of capitalism. Moreover, the cultural values of the frontier, individualism, cooperation, democracy, and a willingness to experiment, also encouraged political rebelliousness. When the pioneers were introduced to ideologies such as that of the Farmers' Alliance or the Socialist party, the Oklahoma frontier quickly became one of the most radical areas in the United States.[18]

The exploitation and domination of the frontier was accompanied by three basic radical ideologies: populism, socialism, and neopopulism. From 1889 to 1907 the only coherent and significant political ideology in the Oklahoma Territory was populism. Then, from 1907 to the mid-1910s, when the abrupt close of the frontier devastated the young state, a more comprehensive ideology, socialism, emerged and dominated Oklahomans' political thought. Finally, after World War I, when most of the state had extricated itself from the frontier, neopopulism or an exceptionally belligerent and anticorporate reformism became the troubled state's most popular political creed.[19]

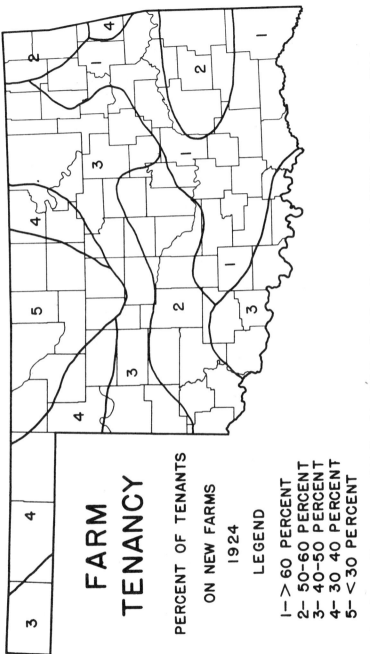

FARM TENANCY

PERCENT OF TENANTS

ON NEW FARMS

1924

LEGEND

1— > 60 PERCENT
2— 50–60 PERCENT
3— 40–50 PERCENT
4— 30 40 PERCENT
5— < 30 PERCENT

Distribution of farm tenancy, 1924. From Meredith Burrill, *A Socio-Economic Atlas of Oklahoma* (Stillwater: Oklahoma Agricultural & Mechanical College, 1936).

Such a chronology is, of course, crude, and the ideologies are inexact categories. Many Oklahomans would not fit neatly into any of the three orientations. Instead, the three groupings are a composite of the options which Oklahomans perceived as being available. They are heuristic devices designed to help illuminate the nature of Oklahomans' political attitudes. The ideologies are less a specific platform than a combination of awareness and orientations. They illustrate the forms of logic and the kinds of values that were produced by the frontier crisis.

This analysis takes the form of an essay that describes the dominant radical ideologies created by the opening and the rapid destruction of the two Oklahoma frontiers. It first shows that from 1889 to statehood, when both territories were frontiers, a complex and also ambivalent agrarian consciousness was produced. It shows that Oklahoma's Populists produced differing degrees of radical consciousness, but it will also show that populism became the state's predominant political ideology. Dissatisfied farmers and workers in both regions realized that they lived in a pioneer society with flexible institutions. Consequently, Oklahomans who hated capitalism but lacked political awareness and more thoughtful radicals worked together to gain control of the political system before corporate powers could become irrevocably entrenched.[20]

This book shows that from statehood to the beginning of World War I the northern and western prairie made considerable progress in outgrowing its frontier status while the southern and eastern hill country failed to modernize or to construct appropriate economic institutions. Neither frontier, however, fulfilled its promise to its farmers and laborers, and both regions produced a new ideology, socialism. In the south and east an especially violent, almost primitive radicalism grew beside a modest yet surprisingly dignified Socialist ideology. In the north and west a moderate anticapitalism, which was capable of slipping into mere reformism, grew in conjuction with a sophisticated, innovative, and idealistic socialism. Whether or not the various kinds of radicals could have taken control of the state and instituted "industrial democracy" is problematical. It is known, however, that a remarkable cadre of Socialist educators established a formidable party organization as well as a flexible program and that from 1912 to 1916 they came within reach of winning at the polls.

Finally, this analysis recounts the closing of the frontier radicalism. It shows that after World War I most of the state adjusted to the demands of the national market system and temporarily found stability by adopting modern methods of production and by instituting reforms. During the same period, however, southeast Oklahoma failed to outgrow its underdeveloped conditions. A few citizens in Little Dixie persisted in attacking capitalism, but they were crushed and dispersed. The final defeat of frontier radicalism, however, did not come easily. In 1922, despite their huge differences, a coalition of wheat farmers, cotton tenant farmers, laborers, small businessmen, Progressives, Populists, and Socialists united for a last desperate revolt and elected John Calloway ("Our Jack") Walton governor. By that time, however, Oklahoma was no longer a malleable pioneer society, and Oklahoma-based oilmen, businessmen, landlords, and bankers who understood the nature of the capitalist system and worked smoothly with the corporate centers in the Northeast and in Europe were in complete control of the state's political and economic institutions. The fragile coalition won a brief symbolic victory and took the first steps toward building a more humane society, but it never successfully challenged the power structure of postfrontier Oklahoma.

At this point two troublesome issues must be mentioned. First, I have tried to avoid falling into the trap of geographical determinism. Nothing in this work is meant to imply that the radicalism of Oklahomans was simply a product of the frontier. Oklahomans' political ideologies were a legacy of the cultures and the socioeconomic systems that were introduced to the wilderness and were altered by the frontier. Credit must be given to nature,

however. We must not neglect the effects of the formidable natural forces, especially the weather, which had the power to dwarf
the influence of established cultural and economic practices.

These dynamics must be kept in mind whenever the reader
comes across a statement such as, "A farmer could not survive on
the prairie with only 160 acres" (or "200 acres" or "a 10-acre plot
of cotton," depending upon the part of the state which is under
discussion). That statement, of course, is not literally true. Farmers from other cultures, functioning in a different economic system, could scratch out a living in that situation (occasionally
they starved when the crops failed, but perhaps the consequences
of such a disaster would be less unacceptable to another culture).
On the other hand, it was impossible for an Oklahoman, regardless of his skill, to survive in such conditions because of the
social and economic system of which Oklahoma was a part.

The second issue which requires clarification involves the term
"frontier." Some of the salient characteristics of the frontier,
such as materialism, exploitation of humans and nature, geo-
graphic and social mobility, and a weakened sense of class, were
extant throughout the United States. These and other characteristics, such as low population density and lawlessness, were common in the Midwest and especially in the South. Historians who
use the concept of the frontier, however, frequently seem to imply that the frontier is more than the sum of these qualities. The
implication is that the pioneering experience creates a form of
frontier culture. If that is the case, a frontier is more than a recently settled place with a small population and few laws and institutions; it is also the home of persons with a shared experience
which prompts certain forms of social interactions and unique
values and attitudes.

Ideally, historians should be able to differentiate between the
importance of the physical conditions characteristic of the frontier and the significance of the frontier culture. In practice, however, that is impossible. (To separate the effects of the physical
and material conditions from those of the culture would require a
concept of mind-body dualism that few would accept.) Histo-

rians discover that the material reality of the frontier makes some kinds of behavior possible and precludes other kinds. On the other hand, they cannot conclude that a certain type of behavior not only was allowed by those conditions but was also produced by them without the assistance of the actor's cultural background. Historians are also baffled by another question about the durability of culture. When the frontier ends, and the physical conditions which accompany it also cease to exist, does the frontier culture expire also?

A historian must recognize that settlers brought a variety of cultures with them. These settlers encountered the frontier not in a simple and straightforward manner, on nature's terms, but in accordance with their own cultural orientations. The frontier altered the settlers' previously held values and attitudes and produced a new culture, a frontier culture. This frontier culture, like all other cultures, was the result of both physical realities and the people's beliefs and preferences. After the frontier closed, however, many of the physical foundations of the frontier culture were removed. The question then arises about the durability of that culture in a postfrontier society. This question is especially difficult in Oklahoma or on similar American frontiers to which the settlers brought cultures that were not far removed from those of earlier American frontiers.

These questions are more philosophical than historical, and they are beyond the scope of this book. They are questions that historians cannot answer in an authoritative manner. Historians, however, must give at least a tentative answer to these questions. The difficulty and the necessity of dealing with these issues can be illustrated by a phenomenon crucial to the study of frontier radicalism in Oklahoma: the effect of the "lawlessness" that allegedly characterized the frontier.

Among the distinctive characteristics of the frontier lawlessness is perhaps the quality which, if it existed, would have been the most influential. This lawlessness, a legacy of the lack of established government institutions, meant that settlers were free to build their own set of institutions that would be responsive to the

conditions that existed in the new world and not on ancient
precedent. Also, the lawlessness was supposed to be a quality
shared by large numbers of citizens. It was, in effect, a character
trait of the frontiersmen's collective personality. This lawlessness
supposedly led to a uniquely American form of democracy where
"God made some men big and others small, but Samuel Colt
made them equal."

Such a concept of lawlessness is of dubious value to today's historians unless it is taken in a poetic fashion. The value of the
concept is enhanced, however, by changing the focus from a romantic vision of the pioneer using his native sense of justice to
replace English legal precedents or the bravery of the gun-toting
westerner. The typical settler was a family member who lacked
the power to aggrandize himself in a lawless society. Frontiersmen,
who routinely stole firewood from government land and who were
in the habit of defending themselves might, as the historian E. E.
Dale, a onetime cowhand and a student of Frederick Jackson
Turner, remembered, be more open to political radicalism.[21] In a
lawless environment the settler was freer to brew moonshine or
retaliate against an intruder, but he had little opportunity to
profit from the environment.

The persons who were freed by the restraints of law and who
had the inclination and resources to take advantage of frontier
lawlessness were the entrepreneurs. Lawlessness, instead of encouraging democracy and innovation, spurred land speculation,
fraud, usury, price-fixing, and monopoly. The major way that lawlessness promoted democracy was by assisting corrupt business
practices that encouraged the growth of populism, socialism, and
other political responses by law-abiding citizens to counter the
"grafters."

The problem with either interpretation of lawlessness was that
the phenomenon was widespread outside frontier Oklahoma, especially in the South. The South also had a tradition of settling
disputes in a personal and often violent manner. Land speculation and price-fixing were equally common there. Industrialists,

landowners, railroaders, and timber owners in the South showed no inhibitions in violating the law to crush strikes or disrupt organizing efforts of blacks and poor whites. Finally, the government was similarly corrupt, and the Democratic party was equally skillful in stuffing ballot boxes to remain in power.

It is at that point that a judicious use of some other principles of the frontier thesis, combined with a recognition of the role of lawlessness on the frontier, can be of value. In the South lawlessness was incorporated into the region's most powerful institutions. Landowners, businessmen, government officials, and Democratic party functionaries were free to break the law. They were invulnerable because they had police power, the militia, and the courts, as well as economic power, on their side. In Oklahoma Territory, however, official lawlessness was not protected. Oklahoma lacked not only a developed legal tradition but also the institutions to enforce it. This lack of police power not only inhibited routine law enforcement but made it impossible for corrupt entrepreneurs to use the law to defraud, disenfranchise, and intimidate the public.

This revised concept of lawlessness is attractive because it helps explain both the rapid rise of populism and socialism in Oklahoma and radicalism's precipitous decline. During the territorial period, when legal institutions were primitive, radicals were free from government-sanctioned repression. After statehood, however, and after the government matured to the point where it had the power to enforce the law, Oklahoma became more like the Deep South. Two results of the development were repression and election fraud equal to those of established society, which helped destroy the political radicalism that had prospered on the "lawless" frontier.

Such an interpretation of the role of frontier lawlessness must be presented in a tentative manner. A historian must avoid slipping into the trap of arguing that there was "just enough" lawlessness to produce a political movement. An understanding of frontier radicalism in Oklahoma, however, requires an appreciation of uncertainty and nuance. In the course of this book the reader will encounter numerous other paradoxes, including the roles of frontier communalism and individualism, materialism and idealism, tolerance and bigotry, cosmopolitanism and provincialism, and humanitarianism and violence in both advancing and destroying political radicalism.

PART ONE

The Oklahoma Frontier, 1889–1907

"And God hath made of one blood all of the races of men to dwell together on the face of the earth." We who descended from the Indian, our forefathers lived here before other races came. We who are Negroes, our forefathers were brought here in chains. We who are descended from the Acadians, our fathers were transported here by force and cast upon the shores to perish in a strange land. We who are Mexicans were lured here by promises of a better life. We came of all races and nationalities to this land to make a home and a better life for our children. We live in a land of plenty, and yet the products of our labor will not support our families and educate our children. We work all the days of our life and are yet cast aside in our old age. There are those who would deny us the God-given right to act together for self improvement.

—Ceremony of the Land

2

The Frontier in the South and East

THE DISTINCTION between Oklahoma's two frontiers is crucial to any study of the state's cultural and political heritage. One scholar argued that by 1900 Oklahoma had developed two distinct cultural areas. Michael Doran wrote: "When the Indian Territory was filled with white homesteaders it did not become a melting pot. Instead it was neatly divided among pioneering whites from the Midwest and the South creating a distinct cultural bifurcation that remains noticeable to the present." Doran explained:

> Because so little cultural mixing occurred the cultural *Milieu* of the neighboring states were inserted virtually intact into the Northern-dominated and the Southern-dominated sections of Oklahoma. Essentially what occurred was the *extension* of the older cultural areas into discrete portions of the new state, with the creation of a distinct border zone between them.

According to Doran, "The boundary between the two regions was a transition belt that runs at an angle across the state from Tulsa to Oklahoma City and west towards the Antelope Hills near the Panhandle of Texas."[1]

The land above the border line was clearly "Jayhawker country," and the area south and east was the distinctive region of "Little Dixie."[2] Doran persuasively documented his hypothesis by charting patterns in migration, voting and party preference, agricultural methods and occupations, income and education achievement, religious preference, and vocabulary and speech.[3]

Doran's study gave only a cursory analysis of the economic history of the new state. Had he carefully analyzed market conditions in the two regions, he could have drawn an even clearer line between the north and west and the south and east. During the late nineteenth and early twentieth centuries a profitable system of wheat agriculture allowed the northwestern and north-central portions of the state to outgrow their frontier conditions and become integrated with the international market. The cotton tenants of the southern two-thirds of the Indian Territory, however, were unable to become partners in the market system. Consequently, the north and west showed signs of progress, while the south and east stagnated and remained essentially an impoverished colony.[4]

If a sociologist were to compare the two regions at any given moment, he might not be able to discern a qualitative difference between them. Both regions were basically agricultural. The farmers in both were extremely poor, relatively uneducated, and very isolated. The social organization of both subeconomies was similar. The strains of facing harsh weather and economic hardship prompted citizens to band together into close-knit families and small communities.

An analysis of the development of the two regions from 1895 to 1907, however, reveals two dissimilar sets of hidden social and economic dynamics which prompted the growth of distinguishable cultural regions. The southern two-thirds of the Indian Territory and southern plains has been called basically a premarket economy. Economic exchanges had not been regularized or institutionalized. Commerce in the southern and eastern portion was a hybrid of a very personalized and erratic system of trade and struggles to obtain wealth. The northern sector, however, was an immature and underdeveloped component of the national market system. The institutions of the north were primitive, and economic exchanges were uncoordinated, but, as will be explained in chapter 3, the members of the northern society understood the workings of capitalism and intended to integrate their territory into the corporate world.

Douglas Hale, an Oklahoma historian, conducted an analysis

of the regions and concluded that the two areas had dissimilar economic structures. He concluded that the settlers from the Midwest tended to settle north of the Canadian River in Oklahoma Territory (he claimed that the midwesterners' frontier roughly followed the paths of today's Interstate 44 and Interstate 40. This includes Tulsa and it fits well with Doran's boundary), and he argued that

> The Midwesterners tended to be more enterprising and progressive, more committed to economic advancement and more aggressive in their pursuit of profit than their Southern neighbors. They became in short, the "movers and shakers" of territorial Oklahoma. They voted Republican and belonged overwhelmingly to northern religious denominations. As farmers, they tended to occupy the best land and increase their holdings. But they were often more interested in townsite development than in agriculture and were more likely to make their homes in towns and cities.

Hale noted that during the territorial days "of Tulsa's business and professional elite 77.4% were born in the Midwest or the Northeast."[5]

Hale contrasted the more knowledgeable midwesterners who settled the northern and western region with the 86 percent of the settlers in the Indian Territory who came from the South and who brought "a complex of attitudes and institutions," which included fundamentalism, localism, a strong sense of family and place, and often a tendency to use violence. He noted further that they placed less value on education than did Americans in general.[6]

Hale's analysis of southern and eastern Oklahoma was not excessively derogatory. Sheila Manes, who has also made a detailed analysis of Oklahoma's regions (she divided the state into three triangles, the northwest, the southwest, and the southeast), concluded that the southeast was economically stagnant and that "the system was inherently exploitative for the renter and unproductive for the small landowner."[7]

The contrast between the southeast and the northwest was

supported by the analysis of Ellen Rosen, a sociologist. Rosen discovered through oral history that settlers in the west were "cash poor" but did not go hungry. She contrasted their conditions with those in the east, where malnourished tenants were victimized by a "pre-capitalist, pre-market" system. The suffering in that region was a legacy of an economy based on an "accumulation of private wealth rather than economic growth."[8]

Angie Debo, who grew up in Marshall, less than fifty miles from Indian Territory, has offered the best explanation of how the southern and eastern region functioned even though landlords as well as tenants were unable to make a profit. She explained that all of eastern Oklahoma was "dominated by a criminal conspiracy to cheat Indians out of their land." She was surprised to learn this as an adult while conducting archival research. She had not realized it while she was growing up in Oklahoma Territory because the "Indian Territory was as far removed from our experiences as though it had been in the Orient."[9]

Research into this criminal conspiracy was an ordeal for Debo. She looked on the society pages of the current newspapers (she did the research in the early 1930s) and saw the names of the wives of the grafters who gained prominence simply through stealing from the Indians. Moreover, she was uncomfortable doing research on such a sensitive subject alone in dark corridors and basements. When Debo remembered what happened to reformers, her vulnerable work environment made her fear for her safety. She persisted, however, and in an award-winning monograph explained the details of an entire social and economic system based on unmitigated corruption. Debo explained that as she conducted her research "everything I touched was slimy" and that the region's business prospered simply by robbing Indians.[10]

An analysis of the economy of southeast Oklahoma can be assisted by an unlikely source, Karl Polanyi. If we accept Polanyi's definition of the market system, the southern and eastern section of Oklahoma was not a part of the market. Polanyi explained that a definition of a market economy "implies a self-regulating system of markets" which is directed by prices and not by coercion. Polanyi noted that "all societies have an economy of some sort" and that even the most primitive cultures have a complicated set of economic arrangements for the distribution and redistribution of wealth.[11] In premarket economies, however, economic transactions require one group simply to confiscate wealth from another. In a market system, however, a set of distinctively political and economic institutions guide exchanges based on prices. Market behavior may or may not be more complicated than premarket behavior, but it has been channeled into routine patterns which conform to social and economic laws and not simply to the dictates of a powerful person or group.[12]

Polanyi further described how a market economy is based on long-distance trade. It is the process of organizing itself so that it can engage in competitive exchanges with distant markets that allows a society to develop a market economy. Long-distance trade, however, must be characterized by a degree of balance and of cooperation. Unilateral relationships where one society expropriates wealth from another or piracy do not qualify as trade.[13]

Oklahomans in the east engaged in a curious form of local trade, but they had few business ties to the national and international corporate system. A few representatives of the Indian Territory had contacts with representatives of the eastern business establishment, but their ties were not the kinds of mutual transaction that Polanyi described as being a characteristic of trade.

A brief summary of the social and economic history of the southern and eastern portion of Oklahoma thus reveals two salient features. In the first place, the region did not develop efficient political and economic institutions. The major corporations that did business in the southeast showed no interest in modernizing the region. They saw Little Dixie as simply a supplier of timber, coal, and cotton that was unworthy of any efforts toward building a diversified economy. In the second place, local entrepreneurs lacked the expertise and the capital necessary to build and operate roads, gin and storage facilities, banking institutions, and the manufacturing concerns needed for a healthy economy. Consequently, local landlords and businessmen dismissed the southeast's major product, cotton, as insufficiently profitable to be worthy of effort. Instead, they came to rely on land speculation, usury, and, not infrequently, criminality to support themselves.[14]

At first glance southeastern Oklahoma appears to have been engaged in long-distance relationships with the international market. Closer study, however, reveals that Little Dixie was an isolated premarket society devoid of distinctively political or economic institutions in which prices were set not by economic laws but by coercion. Although circumstances in the international market may have had a marginal effect on the affluent, the fate of the market meant nothing to the tenants, who had no chance of breaking even. Regardless of the prices that their cotton received in the Northeast or in Europe, in the long run tenants inevitably found themselves in debt and at the mercy of their creditors.

Nor were local merchants and landlords greatly influenced by the strength of the market. Prices for the region's chief crop, cotton, were too low to be a major concern of landlords. Consequently, landowners neglected to improve the methods by which cotton was produced, transported, processed, and sold. Instead, landowners and businesses supported themselves through various activities ranging from land speculation and usury to bootlegging and fraud. As will be explained later, landlords were barely able to earn enough from cotton to pay their taxes, but they could prosper through speculating in cotton lands. Little Dixie's landowners were not, as Socialists later phrased it, in the business of "farming the land." Instead, they "farmed the farmer."[15]

The inability of southeastern Oklahoma to produce a knowledgeable entrepreneurial class and to develop modern economic institutions was of crucial importance. Instead of regularized methods of conducting orthodox business transactions, economic exchanges remained a collection of unpredictable and disorganized personal transactions. Moreover, in such an uncontrollable business world both the wealthy and the criminal had a nearly

An unpaved road in eastern Oklahoma, 1915. Courtesy of Western History
Collections, University of Oklahoma Library.

insurmountable advantage over the poor and the ethical. The result was that Little Dixie's key economic enterprises resembled
piracy more closely than they did marketplace exchanges.

The manner in which the southern and eastern section of
Oklahoma was developed thus differed from the more typical
American frontier success story. In contrast to the dominant
Great Frontier experience, the pioneers who settled the south
and east failed to subdue nature and to appropriate the region's
resources for the market. The frontiersmen who were attracted
by or driven to Little Dixie lacked the expertise, the tools, and
frequently, the desire to transform the raw material of their new
home into economic commodities.

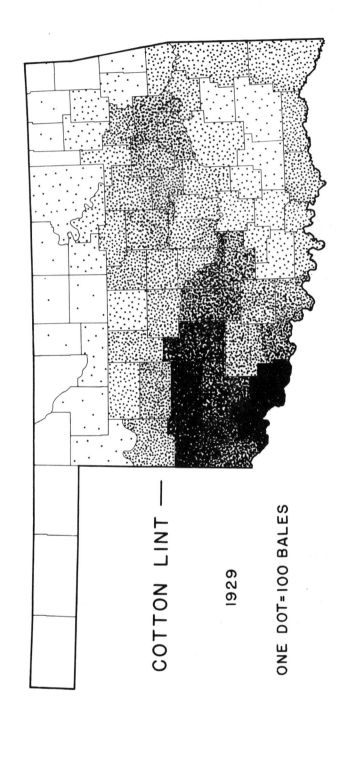

COTTON LINT —

1929

ONE DOT=100 BALES

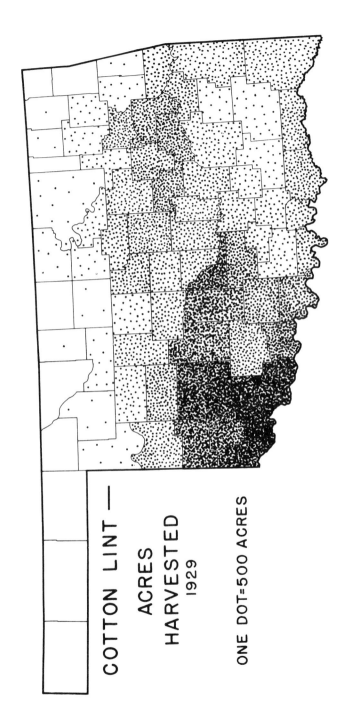

Cotton farming, acres harvested, 1929. One dot equals five hundred acres. From Burrill, *A Socio-Economic Atlas of Oklahoma*.

The first groups to have difficulty coping with this anomalous frontier were the Five Civilized Tribes. Ironically, the Choctaws, Chickasaws, Cherokees, Creeks, and Seminoles who were forced to migrate to Oklahoma were the pioneers best qualified to settle the region in a manner consistent with the principles of the Great Frontier. Although they were much less aggressive in seeking wealth, Oklahoma Indians possessed many of the talents of the most successful of American frontiersmen. Unfortunately, however, the Indians who were participants of the last major American frontier found the exceptionally unrestrained competition overwhelming, and the Five Tribes became the first of many waves of immigrants who either failed to establish or were prevented from establishing a stable or healthy society in the new land.[16]

When the Five Civilized Tribes were moved to Oklahoma in the 1830s and 1840s one Cherokee leader remarked that their new land was an almost exact reproduction of their old homelands in Mississippi and Georgia. The Indians soon discovered that the soil of the new territory was thinner than they had realized and that it was not particularly appropriate for growing their staples, cotton and corn.

Eastern Oklahoma was rich enough, however, to support the 50,000 members of the five tribes. From the 1830s to the Civil War was the golden age of the Five Civilized Tribes. Agriculture boomed, cattle and horse stocks flourished, and wildlife was plentiful. The tribes established good schools and adequate political institutions. Notable progress also was made in building medical facilities, roads, and towns. The Indians consciously patterned their new home after the South of the white aristocracy and established plantations. They bought slaves and built fine homes. Townspeople adopted southern architecture and decorated the streets with magnolia and pecan trees.[17]

The Civil War, however, destroyed this prosperity. Most Choctaws, Chickasaws, and Seminoles sided with the Confederacy and suffered as all nations do when they lose a war. The peace treaties cost them their lands in the western half of Oklahoma. Moreover, half of their livestock was killed or stolen, and they were overrun by refugees. Their most important loss, however, was the collapse of the cotton market. Ironically, the war hurt the tribes who sides with the North more than it did the Confederates. The Cherokees and the Creeks remained in the Union, but only after they had been devastated by a civil war of their own.[18]

From 1865 to 1890 the Indian Nations partially recovered. They reached an equilibrium where subsistance farmers coexisted with the great landlords. These landlords gained power by attracting white tenant farmers to rebuild their fields. Reconstruction in the Indian territories was not as tragic as it was in the Deep South. The Indian was usually a more kindly landlord than his white counterpart. Blacks were not welcomed, but they gained more autonomy, and they were more fairly treated by the Indians. The discovery of coal brought money into the tribal treasuries, and natural resources like lumber and wild game often kept the poor of all races from starving. The Indian Nations began rebuilding their schools and social institutions, and tribal governments usually attempted to be responsive to the needs of the people.[19]

As their economy slowly improved, the Indians rebuilt social, financial, and political institutions that were adequate for their needs. Judged by the white man's standards, their public sector was primitive. Both private and government bookkeeping was incomplete and inaccurate. Corruption was rampant, and social and political disputes were commonly resolved by violence. The Indians' institutions, however, worked reasonably well when the whites did not interfere. Their institutions were designed to protect a communal way of life. Community and government sanctions prohibited the ownership of private property and regulated all business activity. These guidelines were loosely enforced, however, and Indian entrepreneurs were given a good deal of freedom so that they could produce the wealth which supported the tribal system.[20]

The tribes thus formulated a social and economic system whose chief characteristic has been described as "careless hospitality."[21] The hierarchical aspects of both their southern heritage and their tribal cultures merged to create a relaxed but aristocratic social structure. The common people typically deferred to the wishes of their tribe's elite. On the other hand, the Indian upper classes were rarely oppressive. Moreover, the volatility of tribal politics deterred the growth of a single dominant class. Tribal governments were regularly threatened by civil strife which did not necessarily lead to a democratic ideology but did discourage the men at the top of the system from behaving in an arbitrary manner.[22]

Full-blooded Indian businessmen regularly bent their society's guidelines, but they rarely abused the system in ways that seriously damaged the general welfare of the people. Ambitious whites, however, heard about the situation and rushed to the territory to take advantage of its complacency. Even though property ownership was restricted to tribesmen, a white could marry an Indian and thereby gain full rights. Many of the largest lumbermen, landlords, coal and mine developers, and cattlemen were either white immigrants or their children. Their entrepreneurial skills often spurred the local economy by helping the Indians take advantage of their unused resources. These outsiders, however, commonly took advantage of the traditionally lax governmental and legal systems and often divided and undermined the tribes' political institutions.[23]

A large number of Indians had always resisted white immigration. At one point the selling of property to a white man was made a capital offense. Other Indians, however, profited from the outsiders and welcomed them. White entrepreneurs realized that without political support their position would always be precarious, and they joined with the more "progressive" tribesmen to establish a political base. Even when these entrepreneurs used completely legal means to advance their position, their presence was inherently divisive. Consequently, political squabbles led to violence and threatened to become civil war. Moreover, white immigrants, mixed-bloods, and their Indian allies commonly contributed more bribery, fraud, and extortion than had previously existed, and they forced their opponents either to respond in kind or to abandon their political system and the way of life it was designed to protect.[24]

In eastern Oklahoma, as in most other American frontier areas, it was the railroad that made the quick development possible. By the 1880s the Indian Territory was bordered on three sides by states with fully developed railway systems. Had not Indian law slowed the construction of the railroads, the Indians' land would already have been crisscrossed with tracks. In the late 1880s, however, the power of the Indian governments weakened, and the last obstacle to unrestricted railway construction was removed. Subsequently the belated development of a rail system occurred within a decade.[25]

The railroaders who opened the Indian Nations demonstrated a notable disrespect for their hosts. Since the Civil War the railroads had complained to Congress that a few "primitive natives" had obstructed the completion of a nationwide railway system that was essential to the American economy. Railroad lobbyists were consistently insensitive to the welfare of the Indian economic system.[26] For instance, after the outstanding constitutional scholar of the Choctaw Nation testified on the reasons for Indian regulation of the railroad through the territory, C. J. Hillyer, the attorney for the Atlantic Pacific Railroad, described his testimony: "A sleepy-eyed stupid-looking Indian pulled a few scraps of paper from his pocket which were the Tribe's Constitution." Hillyer also commented that it was in the best interests of the United States to allow the railroad to expand regardless of "whether one Indian or 5,000 were killed in the operation."[27]

Even if the representatives of the railroad had honored the integrity of the Indian Nations, the needs of the railroads and the Indians' economy were inherently contradictory. The policy of the Indian government was to allow the introduction of modern business enterprises at a deliberate pace. In an effort to do so, they licensed and taxed white intruders, and they prohibited the railroads from engaging in the lumber or the real estate business.[28] The railroads complained, however, that they could not make a profit unless the development of the Indians' agricultural and natural resources was drastically accelerated. "We might as well lay tracks through 250 miles of tunnel," exclaimed one railroad man in a successful attempt to open the territory to white developers.[29]

Several decades of both legal and illegal pressure by the railroads eventually destroyed the regulations of the Indian Nations. More important, however, the railroads brought hundreds of legal and illegal intruders into the Indian lands. Often the white migrants could not gain a foothold until they bribed Indian officials or tribesmen to allow them to establish a clandestine cattle, lumber, or bootleg whiskey business.[30]

By the late 1880s the railroads were victorious, and within a decade more than 100,000 whites had entered the Indian Nations. Cotton farming doubled, and the coal industry boomed. This production ensured the profits of the railroad industry because it meant that its cars would not move half-filled. The result, however, was that cotton was planted on unsuitable soil, and land was ruined. Indian wildlife and timber were decimated, and the easily mined coal was removed while the less accessible minerals were left behind and permanently lost.[31]

The most visible change was caused by the timber industry. Eastern Oklahoma in the 1880s was a humid, hilly region covered with majestic pine and oak trees. A Texas settler recalled that when his family passed through the Indian Nations it did not need roads because the land was covered with huge oak trees and Kentucky bluegrass. It was almost like going through a green tunnel. There was no underbrush, and the land was completely unbroken. By the earth twentieth century, however, timber companies had changed all of that. The oak trees along the Red River had been almost completely stripped, and work was in progress on the pinelands.[32]

The speed with which the land was stripped is astonishing because the western forests of the 1890s were normally outside the market system. Oklahoma timberlands, however, were not protected by white man's law and thus were an attractive resource to timber buyers in the North and in Europe.[33]

Oklahoma tree lands, however, were under the protection of Indian law. Lumbering for the purpose of building homes and fences was legal, but the harvesting and exporting of lumber were prohibited. The tribal governments rigorously prosecuted when they had the opportunity, but they were unable to slow the timber-smuggling business.[34]

The wildlife in the east was decimated at an equally astonishing rate. Game was the Indians' most valuable resource, and hunting was an important part of their economic and recreational life. For these reasons the Indians expended a great deal of effort in trying to stop poaching. They failed, however, and within a generation three of the most valuable species of game birds were destroyed.

In 1880 there were over a billion passenger pigeons in the Indian Territory. When flocks of tens of thousands flew over, they could block out the sun. The territory also had hundreds of millions of quail and wild turkeys. The quail and pigeons were integral parts of the diet of many poor Indians, and the turkey was being domesticated. White poachers slipped into the territory however, and completely wiped out the pigeons and turkey and almost all of the quail. The intruders smuggled their kill to the packing houses in Chicago. This poaching and smuggling became big business. Two pigeon hunters, on a bet, killed seven thousand birds in one day. Officials of the Choctaw Nation intercepted cargoes of ten to fifteen thousand birds being smuggled out of the Territory.[35]

Another wave of intruders came in the 1880s in search of coal. At first the coal industry did little harm to the Indian society. J. H. McAlester read about the Territory's potential for coal in a geologist's field notes. He went to the Choctaw Nation and took out a mining permit. He persuaded the railroads to extend their lines to the coal fields in the southeast and east-central parts of Oklahoma. When Indians refused to go into the mines,

McAlester imported European immigrants. McAlester paid the Choctaw government fifteen dollars a year for each alien worker as well as royalties on the coal.[36]

At first the arrangement benefited all. Miners were paid a good wage, more than $2 a day, which allowed them to save enough money eventually to buy land. Moreover, coal money spurred the growth of local businesses and attracted entrepreneurs with economic expertise. The royalties and lease payments allowed the Nations to remain solvent. From 1872 to 1897 in the Choctaw and Chickasaw Nations coal companies paid $1 million in royalties and $800,000 in bonuses, fees, and leases.[37]

The advantages of the coal boom were tempered, however, by frequent mine disasters. The Oklahoma mines were the most dangerous mines of any major coal region in the United States. The state's ratio of 2.84 deaths per 100,000 tons of coal mined was much higher than the ratio of either the Pennsylvania or the West Virginia mines. Many deaths were due to the brittle nature of Oklahoma's coal seams.[38]

Perhaps the main reason for the danger, however, was the negligence of the coal companies, which persisted in the foolhardy practice of "shooting into the solid." By 1914, 860 miners had been killed in accidents. Moreover, the mining companies did not give adequate compensation. On one occasion an explosion killed 69 miners and left 250 orphans; the families were told that they could have the by then worthless mine if they wished but that they would receive no compensation.[39]

Despite the danger profits from coal theoretically could have stimulated an economic takeoff. In 1894 the tribal governments collect $29,000 in royalties, fees, and taxes. In 1901 the annual royalty increased to almost $200,000, and in 1905 it rose to $245,858. This capital was thought to be the key to building a healthy economy. It could have financed improvements in agriculture, roads, marketing, and financial institutions. Moreover, the coal boom could have attracted outside businessmen with the skills needed to guide the Indian Nations into a modern corporate system.[40]

The coal bonanza, however, failed to materialize. Throughout the 1880s and 1890s an unknown—but large—amount of royalties and taxes was never collected. Green McCurtain, principal chief of the Choctaw Nation, initiated legislation to compel mining companies to pay their royalties promptly, but the tribe was never able to collect the full assessment. Moreover, when taxes were received, significant amounts of money were lost to graft and lax accounting methods. Despite the hundreds of thousands of dollars paid into the Choctaw treasury by coal miners and the receipt of nearly a quarter of a million dollars in royalties, by 1903 the treasury was bankrupt.[41]

A major reason why coal did not greatly benefit the tribes involved the absentee ownership of many of the mines. The Choctaw Coal and Railway Companies (the largest producer in 1894) was a subsidiary of the Chicago, Rock Island and Pacific, and the Osage Mining Company (the second-largest) was a subsidiary of the Missouri, Kansas and Texas Railroad. Good profits were made with a minimal amount of effort. The companies stripped the most accessible coal and left the rest behind. The mines could have produced much larger quantities, but an increase in productivity would have required more sophisticated mining procedures and a complex system of marketing.[42]

During the mid-1890s the national offices of the mining companies began to take a more active interest in the actual management of the coal industry. The freedom of local managers was curtailed, and a more intense pursuit of profits followed. The new policy was successful. In 1895, the Choctaw, Oklahoma and Gulf Railway reported an income of $332,000 from railroad operation and $559,000 from coal. In 1896 its income from the railroad increased to $557,000, while its income from coal decreased to $536,000.[43]

The large amounts of money earned from the coal industry did not produce prosperity for either workers or local businessmen. The real wages of miners steadily diminished as eastern powers gained control. In 1894, Jay Gould's coal interests announced a 25 percent cutback in wages and an increase in the price of shooting powder. This sparked an eighteen-month strike that impoverished the miners, destroyed the local Knights of Labor, damaged many local merchants, and nearly bankrupted the Choctaw government. Strikers were able to reduce production by 65 percent, but the companies responded by importing strike-breakers and deporting strikers. In 1895 a settlement was reached that restored the previous price for shooting powder and curtailed wages by only 20 percent. In 1898, however, miners reorganized under the leadership of the United Mine Workers and again went on strike. From 1898 to 1900 UMW workers remained on strike, but they were barely able to curtail production, and the strike failed.[44]

In the 1890s a third wave of white intruders was lured to the Indian Nations. They were attracted not by the tribes' natural resources but by their financial resources. The Indians' accounting methods were notoriously poor. Graft and incompetence cost the tribes millions of dollars. White businessmen and professionals, especially lawyers, throughout the Southwest heard of these deficiencies and migrated to Oklahoma in search of quick fortunes.[45]

William H. ("Alfalfa Bill") Murray, who was one such migrant, described the process. The lawyers would settle in an Indian government center to which payments from the federal government were delivered. Murray made his money providing legal services for Indian landlords, but he said that anyone who knew a little law or finance and knew what he wanted out of life would emerge from the economic anarchy of the times a wealthy man. "Any lawyer who did not make money in the Old Chickasaw Nation," Murray dryly commented, "was no lawyer."[46]

At first the newly arrived white lawyer worked closely with the Indian elite. The basic pattern was that the white entrepreneur married an Indian and thus became a member of the tribe. This gave the white the full privileges of Indian citizenship, and, therefore, the opportunity to do business with the tribal governments. The most lucrative prospects were for lawyers, who could

A mine cave-in in McAlester, 1929. Sixty-one men were killed; two men survived. Courtesy of Western History Collections, University of Oklahoma Library.

assist in the tribe's financial exchanges. An attorney with the right political connections could receive a fee of up to 30 percent on transactions of hundred of thousands or even millions of dollars.[47]

The Indian Territory was especially attractive to quick-witted whites during the late 1890s, when the Territory was undergoing a massive process of dissolving and reorganizing its political and legal system. Millions of dollars and thousands of acres of mineral titles and farmlands were changing hands. Although established businessmen might not necessarily be drawn by such financial opportunities, speculators and less orthodox agents arrived in droves. William Murray referred to this new business class as "disreputable Texans" and a "multitude of criminals." Murray evidently did not exaggerate about the character of the immigrants who assisted in the tribes' financial matters and who then became the backbone of the regions' mercantile sector: Archibald S. McKennon, an investigator for the Dawes Commission, discovered that intruders had bribed at least twenty-three of the thirty-two members of the Choctaw Council.[48]

One example of the kind of transaction that made the Indian Territory attractive to outside entrepreneurs was the sale of the Choctaw Nation's western lands. In 1860 the Choctaws ceded the western half of their lands to the federal government for almost $3 million. For nearly thirty years, however, Congress balked at fulfilling its financial obligation. In 1892 the desperate Choctaws hired a group of attorneys at a fee of 25 percent to try to persuade the United States to pay for the land. During the subsequent negotiations it was found that one of the attorneys had gained his position by bribing five Choctaw councilmen. This produced a violent debate within the tribe, but the attorneys defended themselves, saying that it was better for the Choctaws to pay their attorneys generously than to lose the entire amount. At the end of the debate the council raised the fee to 30 percent and gave their representatives the freedom to lobby Congress. In the end the government paid $2,991,450, and the attorneys received a 30 percent fee and another 20 percent for expenses, around $1.5 million altogether.[49]

It was nothing new that money intended to pay Indians for their land was used to enrich white and mixed-blood intruders. A founding father of the Cherokee Nation, John Ross, who was one-eighth Cherokee, had built an empire on plantations, steamboats, and trading posts with $200,000 he collected for managing the Cherokee removal from Georgia. By the 1900s, however, the profits of graft and speculation mostly benefitted recent arrivals, white immigrants, and mixed-bloods who were revamping the Territory's upper class. For instance, Robert Owen, a mixed-blood landlord, earned a 3.5 percent fee for his work in a multimillion-dollar Kiowa land sale and invested it in an estate of 1,000 acres. William Murray had to borrow a few dollars to go to the Chickasaw

Nation. He quickly earned enough money helping Indian land-lords to build a 1,600-acre estate.[50]

White immigrants found various other means of becoming rich by manipulating Indians. Many lawyers became wealthy by repre-senting mixed-blood landlords in legal battles with their tenants. Others cajoled isolated and ignorant tribesmen into surrendering their land. The most infamous group of successful immigrants went into the business of running orphanages. These whites would bribe local judges and have themselves declared the legal guard-ians of Indian orphans. Thus they gained control of each ward's inheritance, which usually included title to 40 to 120 acres of land.[51]

In a society whose people had a short life expectancy and in which accidental death was common, there were so many orphan-ages that the care of orphans became a big business. A govern-mental study in 1913 estimated that 50 percent of these homes were fraudulent (one man cared for five hundred children, and he had to assign them numbers to tell them apart). Moreover, the study said, many of the merchants in the area were financed by the profits from these enterprises.[52]

Henry Everidge, a mixed-blood Choctaw from Frogville, had long been suspicious of the way the two leading businessmen in his hometown made their money. He would argue with his friends that the two leaders could not have made their money legally, and his friends would reply that no businessman was completely honest. Henry was proved correct when the record book of a local judge was found, and it proved that the two town leaders had gained their wealth by defrauding orphans.[53]

The influx of white entrepreneurs thus produced an economy that was a hybrid of orthodox commercial activity and crimi-nality. (Today drug traffic holds a comparable position in some areas of the United States. It is outside the mainstream of con-ventional business, but it is too large to be ignored.) The effect of the situation on the Indians' society was disastrous. During the 1890s, when the United States government saw that criminality was rampant in Indian society, that condition was cited by the Dawes Commission as proof that the system was a failure and as justification for forcing Indians to cede their lands.[54]

The Indians quickly realized that the influx of whites was undermining both their economy and their independence. In the 1880s the conservative Nationalist party came to power in the Choctaw Nation and reimposed the death penalty for selling land to an outsider. A similar reaction occurred in the Creek Nation when an insurgent group of full bloods tried to prevent their tribal leaders from participating in negotiations with the United States government. The tribes, however, usually followed a more moderate course. For instance, the Choctaws quickly abandoned violent resistance; instead they raised the license fees for newly arrived whites from $50 to $1,000 and attempted to write more stringent regulations.[55]

Unfortunately, the power of the tribal government gradually diminished. The United States government did not openly usurp control. Instead, agents of the Department of the Interior pressed Indian authorities to enforce their tribes' regulations loosely. The Indians were caught in a dilemma. If they refused to compromise with white agents, their lands would be taken from them. Consequently, they chose to enforce their laws in a haphazard manner and thus allowed greater numbers of white into their nations.[56]

By the early 1900s new aggressive white businessmen were in control of southern and eastern Oklahoma. William Murray was one of those immigrants but he regretted their influence. The old Indian elites, wrote Murray, were intelligent, dignified, and gracious. He greatly admired their gentility and their remarkable lack of pettiness. Murray, however, claimed that every Indian economic and social notable in the Chickasaw Nation was quickly dispossessed and that almost every one died in poverty.[57]

Murray's charges were belatedly documented in a legal study conducted by the Oklahoma Indian Legal Research Project which concluded that the Seminoles (and the same percentages hold true for the other tribes) had allotted to their membership, 369,854 acres of restricted land which could not be legally ceded from the Indians. The study reported that tribesmen lost all but 29,744 acres through fraud and other forms of theft.[58]

The new elites were composed largely of southerners who aspired to reconstruct the antebellum plantation system. Progressives like Murray and Robert Owen, as well as conservatives like Robert Williams, saw themselves as natural aristocrats who had earned a position in the landed gentry class. They shared much of the Protestant ethic of hard work and thrift, but they had no desire to become capitalists. One of the most ambitious of these landlord-bankers, Robert Williams, had nothing but scorn for capitalists, whom he condemned as "Babbits."[59]

The salient characteristic of members of the new elite was their parsimony. What they lacked in knowledge of society's economic institutions they made up for in a fervent belief in traditional family economics, hard work, and thrift. Murray, however, was upset by their "close-fistedness." The two agents whom he knew best, Williams and E. G. Treadwell, were "terribly selfish, envious and jealous." Murray illustrated Williams's and Treadwell's banking policy with an anecdote about the poor farmer who wanted a loan. The banker said that he would make the loan if the farmer could identify which one of his eyes was real and which was glass. The farmer said that the left eye was glass because he could almost see a tear in it.[60]

An aggressive entrepreneur familiar with the corporate world might have attracted outside capital and built up the region. Other American frontier areas had previously climbed out of poverty. For instance, Iowans were able to attract capital and thus lower interest rates by attracting life insurance companies to the frontier. Insurance companies provided both investments and business expertise which helped Iowa develop the economic substructure necessary for a modern agricultural economy. The same pattern also occurred in Oklahoma Territory. Indian Territory, however, was unable to attract either outside economic guidance or outside finance.[61]

The members of the new white elite were no more aware of business principles than the Indian aristocrats had been. They typically invested their earnings in land and fine mansions. Their estates earned enough profits to enable them to build cotton gins and to establish a few very small banks. The region, however, did not have enough capital to do more than keep pace with the increased production. Consequently, even the boom in cotton at the turn of the century did not help the region outgrow the old South's cotton tenancy system.[62]

Ironically, even though the region produced enormous amounts of cotton, the fate of agriculture was much less important to the landlords than their more profitable concern, speculating in land. The standard rent (one-third of the corn crop and one-fourth of the cotton crop), which was a considerable burden for the renter, was for the landlord an inconsequential sum which barely covered his taxes. Consequently, the landlord supported himself by selling land in the perpetually rising real estate market. The result was that landowners had little motivation to improve the quality of their farms or to invest in institutions necessary for a prosperous agricultural economy.[63]

A corollary of the general pattern of unconventional methods of business in Little Dixie was that the primitive nature of the economy helped impoverish the region. The white tenants were stigmatized because they were less educated and poorer than Indian small farmers. Whites were legally prohibited from owning land or voting, and they did not have access to schools or public institutions. They were admitted simply to perform a function, the cultivation of 80 percent of the region's cotton. The tribe offered them the privilege of renting land, but it assumed no moral or legal obligation for their welfare.[64]

Tenants in the old Indian Nations had not been cruelly oppressed. Under the system Indian landlords could control all the land which they could arrange to have cultivated. They attracted tenants by allowing them to live rent-free for five years as they improved the farmland. With luck a renter could put together a team of mules and some hogs and chickens. Moreover, he could supplement his diet by hunting and earn extra money by cutting

The R. E. Richardson home in Hollis, 1904. Courtesy of Western History Collections, University of Oklahoma Library.

timber. Also, during hard times he was not likely to be ejected from his land.[65]

The quality of life of Oklahoma tenants, however, steadily worsened through the early twentieth century. The landless cotton farmers who immigrated to the Indian Territory had had no experience with the lackadaisical control of Indian landlords. These immigrants were fleeing the world of the Reconstruction South and were firmly entrenched in a culture of poverty. Their children were malnourished, ill-clothed, and deprived of medical treatment. William Murray remembered that when he was growing up on a tenant farm under similar conditions in east Texas he was so thin and pale that passers-by asked what was wrong with him. Because of his inadequate diet he was "tallow faced" and had "stomach worms," and his "vitality was stripped." Young

Murray did not even have enough energy or desire to prompt him to get out of bed. His mother would continually urge him to become active, but Murray "tried to sleep all of the time."[66]

When Oscar Ameringer, a key Socialist leader, visited southeastern Oklahoma in 1907, he described the cotton tenants:

> They were worse fed, worse clothed, worse housed, more illiterate than the Chicago packing house wops and bohunks Upton Sinclair described in *The Jungle*, and whom I had seen with my own eyes while doing my bit in one of their strikes. The Oklahoma farmers' living standard was so far below that of the sweatshop workers of the New York east side before the Amalgamated Clothing Workers and International Ladies Garment Workers Unions had mopped up that human cesspool, that comparison could not be thought of.[67]

Ameringer described his visits in the southern and eastern parts of the state:

> I found a hospitable old hostess, around thirty or less, her hands covered with rags and eczema, offering me a biscuit with those hands, apologizing that her biscuits were not as good as she used to make because with her sore hands she no longer could knead the dough as it ought to be. I saw youngsters emaciated by hookworms, malnutrition, and pellagra, who had lost their second teeth before they were twenty years old. . . . I saw a white man begging a Choctaw squaw man who owned the only remaining spring in that neighborhood to let him have credit for a few buckets of water for his thirsty family.

Ameringer had seen some of the worst poverty in America and Europe, but he was not prepared for the shock of seeing Oklahoma tenants, whom he described as being "as wretched a set of abject slaves as ever walked the face of the earth, anywhere or at any time."[68]

Tenant children's psyche was molded by the violence that pervaded their society. Alfalfa Bill Murray, the son of a Texas tenant farmer, went to work in the lumber mills at age nine. Between the ages of nine and eleven he saw one workman "choked until his tongue hung out," and he saw one workman's eye gouged out. Murray remembered other gruesome events which he said negatively influenced his maturation process. The most notable influence was the public hanging. Murray described the effect on a ten-year-old:

> That sight had a great impression, not for good, upon George [Murray's bother] and me. For two years nearly, we were always trying to hang something. We made a wood scaffold and hung a variety of animals. We hanged a cat. We didn't like it anyhow. For weeks it walked with a bowed neck. We would hang chickens and it would jerk their heads off.[69]

Murray regretted the influence that early exposure to violence had on his childhood, and he did not doubt that it affected his personality. As Murray matured, he considered following his closest friends' path and becoming a cattle thief. His friends were soon killed, and Murray changed his mind. Murray's new career, politics, gave him an opportunity to exercise his self-admitted violent tendencies. In two separate incidents in his early political career Murray beat up his opponents and "stomped" on their faces.[70]

The suffering of tenants was aggravated by segregation. Tenants were not welcome even in local churches. Established churches were controlled by townspeople and wealthier farmers. Tenants were often considered crude, immoral, and unsuitable church members. Even if they had been welcomed, the ill-clothed and awkward backwoodsmen would not have been comfortable attending church.

The gap between tenants and townspeople was so great that weekend dances were segregated. Square dances, which attracted all kinds of people, were such energetic and rough affairs that church members and wealthier parents tried to prevent their children from attending. As a result a uniquely southern institution, the "play-party," developed. The play-party was basically a dance without music. It was designed to be a less exuberant affair than the square dance, with greater controls on alcohol and closer supervision of the participants. The logic was that poor people would shy away from the more restrained affairs.

Tenants, however, were both energetic and flexible, and many young farmers attended both the play-parties and the dances. Sometimes the increased regulations were counterproductive because the young men, knowing that they could not drink near a play-party, would consume an even greater amount of moonshine before arriving, and the drunkenness led to knife fights. There is evidence that tenants and townspeople were often able to forget their antagonisms and enjoy the parties. It is likely, however, that class tensions probably contributed to rowdyism and that the tension encouraged bloodshed.[71]

Such violence was not limited to southern and eastern Oklahoma, of course. (According to Robert Dykstra, however, the level of violence on the frontiers of the Midwest and the West was much lower than is generally believed.)[72] Nor was the brutality that pervaded the region a transitory phenomenon produced by coarse, unrestrained, and intense pioneers. On the contrary, the most violent and inhumane aspects of life in Little Dixie were legacies of a restrictive and deprived social order. The area's most unseemly characteristics were less the results of a wide-open and thus "lawless" frontier than the products of a cripplingly oppressive society that Cary McMilliams was to refer to as a "rural ghetto."[73]

The other form of lawlessness that characterized the region, the lawlessness of the affluent, was a critically important and enduring force. The criminality involved in the initial settlement persisted into the twentieth century, after representatives of outside corporate powers joined the petty grafters who were the region's founding fathers. The sordid state of business activity has been vividly described by Danney Goble. Picturesque examples of illicit business activity included the transportation of a dead body decomposing in a carload of wheat; the adulteration of Muskogee's milk by a half-dozen dangerous chemicals including chalk, saltpeter, boric acid, and bacteria-infested water; and the refusal of the Atchison, Topeka and Santa Fe in Pottawatomie County to pay any of its taxes.[74]

Such lawlessness was only the most noticeable difference between the two regions. The southern and eastern frontier differed emphatically from the frontiers of the North, the Midwest, most areas of the West, and even the Oklahoma plains. It was not settled by ambitious, talented pioneers lured by the promise of freedom and economic security. Instead, Little Dixie was populated by refugees of defeated, impoverished, and often despairing societies such as the former Indian Nations, the Reconstruction South, and southern Italy. Lacking the expertise and the capital to participate in the market, southeast Oklahoma's frontiersmen utterly failed to profit from their new home's natural resources. The result was that the region's pioneers were trapped in poverty, isolation, and brutality.

The experience of the southern and eastern portion of Oklahoma thus agrees with the analysis of Allan Bogue that tenant farmers in the Midwest had access to the proverbial ladder out of debt but that many southern tenants did not. Bogue noted that an agricultural agent argued that if southern tenant farmers were given a farm free of charge in a few years they would be renting again. Bogue agreed with the agent that the reason for such pessimism was lack of managerial ability owing to a lack of education. The biggest problem with applying Bogue's analysis to southeast Oklahoma is that even an educated and skillful farmer would not have been able to keep his land in the "orgy of exploitation" that was the sum of the economy of Little Dixie.[75]

3

The Frontier in the West

THE SETTLEMENT of the prairie and the urban areas of Oklahoma
was not as disastrous as the development of the east, but there
was a good deal of chaos and waste in the Oklahoma Territory.
The Great Frontier may not have devastated the cities and plains
as completely, but it left a good deal of structural damage, which
eventually led to the dust bowl. Hurried, random growth and destructive competition kept settlers from devising adequate means
for dealing with their environment. Consequently, when drought
or depression disrupted the frontier settlement, the system was
patched up in ways that caused even more destruction.[1]

The opening of the Oklahoma Territory was prompted by a
colorful group of activists known as the Boomers. The Boomers,
led by David Payne, a former soldier, government official, specu-
lator, and lobbyist, consisted mostly of modest farm families.
These settlers, however, almost certainly were unknowing agents
of the railroads. The connections between the railroads and the
Boomers has not been conclusively demonstrated, but the con-
sensus is that historian Arrell M. Gibson was correct in labeling
the homeseeker a "stalking horse" of the railroad interests.[2]

Although popular myth has presented the Boomers as noble,
heroic pioneers who defied an oppressive government, the truth
is much less romantic. The first Boomers were fairly well established, and their leader was essentially a soldier of fortune influenced by the railroads. Although they once came close to a gun
battle with a U.S. Army unit, the Boomers were not rebels, and
they were slow to take personal risks to subdue the wilderness.

48

Few of the Boomers were greedy capitalists completely insensitive to the Indians, though they were ignorant of many of the complicated circumstances surrounding the ownership of the Oklahoma plains. Many did not realize that the Indians owned the land. Often Boomers were under the impression, intentionally cultivated by Elias C. Boudinot, a mixed-blood Cherokee attorney who was on the payroll of the railroads, that the western portion of Oklahoma was public domain. The Boomers thought that only the large cattle corporations who leased the lands would be hurt by settlement.[3]

In 1889 public pressure forced the opening of Oklahoma Territory to settlers. Large strips of land were designated for public settlement. The Indians who still lived in those areas and the cattlemen who leased the land were forced to relocate. Then, after a minimal amount of government planning, the central portion of the territory was opened. On April 22, 1889, the first land run occurred. Fifty thousand people took part in the race, and within a year the legal population had increased to 61,000. In 1893 the Cherokee Outlet was opened to settlers. The population of Oklahoma rose from 311,400 in 1898 to 723,441 in 1907.[4]

The land runs were picturesque, but they were unsatisfactory methods of settlement. In the first run 40,000 homeseekers raced for only 10,000 plots. In the largest run for land in the Cherokee Outlet, only one in ten had a chance of winning land, and much of the land was not claimed because it was obviously too dry for a small farmer. Even those who found homesteads were taking a gamble. In fact, the cowboys who had previously worked the range figured that it was impossible to survive on 160 acres. Some of them made the run for the fun of it. If the cowboys found someone foolish enough to want the land, they sold it for a few dollars and had a party with the proceeds.[5]

The homesteaders who raced for farmland were orderly and responsible. There was surprisingly little conflict over claims. The competition for homesteads was vigorous, but the settlers did not take advantage of each other. The plains attracted hard-working

OKLAHOMA

CAPT. PAYNE'S

OKLAHOMA COLONY

Will move to and settle the Public Lands in the Indian Territory before the first day of December, 1880. Arrangements have been made with Railroads for

LOW RATES.

14,000,000 acres of the finest Agricultural and Grazing Lands in the world open for

FREE HOMES

For the people—these are the last desirable public lands remaining for settlement. Situated between the 34th and 38th degrees of latitude, at the foot of Washita Mountains, we have the finest climate in the world, an abundance of water, timber and stone. Springs gush from every hill. The grass is green the year round. No flies or mosquitoes.

The Best Stock Country on Earth.

The Government purchased these lands from the Indians in 1866. Hon. J. O. Broadhead, Judge Jno. M. Krum and J. W. Phillips were appointed a committee by the citizens of St. Louis, and their legal opinion asked regarding the right of settlement, and they, after a thorough research, report the lands subject under the existing laws to Homestead and Pre-emption settlement.

Some three thousand have already joined the colony and will soon move in a body to Oklahoma, taking with them Saw Mills, Printing Presses, and all things required to build up a prosperous community. Schools and churches will be at once established. The Colony has laid off a city on the North Fork of the Canadian River, which will be the Capital of the State. In less than twelve months the railroads that are now built to the Territory line will reach Oklahoma City. Other towns and cities will spring up, and there was never such an opportunity offered to enterprising men.

MINERALS!

Copper and Lead are known to exist in large quantities—the same vein that is worked at Joplin Mines runs through the Territory to the Washita Mountains, and it will be found to be the richest lead and copper district in the Union. The Washita Mountains are known to contain Gold and Silver. The Indians have brought in fine specimens to the Forts, but they have never allowed the white men to prospect them. Parties that have attempted it have never returned.

In the early spring a prospecting party will organize to go into these Mountains, and it is believed they will be found rich in GOLD AND SILVER, Lead and Copper.

The winters are short and never severe, and will not interfere with the operations of the Colony. Farm work commences here early in February, and it is best that we should get on the grounds as early as possible, as the winter can be spent in building, opening lands and preparing for spring.

For full information and circulars and the time of starting, rates, &c., address,

T. D. CRADDOCK,
General Manager,
Wichita, Kan.

GEO. M. JACKSON,
General Agent,
608 Chestnut St., St. Louis.

October 22d, 1880.

A Boomer poster promoting western Oklahoma. Courtesy of Western History Collections, University of Oklahoma Library.

families, not gamblers or persons who were greedy enough to re-
sort to violence. These settlers, as journalist Helen Candee remarked, were held together by "the free-masonry of hard times."
The salient characteristic was neighborliness. Travelers always
knew that, regardless of how impoverished a homesteader might
be, his "latchstring was always out." According to the custom of
the country, a stranger was always welcome to take what he
needed even if his host was not at home, as long as he cleaned up
after himself. Not only did survival depend upon cooperation,
but life would have been unbearably drab without genuine com-
panionship. Homesteaders were often racist and capable of intol-
erance, but during this pioneer period the force of prejudice was
minimal.[6]

The homesteaders should not be romanticized, but there is much
truth to the popular image of these frontiersmen and women. They
were trying to make a living on land that received an average of
22 to 35 inches of rain a year. They had to farm in summer heat
of well over 100 degrees, suffocating dust, fifty-mile-an-hour
winds and subzero winter temperatures. Many homesteaders slept
in sod huts which let in the weather so that they would awaken
to find a layer of snow on them. Moreover, because of a shortage
of wood, they could never adequately warm their huts. Although
sod huts did not adequately protect humans from the weather,
rattlesnakes found them excellent shelter and would crawl under-
neath beds and into the rafters. Allie B. Wallace tells about the
time her family was eating dinner and a rattler dropped onto the
table.[7]

During hard times the pioneers might have to subsist on cof-
fee, molasses, and flour, or they might not have any food at all.
Wallace concluded that the best illustration of the tenacity of the
settlers and their tragic condition was the farmer who continued
his hopeless battle after his mules died and tried to plow his field
with an emaciated cow.[8]

Eastern journalists who investigated life on the prairie were
shocked to discover that homesteaders faced conditions worse
than those in big-city slums. Helen Candee, writing in the *Forum*

A dugout home in western Oklahoma. Courtesy of Western History Collections, University of Oklahoma Library.

magazine, estimated that the total belongings of the average homesteader were worth only $27.50.[9] Another observer wrote in *Harper's* "any man who can afford a hall bedroom and a gas stove in New York City is better off than he would be as the owner of 160 acres on the prairie."[10]

Typically the settler who entered Oklahoma in the Run of 1889 did not stay on the land the first year. According to Angie Debo:

> The homesteader had six months to settle his claim. He seldom stayed. He staked his claim and filed on it at the land office, and he made a few improvements so that it would look as though he had started to develop it. . . . And then, he went back to his old home wherever his home was—and he spent the summer laying by supplies to get started.[11]

The next year, 1890, Debo continued, was a drought year. Potatoes "were the size of marbles," and "hot winds killed the corn." Many survived on kaffir and turnips, but others could not. Their money was gone and their claim had produced absolutely nothing. For that reason the second winter, 1890–1891, was their 'starving time.'" Fortunately, game was still plentiful, and those who could not afford ammunition hunted with traps.[12]

In 1890 the sheriff of Kingfisher County estimated that one-third of the people in the Territory needed relief. Many were reluctant to admit it, however, so he scavenged "odds and ends" from a local hotel and quietly distributed them. Even after a settler had established his farm, a drought, a flood, a blizzard, a tornado, or a fire could instantly destroy years of hard work. One farmer remembered a drought that lasted eighteen months and was broken by ten inches of rain that fell in about two hours. Statistics on the subject are unavailable, but it is known that tornadoes, which could measure a mile in diameter, destroyed hundreds of households. The most feared plague was the prairie fire, which could travel at speed of up to sixty miles per hour.[13]

The weather in Kay County, on the Kansas border, was not as harsh as that in much of the rest of the West, but the blizzard of 1894 demonstrated that even a prosperous region could be rendered helpless by nature. When the snow cleared, rescuers found one family of seven dead in their home. A suicide note written by the father said that the food and wood were gone and that he was going to end the suffering. It was claimed that families on neighboring homesteads were found dead from hunger and cold.[14]

The first half of the 1890s was abnormally dry, and crops were poor. In 1896, however, rainfall was adequate, and a good wheat crop was produced. Then, in 1897, the drought was completely broken, and an excellent wheat crop resulted. The average yield per acre increased from nine bushels in 1896 to eighteen bushels in 1897 and twenty bushels in 1898. Moreover, farmers produced excellent crops of kafir corn and broomcorn.[15]

Farmers in western Oklahoma early realized that a certain amount of diversification was necessary. Farmers could supplement their income by raising a few acres of broomcorn and some livestock, and they could improve their diet by cultivating a vegetable garden and keeping a dairy cow. Agriculture never became a self-sufficient operation as it did in the more fertile and humid areas in the east. The key to success was obtaining enough land to ensure a sufficient wheat harvest to provide income to buy essential commodities.[16]

Wheat agriculture thus required a good deal of financing. Fortunately, after the good crops of 1896 to 1898, many farmers were able to acquire capital. The good crops allowed the homesteader to mortgage his land for $200 to $300 and then invest in farm improvements. Successful pioneers were then able to buy land at bargain rates from their less fortunate neighbors. As outsiders realized that it was possible to survive in Oklahoma Territory, larger amounts of investment capital became available. Consequently, in the late 1890s small wheat farmers were able to obtain five-year loans at the reasonable rates of 8 to 12 percent.[17]

Unlike the tenants in eastern Oklahoma, the homesteaders on the central plains were not completely alone in their struggle. In contrast to the Indian Territory, where the railroads extracted mineral resources, without assisting economic development, the fate of the railroad in the plains depended on the establishment of a stable agricultural community. Consequently, the railroad's policy was to offer financial and educational assistance to the region.

In 1889 the railroads supplied seed at cost to homesteaders who promised to use it only for planting. In 1893 the railroads made seed loans to settlers who made the run for the Cherokee Outlet. The loans were to be repaid at a rate of 1.5 bushels for every bushel of seed loaned. The railroads also offered invaluable counsel. They advertised the success which Mennonite homesteaders had enjoyed in raising hard-shelled Turkey Red wheat instead of the soft-shelled wheat that most settlers had raised when they lived in the Midwest. They introduced windmills and encouraged diversification with broomcorn.[18]

The faith that the railroads expressed in the homesteaders was justified. An estimated 95 percent of the settlers paid off their loans in full. By the turn of the century the counties in the central and north-central part of the Territory had completely outgrown their frontier status, and a stable agricultural economy had been established. Seven towns in the region—Perry, Ponca City, Enid, Stillwater, Kingfisher, Oklahoma City and Guthrie—had become prosperous market centers.[19]

With the relative prosperity of the late 1890s prairie wheat farmers and townspeople acted on their knowledge of economic principles. Farmers diversified their crops and to the best of their abilities adopted more scientific farming methods and technology. They set up an adequate system of county governments, which built roads, and they pressed the territorial governments to build agricultural schools. Most acknowledged the power of the railroads and paid them exorbitant bonuses in return for a scheduled stop at their town. Townspeople resented the power of the lawyers, bankers, and merchants but recognized that they were essential. Eventually most towns advertised for professionals to come to their communities.[20]

The wheat farmers and townspeople did not become wealthy, but they were able to live modestly well. Successful farmers absorbed the homesteads of the failures. Often the towns' business leaders or their relatives were successful farmers. The first bank in Enid was established by homesteaders who pooled their money for safekeeping. They learned to invest it and established a financial institution that was responsive to the needs of their community. Many merchants may have been less cooperative, but during prosperous years the farmers were not helpless, and ruthless exploitation was impossible.[21]

The older areas of the central and north-central wheatlands, however, soon encountered a demographic crisis. It took more people to build the towns and roads than the land could support. As late as 1900 there were only three thousand full-time jobs for laborers in Oklahoma Territory, and the farms could not support a large number of year-round workers. Thus toward the end of the first decade of the twentieth century an out-migration from the central region began. Participants in the runs of the 1890s did not venture into most of the semiarid lands of the extreme west and the southwest. A decade later, however, settlers

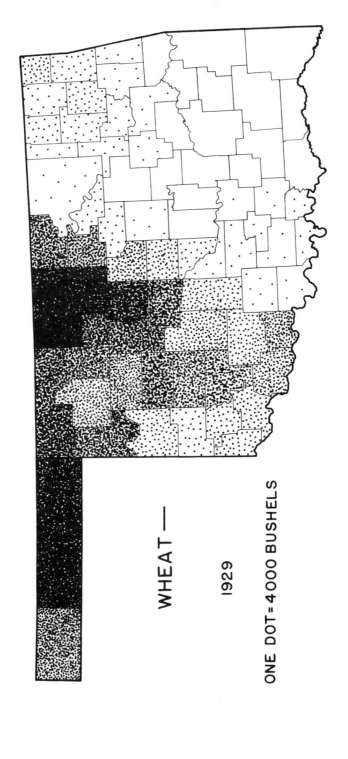

WHEAT —

1929

ONE DOT = 4000 BUSHELS

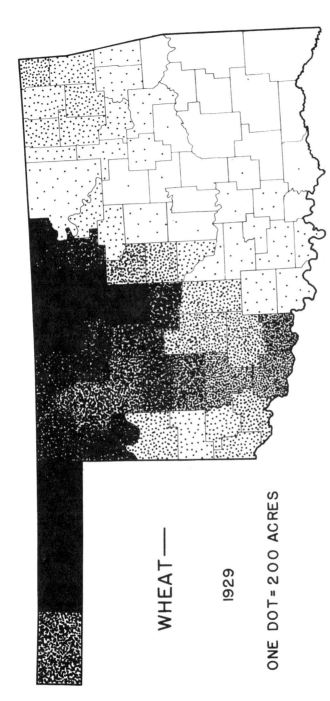

WHEAT— 1929

ONE DOT = 200 ACRES

Wheat farming, acres harvested, 1929. One dot equals two hundred acres. From Burrill, *A Socio-Economic Atlas of Oklahoma.*

had no choice, and the population in the far west rose by 200,000. In these new frontier areas the struggle to subdue the plains was repeated. Whole communities were destroyed by crop failures, fires, droughts, arbitrary actions by the railroads, and economic competition. The struggle was even more brutal than it had been in the slightly more temperate central areas. By 1904 these newer frontiers were in as precarious a situation as those of the first homesteaders of the 1890s.[22]

The towns of western Oklahoma were also established by land runs. Many townspeople were possessed of the same character as their neighbors and relatives who homesteaded the prairie. These runs, however, also attracted gamblers, criminals, specu- lators, and greedy businessmen. In contrast to the relatively orderly and fair runs for homesteads, the races for the cities in- cluded large numbers of "Sooners," persons who slipped into the territory the night before the run. The first days of the towns often were characterized as a junglelike competition. As many as a dozen claimants fought for the same plot. Often a contestant would gain control by hiring a gunman or by bribing a public official.[23]

The history of Oklahoma City provides an excellent example of the land-run method of establishing a city. Settlers came in three waves. The first group was made up of representatives of the Seminole Land and Improvement Company, of Topeka, Kan- sas. They were Sooners who had entered the Territory early and hidden in a gully. When the starting gun was fired at noon on April 22, 1889, they stepped from their hiding places and divided the downtown area among themselves. Then, at 1:30 P.M., the legal participants who had taken the train arrived and found hired gunmen protecting the Seminole claims. For the next few hours, participants on horseback also poured into the city.

The legal and illegal settlers divided into two parties. The Seminole party represented the Sooners, and the Kickapoos were an organization of the legal participants. The Seminole party was led by notables like William Couch, who had replaced the late

David L. Payne as leader of the Boomers, and General James B. Weaver, the former Greenback party presidential candidate. The Seminoles protected both the claims of the first arrivals and the interests of the gamblers, speculators, prostitutes, and gunfighters. The Kickapoos supported the squatters or latecomers who had taken possession of an already claimed lot and advocated the restoration of law and order.[24]

The two groups tried to form a coalition government. The conference, however, degenerated into a mass fistfight. At that, each group formed its own city, hired its own surveyor, and laid out streets. The Seminoles laid out their town in relation to the railroad track, which pointed slightly to the northeast. The Kickapoos laid out their town in relation to due north. Consequently, the main streets that were supposed to connect the two groups failed to meet. (Even today Oklahoma City motorists have to contend with a jog in the streets which connect the north and south areas.)[25]

The Kickapoos eventually gained political control, but the Seminoles retained economic control. The power structure came to be based on a coalition between the town businessmen and the leaders of the vice industry. Some businessmen felt that the economy needed the financial input from gambling and prostitution, so they supported a coalition led by a town builder, a railroad man and "Big Anne," the proprietor of the largest house of prostitution in the city. Periodically the Kickapoos mobilized the large majority of the voters and led a successful crusade against the advocates of a "wide-open city." The political power of the Kickapoos, however, was never strong enough to displace the economic power of the Seminoles permanently.[26]

Oklahoma City and similar communities soon achieved a degree of orderliness. These towns then promoted themselves as lucrative places for economic growth. Towns stabilized themselves, however, to compete with their neighboring communities.[27] This phenomenon, called boosterism, was for the towns a life-and-death struggle. Each town advertised itself as the best location for a railroad stop, a government center, a business enterprise, or a marketing center. Unfortunately, the town that lost collapsed, and the energy expended to build the town was wasted.

The growth of South Enid and the death of North Enid were the best examples of the colorful but destructive institution of boosterism. In 1888 the federal government conducted a study to decide where the county seat of Garfield County should be established. They kept this information secret so that speculators could not buy the best land and take advantage of the rest of the settlers. The railroads, however, had plans of their own. They had also designated certain towns to become transportation and economic centers. Moreover, the railroads refused to defer to the government's plans. They initiated a competition between their towns and the government's towns by refusing to stop their trains at the government centers.[28]

Settlers thus had to decide which side would eventually win and join the competition. During the 1893 land run many of the homesteaders rode the train to the railroad stop at North Enid, while the rest chose to leap from a train traveling fifty miles an hour and settle at the government's townsite at South Enid. South Enid townspeople found themselves stranded. The only way a traveler could reach South Enid was either to jump from the speeding train or leave the train at North Enid and try to get a ride south. North Enid residents, however, refused to rent buggies to people trying to go to South Enid. South Enid residents responded by coming to North Enid to give travelers rides, but North Enid residents retaliated by cutting the reins on their buggies.[29]

The people of South Enid filed a lawsuit and asked Congress to require the trains to stop at South Enid. There was legal precedent for such an action, but the judicial process was lengthy, and the railroads were strong enough to delay congressional action. The only recourse for South Enid residents, then, seemed to be violence. They established barricades on the tracks and began sabotaging trains. Both sides armed themselves, and guerrilla warfare was planned. Fortunately, the imminence of violence prompted Congress to act. South Enid was designated the railroad stop and prospered; North Enid stagnated.[30]

The Enid "railroad war" was extreme, but it was not atypical. Even the large towns, Oklahoma City and Tulsa, were thrown up in an unsophisticated manner. Tulsa gained prominence by out-boostering its neighbor, Sapulpa, and Oklahoma City defeated its competitor, Guthrie. Similar boostering battles occurred between Eufala and Checotah, Sayre and Erick, Westville and Stilwell, Kenton and Boise City, Tecumseh and Shawnee, Grand and Arnett, Lehigh and Coalgate, and Mountain Park and Snyder. Fatalities occurred in the disputes between Eufala and Checotah and Mountain Park and Snyder.[31]

The Territory's cities attracted a class of entrepreneurs who possessed not only cunning and competitiveness but also an understanding of economics. Northern Oklahoma was settled by merchants who understood how corporate capitalism worked. Northern businessmen may or may not have been more benevolent than their southern counterparts, but they were more sophisticated. Rather than squeeze the highest possible profits from each person, merchants competed to attract farmers as steady customers; northern merchants had both a better understanding of economics and more financial resources.

One example was W. J. Hammer, an immigrant from Indiana, who used his superior understanding of business procedures to turn a tent-based hardware store in Oklahoma City into a $2 million enterprise. It was claimed that Hammer "never refused credit to an 89'er." Hammer's credit policy, however, was based on more than charity. Hammer followed a careful strategy in which he purchased a stock of tin pans, saws, screws, hammers, nails, and lanterns and contracted with a driller who agreed to build a water well on the night of the land run. Hammer participated in the land run, but when he arrived, he saw that the best lots were already taken. Hammer chose a lot that was held by a gun-carrying adventurer and bought the site and the services of the gunman for $25.00. The next morning Hammer's well was functioning, and he had a hardware store open for business.

Many shortsighted profiteers earned the enmity of settlers by selling water for 10 cents a cup. Hammer, however, gave water away.
Moreover, he was one of the few merchants who would extend
credit to honest-looking family men. Hammer's generous policies
attracted large numbers of customers, who gladly paid exorbitant
prices for his merchandise: $1.00 for a tin pail, $0.50 for a wash
basin, and $0.25 for a tin cup.[32]

Norman Crockett studied the histories of 100 businessmen of
Oklahoma Territory and produced a composite portrait of the
Territory's entrepreneurial class. Crockett discovered that Oklahoma business pioneers were exceptionally mobile. Most were
men in their forties who during their late twenties and early thir-
ties had migrated to a state neighboring Oklahoma. He also
found that these entrepreneurs commonly shifted types of business
activities, indicating "a quest for opportunity and profit rather
than a strong commitment to one particular line of business."
Crockett argued that Cassius Cade, of Kingfisher, and Hiram
Diehl, of Lawton, "represent typical examples of the wanderlust
of a number of early Oklahoma businessmen." Crockett outlined
their careers:

> Cade, born in Ohio in 1856, moved to Kansas in 1879, to Colo-
> rado in 1881, back to Kansas in 1884, before taking part in the
> rush into the Unassigned Lands five years later. Diehl, a Canadian
> by birth, operated a lumber yard in Clark, South Dakota in 1888
> before turning to hardware merchandising. In that line he located
> in Oklahoma City during the run of 1889 and joined others in the
> founding of Enid during the opening of the Cherokee Outlet in
> 1893. Diehl temporarily relocated in Comanche in 1900, finally
> establishing a hardware store in Lawton the following year.[33]

Crockett discovered that many businessmen operated on a shoe-
string. One, who immigrated from Wichita, invested his entire
savings in a shipment of bananas to sell in Guthrie, hoping that
he could use the proceeds to begin a fruit-and-vegetable business.
Crockett concluded that "on the average no one settler appears
to have carried a large sum of money" to the new territory. He
discovered a few exceptions, such as Fred Boling, who made
the run with $1,100 concealed under his belt, and a group of

four businessmen who came to Apache with their combined as-
sets of $3,500 hidden under their wives' clothing. The much
more common pattern, however, was for a group of hopefuls to
combine their meager savings and form a spur-of-the-moment
partnership.[34]

Crockett argued that the Territory's first businessmen demonstrated "a peripatetic nature equal to the western land specu-
lator." They rarely had a history of steady participation in any
single business, and they were short of capital. These entrepreneurs, however, were serious and competent businessmen. Most
were midwesterners who had witnessed the process by which a
pioneer region developed into a member of the national market.
Their geographical and career mobility gave them a great reser-
voir of business experience and a knack at adjusting to unusual
circumstances. The new cities provided great opportunities for
speculators and gamblers, but they also provided great opportunities for bankers, hardware merchants, grocers, construction firms,
and lumber companies, and Crockett concluded that the frontier
attracted an unorthodox but stable and competent group of businessmen who guided the development of Oklahoma Territory.[35]

The third enterprise which helped northern Oklahoma modernize was the petroleum industry. Oil could conceivably have
had the negligible effect upon the developing region that coal
had had on the premarket southern region. In the 1890s oil was
controlled by a powerful eastern trust that attempted to monopolize Oklahoma oil as Oklahoma coal had been. It would have
been next to impossible for a single entity to have completely
controlled the drilling of oil. The big profits from petroleum,
however, were derived from transporting, refining, and marketing it, and at one time it appeared that Standard Oil would be
able to dominate much of the drilling and the processing of
petroleum.

If Standard had been able to control the oil fields, its operations could have been very similar to those of Jay Gould in coal
mining. Instead of dealing with local bankers, Standard could
have brought in its own investment capital, provided its own
crews to lay pipelines, and imported drilling teams and rig work-

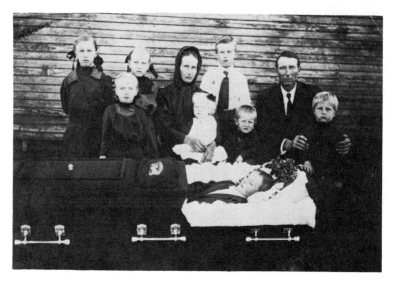

A family of homesteaders in western Oklahoma mourn the loss of a child.
Courtesy of Western History Collections, University of Oklahoma Library.

ers. Moreover, the workman's salaries would not have gone to
local merchants because Standard would have built temporary
company towns and stores.

In 1904, Standard Oil controlled 84 percent of the nation's oil
production. During the first years of the oil boom, it appeared
that Standard and its subsidiary, Prairie Oil and Gas, would also
dominate the Oklahoma oil fields.[36] Even if independent drillers
had access to pipelines and refineries, they were at a disadvan-
tage that initially seemed to be overwhelming. The oil fields were
almost completely unregulated. It was easy for Prairie to use intimidation to cut competition. According to oil-field folklore,
the big powers like Standard and its subsidiary sometimes used
physical intimidation. Prairie, however, had enough resources to
threaten smaller companies without using illegal means. It also
had the resources to survive the large number of setbacks which
were inevitable. The subsidiary could withstand low prices simply
by pumping larger amounts of oil. It could hire the best geologists
and drilling teams and adopt newer techniques.[37]

It took a brave independent to compete with a larger company. A major oil company would commonly offer to buy out a wildcatter. If the wildcatter refused to sell, then the more powerful company would try to drive him out of business. One tactic was to buy the land neighboring a lease and drain the oil and the gas pressure until the wildcatter's well was ruined.

Standard, however, was not able to control the Oklahoma oil fields permanently. It dominated the petroleum industry in the 1890s, when almost all of the nation's oil was pumped from fields in Pennsylvania and West Virginia. As the frontier expanded to California, Texas, Louisiana, and Oklahoma, Standard failed to demonstrate the flexibility necessary to monopolize such a far-flung empire. The pools in the southwest were so large that new fields were continually being opened. Before Standard could take control of a new field, large numbers of independents would be established.[38]

The key to the development of the Oklahoma petroleum industry was the wildcatter. Independent companies controlled by Oklahomans were necessary to establish an industry that would benefit the state. Oklahoma's available oil reserves were not necessarily that much greater than its coal reserves; the difference was that Oklahoma oilmen became participants in processing and marketing and thus helped Oklahoma fit into the international market.[39]

The wildcatter, who played such an important role, embodied the central dynamics of the Great Frontier. One historian has pointed out that the early-day independent oilman was as typical of the American frontiersman as the gold prospector. For both psychological and economic reasons wildcatters were not content to fit into an existing position in an established industry. They were innovators and adventurers who had to create a new economic system.[40]

Since the wildcatter was both a key causal factor in the economic history of Oklahoma and a symbol of the state's frontier culture, a sketch of the wildcatter's personality is essential. Every Oklahoman is familiar with the romantic imagery of the wildcatter. According to the mythology, the wildcatter was basically a gambler. Allegedly he was individualistic, courageous, and self-made. Since the wildcatter was the product of his own efforts, through hardship and success, he remained democratic. Moreover, because he had to earn his wealth, the independent was more innovative and skillful than his larger competitors.[41]

It was no coincidence that wildcatters were often excellent poker players. If they had not enjoyed taking chances, they would have found another career, because oil prospecting, as one wildcatter said, "was not an industry but a gamble." Tom Slick, "Prince of the Wildcatters," was also a famous poker player. His all-night poker games were seen as a ritual. Countless legends grew out of Slick's games, as well as E. W. Marland's and Harry Sinclair's.

Oil wildcatters operated in a basically fluid, democratic environment. The Oklahoma oil-field variety of democracy, however, did not always have the pristine and ruggedly individualistic quality that infused James Fenimore Cooper's novels. For instance, E. W. Marland was reared by aristocratic English parents. He sought to attract "gentlemen" to his company, and he built polo courts for his employees' recreation. Even the aristocratic Marland, however, was forced to adjust to the democratic aspects of the fields. Once, early in his career, Marland was watching roughnecks wrestle with a jammed pipe. One worker looked up at him and yelled, "Give a hand, fats. We'll pay you just as we would a real man." Marland never felt comfortable with the lack of respect for class distinctions, but conditions forced him to abandon his aloofness. In fact, at the time of Marland's first strike in Oklahoma, he was in a muddy ditch with his pants off, laboring beside his employees.[42]

The corollary of the myth of the democratic wildcatter was that his intimate connection with the grimy realities of drilling made him more competent, independent, and flexible than his counterparts in the major oil companies. Marland struck oil in the Osage at a time when Standard Oil accepted the conventional wisdom that the Oklahoma plains were former seabeds and could not produce oil. A Standard official once scoffed that he would drink all of the oil found west of the Mississippi.

The wildcatter's familiarity with his workers and his pragmatism probably made him a more skillful prospector than his
theoretically more sophisticated competitors. A contemporary
said that Marland's geologist "may not have been the country's
greatest oil geologist, but he sure was the country's greatest poker-
playing oil geologist!"[43] "Poker-playing geologists" were the backbone of local wildcatter's companies, but they were rarely found
on the staffs of the major companies.

The dominance of the wildcatter, however, was short-lived.
Although independents controlled much of the production, a
pattern soon developed in which the returns from processing and
transporting the oil yielded roughly twice the returns on a comparable investment in drilling.[44] If an independent was to survive
the dramatic fluctuations in oil prices, he must share in the profits from the marketing of petroleum. As will be explained, an
entirely different set of qualities was required to compete with
established oil companies in transportation and processing from
those required to find and drill for oil. Consequently, in marketing, the flamboyance and intuition of the early days were supplanted by a reliance on orthodox business principles.

The opening and the closing of the oilman's frontier illustrate
the key dynamics of the plain's frontier and the Great Frontier. The Western world's corporate economy demanded that
petroleum be produced as quickly as possible, and oilmen enthusiastically responded. Oklahoma's reserve could not have been
exploited in just a few years except by daring, resourceful, and
often ruthless frontiersmen. Both the creative and the destructive energy of these pioneers is astounding. Oil-field workers and
their employers deserve their reputations for skill and courage.
The reputation of the "oil patch" for cruelty, however, is equally
well deserved. Many of Oklahoma's oilmen held workers, society,
and the earth in contempt. The result was dozens of needless
deaths, periodic depressions, and the waste of incredible quantities of oil.[45]

It is much more difficult to compare and contrast the western
plains and the eastern hills as they existed on the eve of state-

hood than it was to distinguish between the two areas after they became settled. From the beginning it was clear that the two frontiers differed culturally but the crucial difference between the regions' relationships with the markets had not been developed completely. It could not have been predicted with certainty that the plains were destined to be integrated successfully into the market while the hill country remained in isolation. Even in 1907 much of the prairie was still uninhabited. At the same time it was not obvious that the considerable natural resources of Little Dixie would fail to attract investors who wished to build a stable community. By statehood, however, the two frontiers had evolved to the point that it began to seem inevitable that the plains would join the market while the hills were left behind. Then, as the bifurcation became more obvious, businessmen, as well as the farmers and workers with the skills and money that the frontiers needed, tended to favor the northern and western regions. This further reinforced the pattern in which the prairie conformed to the basic dynamics of the Great Frontier while the hills stagnated.

The farmers and laborers of the two sections, however, were not yet ready to acknowledge the inevitability of the two processes, and they produced two comparable forms of anticapitalist political radicalism. The social segregation which accompanied tenancy, along with economic and political injustices, combined to make Little Dixie an ideal environment for radicalism. Its citizens not only were impoverished and exploited but also possessed an intense distrust of outsiders and a strong faith in the value of self-defense. Similarly, the westerners, who also had many economic and political grievances, were equally independent and strong-willed and were quick to resist anyone, either cattle thieves or corporate powers, who challenged their way of life. Consequently, both frontiers produced powerful agrarian movements which opposed many of the fundamentals of capitalism.

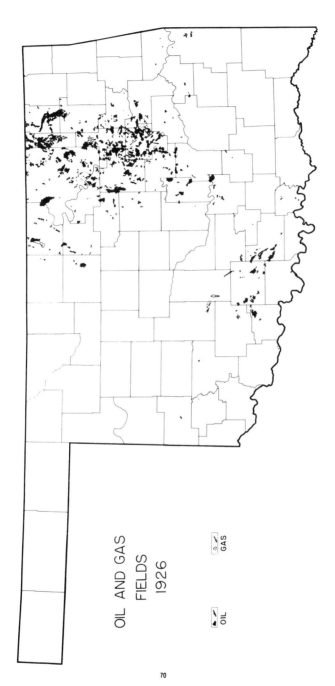

OIL AND GAS
FIELDS
1926

OIL

GAS

Oil and gas fields, 1926. From Burrill, *A Socio-Economic Atlas of Oklahoma.*

4

Frontier Populism

ANY ANALYSIS of the meaning of Oklahoma Territory's political history must begin with the fact that the region was a frontier. Businessmen and political activists alike functioned in a malleable and dynamic environment. Patterns of political behavior had not been institutionalized, and various power blocs, businessmen, landlords, organized farmers and labor, and professional politicians were confident of their ability to influence the Territory's power structures significantly. The result was that Oklahomans were especially amenable to far-reaching and even revolutionary political creeds.

Frontier conditions also produced the opposite effect, a tendency to ignore political principles and to concentrate on obtaining short-term personal gains. Settlers were preoccupied with survival. At times resistance to dominant powers, the railroads, utilities, and agricultural and financial brokers, seemed to be an immediate threat to the very existence of farmers and workers. Consequently, frontiersmen seriously considered the most far-reaching of radical political programs. Pioneers could also be inundated with mundane concerns such as winning access to a railroad or obtaining a government construction project. The survival of entire communities often depended upon campaigns for pork-barrel projects which were completely antithetical to the revolutionary political ideals. The result was a divided consciousness that recognized the immediate need for thorough change but also saw the need to ignore all but the most concrete results of short-term projects.[1]

The political history of the two Oklahoma frontiers thus confirms Walter Prescott Webb's assertion that the American West was politically radical for two reasons: because settlers suffered from intense economic deprivation and because the new land provided a "testing ground" for new political solutions. But the plains were a "lawless" area, where pioneers were continually tempted to concentrate on their own economic future and abandon efforts to remake society.[2] Consequently, Oklahoma frontiers produced a complex form of populism which included both a short-lived protest by aggrieved settlers and a radical vision of a humane, cooperative society.

The reason why the "lawless" frontier was a fertile ground for populism was more complicated than Webb implied. The lack of written legal codes and the propensity of settlers to take care of their affairs on their own probably assisted somewhat in the growth of frontier radicalism, but the contribution of these cultural factors was minimal. On the other hand, the lack of an established legal system, functioning police forces, an effective judicial structure, and a state militia assisted the growth of populism in Oklahoma Territory. Not only did citizens have to handle legal problems without the benefit of the government's legal, judicial and police power, but employers, landlords, bankers, and party officials had to handle disputes with strikers, agrarian reformers, and members of insurgent political groups on their own. Moreover, in predominantly rural Oklahoma Territory, where the great majority of citizens were small farmers and workers with close personal ties to each other, outnumbered representatives of party officials had to handle disputes with strikers, agrarian reformers, and members of insurgent political groups on their own.

As a result of Oklahoma Territory's pioneer status, political disputes were much more peaceful on the lawless frontier than in the South and even in the Midwest. Citizens in the South and in Indian Territory were even more inclined to rely on vigilantism than were those in the Oklahoma Territory, but their ethic of lawlessness was nearly useless in dealing with established governments. More often than not, the law served to make the Populists' opponents invulnerable. This was certainly the case in Indian Territory, where the established tribal governments worked closely with corporate interests to undermine challenges to the status quo. Although the region's farmers and laborers were denied the vote, corporate powers who had bribed tribal officeholders had access to the government and its police power. Moreover, they were free to import Pinkerton detectives in the event that the tribal police needed reinforcement. The result was that the Indian Territory's Populists, whose numbers were probably equal to their counterparts in the West, remained powerless while Populists in the Oklahoma Territory had power comparable to that of the Democrats and the Republicans.[3]

Oklahoma Territory Populists, although they faced relatively little political repression, were acutely aware of the criminal nature of many of the territory's corporate activities. The *People's Voice* (Norman) commented that

> if this republic ever falls it will fall through having too "strong" a government. The calling out of troops to put down labor trouble breeds contempt in the hearts of those who earn their bread in the sweat of their face. The past year has shown the people that the strong arm of government is all on the side of the moneycrats and grabocrats. . . . the constitution and laws of our land are trampled under foot every day by the corporations of this country; yet none of our big daily papers denounce them as "traitors" or "anarchists."[4]

Similar attitudes were presented by the *Oklahoma Representative* (Guthrie), which explained that "in former times the brigands protected themselves with arms; in modern times by securing immunity by law." The editor also wrote that "the miners of the Choctaw Nation, I.T., had been put out of the territory by the U.S. Army," an action which he condemned as an example of "the lash of government." It illustrated "a shocking state of affairs in the Indian territory where man is chattel and crime holds command."[5]

Despite a variety of diversions, at times territorial Oklahoma produced a vibrant Populist movement. The People's party provided the balance of power throughout the territorial era. In the election of 1890 the Populist candidate for territorial representative to Congress received 1,464 votes compared with 4,398 for the Republican candidate and 2,543 for the Democratic candidate. Populists elected four of the twenty-six members of the territorial house of representatives and one of the twelve senators. Populists exerted greater influence than would be expected by their numbers because they were able to elect Populists George Gardenhire of Stillwater as president pro tempore of the senate and Arthur Daniels of Frisco as speaker of the house.

Throughout the decade Populists controlled at least one legislative leadership position, and they steadily attracted voters. The Populist vote for representatives rose from 18 percent of all votes cast in 1890 to 21 percent in 1892. In 1894 the Populist candidate received 15,985 votes (33 percent) compared with 12,050 for the Democratic candidate and 20,499 for the Republican. During that election Populists won seven house seats and five senate seats, while the Democrats won only three seats in the house and one in the Senate and Republicans controlled sixteen in the House and seven in the Senate.

In 1896 the Populists fused with the Democrats and gained unquestioned control of the territorial political system. Populist James Callahan was elected territorial representative by a margin of 27,435 to 26,267. Fusionists controlled the house by a margin of twenty-three to three and the senate by thirteen to zero.[6]

As in the rest of the South, fusion brought temporary success, but it also produced a schism that eventually destroyed the People's party. The former midwesterners who lived in northern Oklahoma generally favored fusion, but the embittered Texans and southerners often did not want to have anything to do with the Democratic party. They remembered how James Hogg had disrupted the Texas Alliance, and they knew that large numbers of Oklahoma Democratic leaders were former Hogg supporters. During the 1898 convention antifusionists walked out and held a rump caucus.

The 1898 election allowed the Republicans to reelect Dennis Flynn by a margin of 28,453, to 19,088 for the fusionist candidate and 1,263 for the middle-of-the-road Populist candidate.

They also regained control of the house by eighteen seats to eight to two and the Senate by eight seats to four to one. In 1900 another attempt at fusion allowed Populists to regain the Senate (eight seats to five), and their candidate, Robert Neff, almost defeated Flynn (Neff lost, 33,529 votes to 38,253). During the last seven years of the territorial era, however, populism ceased to function as an independent force.[7]

During the last years of the territorial period the People's party was replaced by the Farmers' Union, the labor movement, and the Socialist party. The Farmers' Union was the most important heir of the Populist party. For the most part the Farmers' Union was more moderate. Its members were not convinced, however, that modern corporate capitalism was salvageable, and consequently they took steps to lay out an alternative approach. Farmers' Unionists, who had great faith in the power of education, lobbied for the establishment of agricultural colleges and scientific stations. Their newspapers informed the farmers about available technology and new methods of cultivation. They formed cooperatives and reorganized marketing procedures in the small towns, and they established programs that pulled cotton from the market in an effort to raise prices.[8]

Oklahoma Farmers' Union newspapers reflected a flexible, quiet, but strong class consciousness. They did not rigidly define who was or who was not a member of the working class. They carried advertising for banks and businesses, and they engaged in boosterism. On the other hand, unionist papers repeatedly made subtle jabs at big-city capitalists. Their most effective way of sniping at agents of the upper class was a thorough reporting of large numbers of divorces and scandals involving economic notables. At the same time they presented evidence not only of an antibusiness sentiment but also of working-class consciousness. Many papers carried weekly columns on labor activities throughout the world, and they commonly contained editorials and lectures on why the farmer was a member of the working class.[9]

The complaints and proposals of the surviving Populists and their successors in the Farmers' Union were reasonable, but they lacked an adequate unifying framework. Their statements of purpose were intelligent, but they were not concise enough to serve as an effective political creed. Consequently, the members were vulnerable to the arguments of Democrats who counseled patience on the grounds that their poverty would be alleviated as soon as Oklahoma became a state.[10]

Since Populists had been severely defeated in their attempt to control the political system, Farmers' Unionists concentrated on controlling the market by establishing a system of farm cooperatives. In the west, where arbitrary actions by railroads and grain-elevator operators hurt farmers but where the climate was a greater threat than the middlemen, cooperatives were often successful. In the east the farm cooperative program was a complete failure. Farmers were unable to raise enough capital to maintain co-ops, and they failed within a year or two. Howard Meredith, however, has uncovered evidence that Farmers' Unionists in Indian Territory had some success in collective buying and selling. They agreed to abandon efforts to establish cooperatives in competition with private merchants in return for the opportunity to buy and sell in bulk.[11]

The Farmers' Union was most successful in its efforts to cooperate with labor. For the most part, farmers and unions appeared to be natural competitors because higher prices for farmers lowered the standard of living of workers, and high wages for laborers threatened the farmers' precarious profit margins. Both groups, however, felt threatened by the railroad and the powerful extractive industries. Moreover, the low population density and the personal nature of economic and political interactions on the frontier helped promote good relations between farmers and labor. Most workers lived in small towns and came in close contact with farmers. In the rural areas laborers dreamed of the day when either they or their children might own land, and farmers prepared for the possibility that they or their children might be forced to become laborers.[12]

The solidarity achieved between farmers and laborers was no small accomplishment. Even the moderates, however, proved to be willing to take risks for their political principles. For instance, when the Theodore Roosevelt administration, in an attempt to silence subversive newspapers, revoked the second-class mailing status of the *Indiahoma Union Signal* (Shawnee), the farmers counterattacked fiercely. Although the paper was told that it could have its status restored by altering its editorial content, the *Union Signal* accepted the increased costs and issued a special edition with the headlines "Required Stamp for Second Class, Same Stamp Used to Keep the *Appeal to Reason* out of Canada." The article below the headline reported that

> the *Appeal to Reason* [a famous Socialist periodical] has been denied admission to the mails of Canada because it published an appeal by Eugene V. Debs to working people. This shows us the spirit of the oppressor is in the air and that it still lives.
>
> If the *Signal* yields now it will be a sign that farmers have surrendered their free-born rights and accepted the collar of the tyrant.[13]

Two weeks later the *Union Signal* published a cartoon strip depicting a postmaster accompanied by a hypnotized Associated Press correspondent trying to persuade a hard-working farmer to accept their stamp of approval. The hypnotized AP correspondent agreed, saying, "It cured me." The outraged farmer replied, "You'd lock my mouth for one cent a week." He then rolled up his sleeve and knocked out the postmaster.[14]

For two months the *Union Signal* was filled with similar cartoons, articles, and letters voicing outrage. It also received numerous donations to help defray the extra postage. Then, after it appeared that the paper would be able to survive the increased costs, the postmaster conceded defeat and restored the paper's second-class status. Of course, such a conflict was small compared with the struggle which was to come, but the key point is that the Farmers' Unionists did not have to take the risk of identifying themselves with the dreaded *Appeal*. They chose not only to make a stand (at the risk of losing their paper and perhaps their organization) but also to link their precarious situation with that of the *Appeal.* Such a position could hardly be expected by persons who were afraid to be ostracized by respectable society.[15]

Both farmers and laborers were pessimistic about their chances for reform while they were under territorial jurisdiction. They saw the coming of statehood, however, as a unique opportunity to build a new society. These reformers were Jeffersonian Democrats who had great faith that a strict constitution could protect democracy and freedom and control business efforts to monopolize the free economy. Consequently, the Farmers' Union and the labor unions began a two-year effort to draft a constitution that would be a blueprint for a just society.

The drive for statehood illustrates another way in which frontier conditions assisted in the growth of populism while also nurturing the seeds of its destruction as a revolutionary force. Especially in the Indian Territory, where poor whites had absolutely no democratic rights, Populists concentrated on preparations for statehood. They successfully maneuvered to gain control of the procedure for writing the state constitution. This strategy promised to advance Populist principles by establishing from the start a government that was responsive to the people, but it did so at the cost of having populism absorbed into the system of traditional power politics. Indian Territory activists had reason to be pleased with the trade-off, however, because the previously disenfranchised had no power as an independent organization but had a strong chance of capturing the Democratic party once Oklahoma became a state.

The Indian Territory Populists' greatest success was the Sequoyah Convention of 1905. The convention's ostensible purpose was to draft a proposal for statehood that would protect the interests of the tribal government as well as the Democratic party. Its most noteworthy result, however, was to capture the Democratic party and the campaign for statehood for populism. The convention was thus "one of the earliest and most coherent expressions of the emerging reform agenda." Moreover, it was approved by 86 percent of the newly formed electorate.[16]

The Sequoyah Convention endorsed a platform for statehood which was almost identical to the Shawnee Plan which was later drafted and approved by a coalition of the farmers and workers. It called for strict corporate regulation, forbade trusts and monopolies, outlawed price discrimination, and mandated tax equity. Moreover, it eloquently affirmed humanitarian and pro-labor principles.

In the fall of 1906 a coalition of farmers, unionists, fusionists, the surviving middle-of-the-road Populists, traditional Democrats claiming to have converted to reformism, and Socialists met in Shawnee to plan their strategy for the Constitutional Convention. The Shawnee convention concluded with a list of demands which were to be included in the state's constitution. The demands were as follows:

Initiative and referendum
Mandatory primary and Australian ballot
Civil law always to be supreme over military
The right of the state to engage in any industry
Abrogation of the fellow-servant rule
No limit on damages recoverable for death
Eight hours work on all public projects
An elective corporation commission
Compulsory education and free textbooks
Elective mine commissioner, commissioner of labor, and
    commissioner of agriculture
No children under 16 in mines and factories
No convict labor except on roads
No corporation to be allowed to do business within the state
    without first having secured a state charter
No gambling in farm products
No irrevocable franchises [17]

Although their decision to work within the orthodox political system undermined the Populists' ability to offer a distinct radical alternative, their strategy must be seen as a great success. By 1907 populism had been dead seven years, and even if Oklahomans had resurrected the crusade in their own state, they would have been alone and powerless on a national level. In return for their compromise, however, they were able to guide the drafting of an excellent constitution. In addition to the adoption of all but one of the major principles of the Shawnee plan, the constitution also mandated pure-food-and-drug regulation and a department of charities and corrections. It also encouraged direct democracy and municipal ownership of utilities. Moreover, it protected the rights of Oklahomans to "life, liberty, and the pursuit of happiness."

With a few exceptions, the Shawnee coalition was able to obtain its goals (the biggest disappointment which the most radical agrarians suffered at the convention was that the affirmation of the state's right to engage in any industry was amended to exclude state participation in agriculture). On the whole, Oklahoma agrarians produced a praiseworthy constitution which labor leader Samuel Gompers lauded as the most "progressive" in existence and historian Charles A. Beard complimented for its "spirit of fierce opposition to monopolies."[18]

The greatest achievement of the convention was the restraints on corporations that were included in the Constitution. The document's longest article (longer than the entire federal Constitution) was article 9, which dealt with corporations. It required corporations to be chartered by Oklahoma, prohibited political contributions by corporations, and required railroads to divest themselves of mining operations, reduce rates to two cents a mile, and pay taxes on rolling stock and movable property at the same rate as personal property. It then stipulated that these principles were to be enforced by a corporation commission whose members were to be elected by the people.[19]

The coalition of farmers and laborers remained potent after the adoption of the constitution and continued to institute reforms in the first two legislative sessions. During these first years of statehood they were able to obtain a 2 percent gross revenue tax on oil pipelines, coal mines, and telegraph lines plus an extra 0.5 percent tax on oil companies, railroads, utilities, and telephone companies and a progressive income tax. They also increased assessments on the railroads' and utilities' property by as much as 400 percent, instituted a banking code, and established a program to guarantee bank deposits.

The initial success of the territorial Populists should not conceal the fact that they possessed differing levels of sophistication in their politics. The radicalism of some Oklahomans may have been merely an atavistic protest. They had never questioned the principles of capitalism as long as the economy was strong, but when the Oklahoma frontier reduced them to poverty, they responded bitterly. Such activists blamed conditions on a conspiracy of bankers and monopolists who disrupted natural cycles that governed economic reality. They believed that if "grafters" were removed prosperity would return and the simple agricultural system of their childhoods would be restored.[20]

Other Oklahoma radicals had a much more profound vision. These Populists also attacked monopolists and bankers, but they had a much more sophisticated awareness of political and economic reality. Level-headed Populists feared that the corporations which had come to dominate industrial America would also absorb the nation's agricultural economy. They dreaded the possibility that absentee owners would abuse citizens, damage the land, and destroy the rural American's way of life. According to their ideology, the corporate powers which had massacred the buffalo and destroyed the Indian's culture threatened to do the same to the Oklahoma farmer and laborer. These agrarians hoped both to curtail the powers of corporate monopoly and to build a more humane and democratic world. Consequently, they tried to prevent abuses by nationalizing railroads and utilities and to create social justice by defending the rights of Indians, blacks, and women and by promoting schools and social-welfare institutions.[21]

Two studies, Lawrence Goodwyn's *Democratic Promise: The Populist Movement in America* and Sheldon Hackney's *From Populism to Progressivism in Alabama*, are especially helpful in an analysis of agrarian radicalism in Oklahoma. Populism, argued Goodwyn, should be viewed not merely as a political creed but also as a "new way of looking at things—a new culture." This culture was a democratic movement toward a cooperative way of life. Moreover, it was a collective affirmation of the dignity of the people.[22]

Sheldon Hackney agreed that populism must be analyzed as both a political and a social phenomenon and borrowed conceptualizations from social psychologists in an effort to do so. Hackney, however, drew a more ambiguous picture of the Populists. He noted that they advocated democratic and cooperative reforms with a fervency that indicated that Populists were potential revolutionaries. Hackney acknowledged that the Populists were Jeffersonian Democrats, but he noted that they shared that ideology with their bitter enemies the Democrats. Moreover, Populists, when they gained the power to work toward a cooperative society, revealed an "ambivalence" about the competitive system.[23]

The inability of the agrarians to formulate a concise creed undermined their political effectiveness. Populist party representatives engaged in "bizarre" legislative actions that did not conform to their rhetoric. The record of Populist government officials thus prompted Hackney to conclude that "if the Populists were not revolutionaries, neither did they behave like reformers. They repeatedly showed a willingness to vote against reforms to which they had pledged."[24]

Hackney argued that Alabama Populists must be explained as loyal members of their communities who were injured by economic change. They did their best to follow the norms of their society, but they were denied the rewards that were promised for conscientiously conforming to the system's rules. Agrarians reacted bitterly and rejected the social structure that had abandoned them. Unfortunately, however, Populists lacked an adequate political ideology. They responded to economic hardship by attacking an alleged "conspiracy" of politicians. Alabama Populists temporarily displaced the "fraudocrats" who had oppressed them, but, once they gained power, they had no vision of an alternative system.[25]

Goodwyn rejected Hackney's disparaging analysis of populism. He argued that Alabama was a special case and contended that

Hackney drew too heavily on the record of the Alabama legislature. Goodwyn argued that, on the contrary, the Populists developed a profound political analysis, one that was far more sophisticated than the analysis of the day's established economists.
According to Goodwyn, confusion arose because historians in-
discriminately list persons as Populists even though they were not
members of the party and had little or no sympathy with its
creed. For example, Governor Reuben Kolb of Alabama was, at
best, a reluctant Populist. Consequently, it is unfair to test the
strength and the profundity of populism by the results of the administration of an ambivalent Populist.[26]

Goodwyn argued that Populists will be characterized as "atavistic" or "paranoid" only if we unfairly group them with non-
Populists and anti-Populists like James Hogg, Ben Tillman, and
William Jennings Bryan. It was the members of the Farmers' Alliance, supporters of the Omaha platform and the reform process,
who collectively represented the "culture that was the essence
and passion of the people's movement."[27]

Goodwyn's work is valuable for students of Oklahoma agrarianism because the alliance was a force in territorial Oklahoma.
Moreover, most Oklahomans immigrated from areas where either
the Farmers' Alliance or the Agricultural Wheel was powerful.
Fifty percent of the settlers in Indian Territory and 30 percent of
those in Oklahoma Territory migrated from Kansas, Arkansas, or
Texas, where populism was the most powerful. Southern populism originated on Oklahoma's southern border, and populism
was strongest immediately across the northern border in Kansas.
Oklahoma settlers encountered the same geographical and economic hardships that were faced by Populists in Kansas, Texas,
and Arkansas, and they read the same reform newspapers.

Oklahoma's agrarians, however, were also strongly influenced
by the activists whom Goodwyn excluded from his study. Large
numbers of the 80,000 Texans who settled in Oklahoma were
supporters of Governor Hogg. Another 12,000 migrated from
Alabama, the state in which agrarians supposedly acted in a "bizarre" manner.[28] Goodwyn may be correct when he argues that

William Jennings Bryan was not a Populist, but for more than a decade Bryan was revered by impoverished Oklahoma farmers. For this reason any analysis of Oklahoma agrarian unrest must also draw on Sheldon Hackney's study of populism. The agrarians whom Hackney describes may not embody the fullest and most sophisticated form of populism, but they were very similar to many Oklahoma agrarians.

Both varieties of populism existed in Oklahoma, and both were hampered by the territorial status of their new home. Populists in eastern Oklahoma were completely disenfranchised. They lived in Indian Territory as guests, and they could not vote. The powerlessness of poor whites was illustrated in the coal strike of 1879. The coal company and the Choctaw Nation resisted the strike by revoking the strikers' licenses to work in the territory and deporting them. A similar situation applied to white tenants, who not only were denied the rights of citizenship but also could never own land or even send their children to school.[29]

Western Oklahoma Populists were better able to resist. For instance, the WF&HW Railroad violated an agreement and tried to set up the town of Kay as a railroad-controlled competitor of the legally established town of Eschita (present Grandfield). After two years of political conflict the residents of Eschita won the support of President Roosevelt, and Kay was dismantled. In another victory citizens became aroused by a railroad tragedy that occurred in 1906. A railroad-constructed bridge whose foundation was built on shifting land collapsed and killed a large number of people. The resulting public outcry forced the railroad to provide a secure foundation for the trestles.[30]

During the 1890s "Free Homes," an issue unique to Oklahoma Territory, were the major issue of Oklahoma's farmers. The overriding concern of the homesteaders was that they would not lose their land because they could not afford to pay their claim fees. This preoccupation undermined the Populist party. Once, in 1896, a Populist territorial congressman was elected. Oklahoma's voters, however, usually felt that they must vote Republican because Representative Dennis Flynn, who made "Free Homes" his major issue, seemed to be best able to persuade the Republican administration in Washington to waive the homesteading fee.[31]

Consequently, both types of agrarians in the Twin Territories participated in two dissimilar forms of political endeavor. Citizens were equally concerned with orthodox political disputes centering around local interests and with agrarianism. Populism was a dominant force in territorial politics, but it competed with the drive for statehood and battles for political patronage. Historians are generally interested in movements like populism, which represent efforts to alter social and economic structures, but the people who lived in the 1890s were equally concerned with more mundane affairs, such as creating jobs by building roads and courthouses and gaining political rights which modern-day Americans take for granted.

The narrow disputes that characterized territorial politics often prompted awarenesses that led to class-conscious political movements such as populism and socialism. For instance, orthodox politicians who were primarily interested in gaining economic benefits initiated competition between towns. Often one town would be supported by the railroad or other business interests. The conflict could then become a symbol between corporate powers and the people. In the Guthrie–Oklahoma City dispute over the site of the state capital, the North Enid–South Enid conflict, and the Kay–Eschita battle, Guthrie, Enid, and Kay became symbols of exploitative capitalism. In fact, the progressive wing of the Republican party first gained publicity and influence by siding with the people of Eschita, the Socialists won early recognition by supporting South Enid, and the Populists gained control of the leadership in the legislature by endorsing Oklahoma City's efforts.[32]

A similar situation occurred with the drive for statehood. Oklahomans who resented their territorial status saw themselves as an exploited colony. They realized that the territory's railroad rates, grain elevator charges, and interest rates were higher than those in the surrounding states. Consequently, Oklahoma farmers and businessmen alike saw statehood as an opportunity to

An attorney's office, Guthrie, 1889. Courtesy of Western History Collections, University of Oklahoma Library.

expel "carpetbaggers." The People's party recognized that the resentment of eastern corporate powers did not necessarily lead to class consciousness, but they accurately perceived that such resentment could become the basis of an awareness of the exploitation inherent in both states and territories in a capitalist system.[33]

The concern over local politics, however, also diffused ideological awareness. Domestic politics was, in part, a recreation that drew people's attention from radicalism. It also provided a hope of obtaining a benefit, such as a railroad depot. Most important, local politics encouraged disunity among working people. Boostering campaigns often resulted in a situation in which a worker in Oklahoma City thought that he had more in common with his town's banker than with a fellow worker in Guthrie. Similarly, the drive for statehood prompted greater cooperation between a small Oklahoma farmer and his merchant than a farmer in Kansas.[34]

The best summaries of the ideological attitudes that characterized this version of agrarianism can be seen in statements by
many moderate members of the Farmers' Union. They rejected
the revolutionary goals of populism and tried to build a nonpolitical organization. They sought to replace class-conscious
efforts to remake society with a program based on cooperation.
By establishing a cooperative system for purchasing supplies and
marketing crops, they would achieve economic justice for farmers and rural Oklahomans, if not for a larger constituency.[35]

Perhaps the best illustration of the ideology can be found in
the *Indiahoma Labor Signal.* The *Signal* was the official paper of
the Farmers' Union. It reflected the cautious politics of activists
who had been beaten badly in previous crusades. Their earlier
defeats prompted them to distrust politics and fear class-conscious
struggle which could spur repression. It should also be noted that
these moderates were more timid when they were fighting for
common laborers and tenants than when they were working
for skilled workmen and small landowners. The fact remains,
however, that writers for the *Indiahoma Labor Signal* expressed a
legitimate form of anticapitalism which fell short of being a
revolutionary ideology but which represented the antagonism of
Oklahoma's working class toward corporate capitalism.

After a sharp debate the majority of the Farmers' Union agreed
with S. O. Dawes, who urged them to try to influence the market
but not the political system. Dawes reflected the majority's opinion when he wrote, "I saw the Farmer's Alliance, the child of the
Grange, gradually rise in the beauty and glory of a well established institution . . . [and] become a cesspool for the political
frauds and grafters of the age." Dawes then contrasted the wage
scale of professionals with that of common workers and farmers.
He argued that the system obviously placed a "premium on
brains." The solution, then, was to "get into the Brain Business
and get some of those premiums."[36]

After the union completely renounced politics, it remained a
useful organization but was hardly a radical movement. It organized wheat farmers, who held their crops until prices rose five
cents a bushel. It pressed the Southern Cotton Association to lis-

ten to the problems of poor tenants, and it encouraged Oklahomans to hold their cotton until prices rose to eleven cents a
pound. It began "Acre Clubs" in which member farmers agreed
to plant one acre with a new crop. The members then kept careful
records on the crops and discussed their results. Such programs
were valuable, but they represented a rather ignominious end for
an organization which had once been a formidable power.[37]

Populists and radical members of the Farmers' Union advanced
a more drastic form of agrarianism. The Oklahoma Populist party
included thoughtful activists with a program to restructure completely their corrupt society. Their ideology was based on a broad
view of history. Oklahoma's Populists were aptly described in
George Tindall's summary of southern Populists, who had a "truly
radical if amorphous critique of the existing society, which in
some ways paralleled that of the Marxists."[38]

The Oklahoma Populists based their ideology on a broad view
of history that was heavily influenced by the values of Thomas
Jefferson and of Christianity. Their historical philosophy was sup-
plemented by research into economics, which led them to a program for breaking trusts and restoring balance to the nation's
economy. The world-view of Oklahoma Populists resembled that
of the southern Populists studied by Bruce Palmer, even though it
is probable that a high proportion of Oklahomans agreed with
the radicalism of the Texas Populists rather than the compro-
mised attitudes of the Alabama or North Carolina party. They
wanted to create a simple market society where all persons, black
or white, had an equal chance for a decent living based on productive labor and not ill-gotten gain. They desired a "personal"
government that was small, economical, and sensitive to the
needs of the people and not the grafters. Oklahomans also combined the beliefs of Andrew Jackson and the Jeffersonian Democrats and devised a philosophy in which civic virtue came not
from having a close attachment to the soil but from being a
producer. They would have wholeheartedly endorsed the editor
quoted by Palmer as writing that populism was the "morals of
Christ and the politics of Thomas Jefferson."[39]

On the other hand, there was a distinctly northern flavor to

much of Oklahoma populism. Settlers brought with them the analytical populism whose ideas were traced by Chester M. Destler
from the intellectual centers of the Atlantic seaboard to the
farms of Illinois and the rest of the Midwest.[40] Moreover, the informed opinions of Oklahoma farmers and laborers were consistent with the midwestern populism that Norman Pollack described as "a kind of folk-wisdom" that was an "extraordinarily
penetrating critique of industrial society." Pollack further described populism as a "profoundly radical phenomenon" that was
"primarily an agrarian movement, although it also contained
significant support from industrial labor, social reformers, and
intellectuals."[41]

These Populists recognized the existence of the town and
country split that was prevalent throughout America but was especially influential in Kansas, Nebraska, and western Oklahoma.
Robert Miller has demonstrated that pioneers who traveled by
train to Oklahoma settled near towns and tended to vote Republican. Oklahoma populists, however, typically arrived in the Territory by more economical modes of transportation and settled
on less valuable land away from marketing centers.[42]

During the 1890s, when populism was an effective force, the
radicals who had influence (unlike their counterparts in the
Indian Territory, who were almost powerless) came from Kansas.
As was true in Kansas, Nebraska, and much of the Midwest,
populism grew out of the economic conflict between the more
cosmopolitan, market-oriented towns that grew along the railroads and the noncosmopolitan, less business-oriented farmers,
who were too distant from railroad towns to profit from the market. These were farmers who were mortgaged not because they
had attempted to speculate but out of necessity. They were isolated, and their land and crops were of lower value. Also, in
Oklahoma as in Kansas they were likely to cultivate corn, which
was the pioneering crop, rather than wheat, which was the commercial crop.[43]

Populists, who were on the periphery of the market and as a
result were not unduly victimized by short-term downturns like

the depression of the 1890s, desired to do more than protect their own personal or economic status. They wanted to create a more humane world. They were outraged by the viciousness and the corruption of entrepreneurs who guided the development and the destruction of the frontier. Populists condemned the grafters for stealing from them and their neighbors, but they also hated the entrepreneurs' disgraceful treatment of nature and natural laws. Even a Farmers' Unionist like William Murray was outspoken about the rape of the environment and frequently pointed out the cruelty of the system that massacred the buffalo and forced settlers to abuse their farmland. A detailed analysis was presented in the *Enid Coming Events* (a pro-fusion newspaper whose editor's radicalism could not be doubted and which ultimately became a Socialist paper). In an article headlined "Plutocracy and Revolution," published on July 4, 1895, the editor wrote the following"

> A system that permits such accumulation and then surrounds the possession of such wealth with all the power of the state for the purpose of protecting such conditions, is not only demoralizing but is unnatural. The oceans have their streams and tides which not only carry life along with them but are constantly equalizing the temperature. On land we have our storm period of tempest and cyclone. The storm period is necessary to "obviate" droughts in a more "speedy" manner: Again, nature is at work in the earth and we see the handiwork in the earthquake, the volcano and other eruptions that have thrown up whole mountain ranges. The growth of mountains, however, produces a need for a grand leveling or equalization of the surface which is accomplished through action of wind and water.
>
> This whole plan of nature seems to carry until man is reached. He piles up nature's bounties, taking as it were the sand from the valley and leaving it on the hill thus causing the inequality to become greater.[44]

The writer then explained that in the past society had means of periodically dispersing the excess accumulation of the greedy. Modern man abandoned such institutions, and the role of leveling inequality between man and man has been fulfilled by revolutions. For instance, after the greed of George III created the American Revolution, "there were neither paupers nor millionaires." The growth of plutocracy, however, led to the abuse of nature and cruelty toward human beings. The writer concluded his naturalistic analysis with the following statement:

> Plutocracy gathers from every nook and corner of the earth and piles the accumulation in one place. Revolution scatters the congestion to the winds of heaven. One is but a product of the other. Prevent immense accumulation in the possession of a few and revolution is unnecessary, and impossible.[45]

The most important components of the Oklahoma Populists' ideology, whether they came from the South or the Midwest, were the hatred and fear with which they viewed the corporate system. Even when agrarians were unsure about the details of their program, they could agree on its first principle, anticapitalism. The hatred of capitalism was expressed in 1906 by the *Stillwater People's Voice*, which compared the capitalist to an "egg-sucking dog" and pledged to destroy it even if it had to "chop off its tail just behind the ears" or to "chain and starve it."[46] Populists argued that "the contest in this country is between producers and accumulators, between the men and women who, by their labor produce the wealth and those who by manipulation, seek to obtain possession of it." These "parasites," whether they were labeled as "grafters" or "capitalists," were condemned as "The non-producing vampires of society, the bankers, the Shylocks, the corporation cormorants, who have muzzled the toiling ox as he 'treadeth out the corn.'"[47] Equally strident views were occasionally expressed by the more belligerent members of the Farmers' Union, as in an article in the *Indiahoma Union Signal*, in 1905:

> The grafter is as destructive to a state as a blight or a drought. He kills prosperity and brings want and destitution as certain as a crop failure. . . . The grafter is a pirate, a usurious robber, a cruel merciless animal without heart or soul, conscience or kindness.
>
> The Farmers' Union is a society for the protection against the grafter because it requires an organized movement to exterminate him.[48]

Populists feared that capitalism, the relatively recent intruder, threatened to destroy America's heritage of democracy and freedom. According to an article entitled "Capitalism vs. Labor" in the *Alliance Courier*, October 11, 1895, Abraham Lincoln shortly before his death saw that "the possible concentration of the wealth of the country in the hands of the few as a greater menace to our institutions than the civil war had ever been. His forebodings have been proved correct. A dozen men or the corporations they represent control one half of our country."[49]

Populists responded to the capitalist threat with "A New Declaration of Independence":

> When the despotism of usury and a usurping money power turns the useful toiling masses into slaves for its own greedy gratification, then justice and loyalty to each other, and to God, commands them to throw off the yoke. . . . This history of plutocracy is a bloodcurdling revelation of bribery, corruption and sneaky deception.

The declaration listed a number of charges against plutocracy, including the following:

> It has purchased representatives of the people to prevent the passage of laws for the benefit of the masses.
> It has combined with the English money powers to enforce the people into debt.
> It wants to train up our boys to be soldiers instead of useful citizens.
> It discourages independent thought and originality.

The declaration concluded with these words:

> We have been proud of the wealth of our country and pointed to our rich men as examples, . . . but we have at last discovered the perversions of wealth. . . . We must in self-defense "hold them, as we hold the rest of mankind—enemies in war, in peace, friends."[50]

Populists hoped to defeat the "money powers" with the help of a political platform based on a controversial but surprisingly sophisticated economic program. Populists claimed that in the previous twenty-five years the nation's currency supply had dropped from forty to fifty dollars per capita to one-quarter that amount. The precipitous decline was not due to misfortune or miscalculation. Instead, it was a legacy of the "money trust," or a combination of bankers with "the power of expanding or contracting the currency" so that they could "raise or sink prices at pleasure."[51]

The key to the program was a stable currency that could not be manipulated by speculators, monopolists, and bankers. "Money must be stable over long periods of time," wrote the editor of the *Alliance Courier*, "not just from Saturday to Monday."[52] The solution was not the "free silver panacea or the gold standard." Instead, Populists argued for the principle of "fiat money." This meant that specie was simply a medium of exchange and had no intrinsic value (one Populist challenged doubters to drill five holes in a gold coin and a dollar bill and see which one the banker would accept).[53] The effect of their subtreasury plan, along with the other reflationary proposals, was to take control of the money supply from the corrupt bankers and give it to legally elected government officials.

John Simpson, a long-term president of the Farmers' Union, believed in some of the most radical of Populist principles and later became a very effective spokesman for the agrarian's monetary philosophy. According to Simpson:

> The only legitimate function of money is what we have described, a medium of exchange. . . .
> Men motivated by greed and avarice have found that money could be used to lend. This was the first diversion and perversion of the legitimate use of money. . . . Our latest grants of finance have further diverted the use of money by using it as a commodity in which they gamble. Interest was too slow for them. We have not solved the money problem until we destroy the interest system and stop gambling in money as a commodity.[54]

In an article entitled "An Honest Dollar," written in 1921, Simpson explained:

> An honest dollar is one that retains approximately the same purchasing power over a long period of time. A dishonest dollar is one which purchasing power fluctuates violently and during short

periods of time. The degree of fluctuation determines the degree of dishonesty in the dollar.[55]

Simpson later argued that the panic of 1919 was an excellent illustration of how capitalists manipulated the money supply. He explained that during World War I the U.S. Federal Reserve allowed the money supply to increase to a natural level. The result was that the bankers grew a "big crop of money," and the prices they received for their money dropped. The Federal Reserve then allowed bankers to destroy "bales of money."[56]

Populists were also concerned with the concentration of power in the hands of the great railroads and utilities. Consequently, nearly each issue of Populist papers published charts showing the cost of operating railroads and utilities in the United States and in other countries. These charts showed that nationalized railroads in Australia, Belgium, Hungary, and Germany provided better service than the privately owned American railroads and did so at lower cost. The papers also included elaborate charts comparing the quality of the American postal service to the quality of service provided by privately owned telegraph and telephone companies, invariably to the detriment of the American companies.[57]

Toward the end of the territorial period many Populists became disillusioned and began to reconsider socialism. They had previously been sympathetic to Socialist ideas, but they had been unwilling to take the great leap of faith. During the first decade of the twentieth century, however, large numbers of Populists endorsed socialism.

Even moderates in the Farmers' Union were reluctant to criticize socialism, as was illustrated in an article in the *Indiahoma Union Signal* advocating socialism because its essence was "cooperation not isolation." The writer explained his position:

> When the people really wish to try the socialist system they will find means to carry out their wishes just as they changed the feudal system and from the [illegible] system to the wage system, and now will change to the co-operative system.

What methods we shall take to get there will depend on the

evolution of ideas, but in this as in every other change "where there is a will there is a way." Socialist statesmanship must succeed capitalist politics. The wisdom of the people will evolve the methods by which the people shall come into their own.[58]

Even Farmers' Unionists who refused to endorse socialism occasionally adopted a charitable position toward it. Perhaps the most radical positions taken by the moderate *Union Signal* were expressed during the campaign of Pat Nagle, a former Grover Cleveland Democrat who later became a Socialist, for territorial representative. The editor of the *Union Signal* did not abandon his faith in cooperation, but he endorsed Nagle and then responded to a Socialist member of the Farmers' Union by acknowledging:

> I am well aware that the courts of law and all of our institutions are built upon the ownership of property and that the established order is opposed to workers.
> You may never see this socialism but you can help bring it about. If a voter understands true principles of cooperation it is a very easy matter for him to analyze political programs and to ally himself politically.[59]

Two weeks later the *Union Signal* printed a campaign statement by Pat Nagle which foreshadowed his switch to the Socialist Party:

> Every man must ally himself with one class or another. There is no middle ground. If we lose this fight our sons will curry their [upper-class people's] horses, our sons will oil their automobiles, our sons will hold their stirrups when they mount and they will tread on their backs and our sisters will go to hell.
> We must not look for relief to Presidents and Congresses. We must look to ourselves for relief. Every man in our class must enlist.[60]

Numerous other statements issued between 1905 and 1907 indicate that the contributors and readers of the *Union Signal* were on the verge of not only endorsing an anticapitalist position but also supporting a radical political solution. The editor would then pull back and call for a thorough moral reformation in a way that indicates that his call for a complete ethical reformation served as a substitute for a revolutionary political program. For instance, the editor wrote:

> The Farmers Union makes the claim that there is something radically wrong in our industrial and commercial world. When men, women, and children go hungry and poorly clothed in a country where overproduction is the cry half of the time, there must be something out of joint somewhere.[61]

A year later, in an article entitled "The Passing of Commercialism," he wrote:

> Commercialism has repudiated Christianity. It committed itself irretrievably to government by force, by navies, by standing armies, militia, armed secret service, police, and fighting and boycotting unions. Commerce is warfare pure and simple. It coins the dollars and demonitizes manhood.[62]

The editor also attacked the modern corporate system as "a vicious one" and he said that "we need to change it." Instead of endorsing an overtly revolutionary political program, however, he called for "cooperation." He then challenged farmers and workers to lead "pure" lives. Rather than placing the blame for cruelty and oppression in the world solely on the capitalists, he reminded his readers that "we are all robbers. Every one of us!" At that point it became clear that his righteous indignation might lead to a personal religious "leap of faith," but it did not lead to a revolutionary political ideology such as the populism of the alliance of Socialism.[63]

The *Ardmore Alliance Courier* editors and contributors, however, were bolder in their appraisals of socialism. These Populists replied to anti-Socialists by printing a major article entitled "Anarchy and Socialism: Not the Same but Exact Opposites." They argued that "Populists are opposed to anarchists but we are not opposed to socialism." They commented that "we are inclined to pronounce socialism as a force of the future, but reforms of this age may help the next generation to attend greater ones." They continued:

> The Declaration of Independence and the Omaha Platform contain probably as much socialism as will be realized in the next one hundred years. However, if the world should be converted to prac-

tical Christianity sooner than that, and render socialism possible, so much the better."[64]

Another article in the *Alliance Courier* presented an even more radical position:

> Has not capitalism held sway for half a century? Has not that system concentrated more of the wealth created by labor into the hands of a few in the last fifteen years than the monarchs of Europe in the last four hundred years? Is not the present starving condition of the masses due to that system? Socialism means that all special privileges shall be repealed. It means that all monopolies shall be abolished and their functions performed by the government and their benefits distributed to the children of the land without favoritism.[65]

Most of Oklahoma's agrarians stopped short of developing a truly revolutionary Socialist consciousness. In fact, it is doubtful that many of Oklahoma's Populists completely understood the revolutionary principles of the Farmers' Alliance. Oklahoma populism was always characterized by both a faith in a complete restructuring of society and doubts that it was possible to do more than reform an avaricious system. The defeat of the movement did not, however, dampen the dedication of many Oklahomans. The revolutionary side of frontier populism remained dormant for only two or three years before reappearing within the Socialist party.

PART TWO

The Closing of the Oklahoma Frontier, 1907–1916

We have given freely of our labor. Our talents have been put to work for the good of humankind around the world. But of the good things of life, we have not shared. We have been oppressed by the strong and powerful. We have lived in the midst of plenty but we have often gone hungry. By sweat and tears we have labored to make America great, free and noble.

—Ceremony of the Land

5

Southern and Eastern Oklahoma

LIFE in the Indian Nations during the late nineteenth century and in the Indian Territory in the first years of the twentieth century was difficult enough, but with statehood conditions worsened. Small farmers had been forced to contend with thin soil, boll weevils, unpredictable weather, chronic shortages of money, and arbitrary acts by landlords and merchants. After statehood they also had to face overpopulation, a growing soil-erosion problem, depression, and landlords and merchants who appeared to be greedier than ever. Consequently the percentage of landless farmers doubled from 1900 to 1910, and the conditions of the tenants became desperate.[1]

The first problem that confronted eastern and southern Oklahoma was overpopulation. Between 1890 and 1910 the population of Indian Territory increased from 180,182 to 783,800. A population density of 2 persons per square mile in 1890 increased to 11.4 in 1900 and to 23.9 in 1910. Although the average population density of the entire region was still less than the United States average (30.9 per square mile in 1910), by the second decade many areas were overcrowded. Approximately one-fifth of eastern Oklahoma was either too hilly or too heavily forested to support an agricultural community. For instance, in 1910 only 10 percent of hilly Latimer County was farmland, but its population was 11,321 (up from 9,340 in 1907). Moreover, nearly 40 percent of the land of the old Indian Nations was involved in title disputes which kept the land partially or entirely out of production. Consequently, only 30 percent of the land in eastern Oklahoma was farmland. At the same time 90 percent or more of the land in several western counties was in production.[2]

By statehood many of the old cotton-growing areas were full, and a modest out-migration had begun. From 1900 to 1910 population decreased in six counties in the old Chickasaw Nation.

Population growth was in the town, but the population of the farming regions remained static. For instance, in Marshall County the urban population increased by 260 percent. By 1910 one-third of the county lived in towns of 2,500 or more. The county's rural population, however, increased by only 91 percent. Moreover, the poorest and most isolated farmland showed the sharpest decrease as an estimated 500 tenants left the county between 1914 and 1916.

The phenomenon that produced the massive in- and out-migrations was cotton production. From 1907 to 1914 the price of cotton rose, while the incidence of the boll weevil decreased, and hundreds of thousands of acres of Indian land were opened for production. This increased cotton productivity did not, however, bring any more prosperity to white tenants than the cotton boom of the 1870s and 1880s had brought to the small Indian farmer. Tenants who worked newly opened land faced the same frontier conditions encountered by pioneers in the early 1890s. They were rarely able to produce on a scale necessary to support a family.[3]

Tenant farmers who lived in settled counties faced even worse conditions. Forty years of erosion and single-crop agriculture had damaged the soil to the point that land that had once produced one to one and a half bales an acre now produced from one-half to one-third bale. Henry Everidge recalled that on many upland fields in Choctaw County, where for seven decades the land had been abused, it might take seven or eight acres to produce a bale.[4]

One articulate farmer who was forced to leave the black soil of east Texas for southeastern Oklahoma described the destruction of the region's farmland. Initially he was pleasantly surprised by the sandy soil. "At first, I had no trouble getting ¾ to 1 bale an acre," he wrote. A few years later the tenant lamented that "the

lands that did not wash away are blown away. Most pioneer
settlers have left this section of the state, some renting out and
some have moved out because their farms have washed out in
ditches so that cropping was unprofitable." The tenant concluded, "There has been too many butchers of the soil here."[5]

The third problem that undermined the economy of eastern
and southern Oklahoma was that the coal-mining and timber industries stagnated from statehood to the beginning of World War I.
Coal mining had never been an unmixed blessing, but the down-
turn in mining activity placed a severe burden on citizens who
had to provide basic services and relief to underemployed miners
and their families. Coal production peaked in 1907 with an annual output of 3 million tons and then slowly declined to less
than 2 million tons in 1915. During that period 6,000 to 8,000
miners were continually underemployed. From 1910 to 1915 the
average miner in eastern Oklahoma worked 213 days a year in
contrast to a nationwide average of 245 working days.[6]

At the same time the timber industry was disrupted by the
chaos that accompanied the transition from Indian to United
States government control. There was confusion over ownership
of the timberlands. The United States government scheduled
auctions of timberlands for 1910, 1911, and 1912, but each time
either the sale was cancelled or the results of the bidding were
nullified by the U.S. Department of the Interior. As a result timber companies delayed most of their aboveboard operations until
1915, when the land was finally made available for lease. Unfortunately, however, the federal government was unable to deter
large timber companies from buying thousands of acres at what
Victor Harlow concluded were "bargain rates."[7]

Confusion over the ownership of lands also prevented investment in other business activities necessary for a smooth-working
economy. Early in the second decade of the twentieth century
boosters in Ardmore and Madill had ambitious plans for building
cotton-oil mills, a broom factory, and a textile factory, but their
plans were based on the hope that white investors could buy land
from its Indian owners. In 1912, however, the United States Su-

Students chopping wood at Euchee Mission, Sapulpa. Courtesy of Western History Collections, University of Oklahoma Library.

preme Court ruled in favor of government regulations prohibiting the sale of allotments by fullblood Indians.[8] In the long run those regulations were probably good for the Indians, but the short-term effect on pre–World War I Oklahoma was disastrous. Since there was little opportunity for investment in reputable business activity, speculation and criminality continued to be inordinately significant sectors of the economy.

The key legacy of the failure of eastern Oklahoma to develop a commercial sector was that the region continued to lack capital and a banking system to disperse it. Scales has explained that "banks" in early Oklahoma did not conform to the contemporary notion of a bank. They certainly were not stable financial institutions. In 1907 when the state bank examiner attempted to audit the books of the seven thousand Oklahoma federal and state banks, he could not find a number of them. Especially in the eastern part of the state banks closed frequently and moved to new locations without even notifying the state banking commission.[9]

In 1914, Carl Williams, editor of the *Farmer-Stockman* (Oklahoma City), undertook a study of problems in the state's banking

system and concluded that most of the state's small financial institutions should not even be called banks and that they should
consolidate into concerns that had a chance of becoming durable
agents for distributing money. Williams noted that the typical
bank had a cashier with a salary of $100 a week and an assistant
with a salary of $75 a week. Williams noted that, even without
the cost of rent and maintenance of the bank building, the two
salaries created an overhead far beyond the means of the great
majority of rural banks. Williams calculated that the typical bank
had only $10,000 in capital and thus faced an impossible goal of
loaning $45,000 a year while keeping the interest rate at 10 per-
cent.[10] For example, a town had three banks with the combined
capital of $60,000 and deposits of $25,000. Because the banks
needed three buildings and three staffs of employees, they were
forced to charge an average of 14 percent interest on loans. If the
three banks would merge, wrote Williams, they could afford to
lend money at 8 percent interest.[11]

High overhead, ignorance, a shortage of money, and the risky
nature of banking on the frontier all contributed to the problem,
but another more insidious factor was also at work. Williams was
slow to blame bankers for usury, but by 1912 the evidence was
changing his outlook. "I am not writing this to stir up sentiment
against the banker, there is enough of that already—" wrote
Williams, as he began an article on usury in Roger Mills County,
in far-western Oklahoma. The lack of capital was not a problem,
for Roger Mills was a relatively wealthy county. Williams noted
that the combined wealth of its top 115 citizens came to over a
million dollars but that most of the county's farmers endured usu-
rious interest rates. Even in prosperous counties interest rates
ranged from 12 to 60 percent, and the average was 25 percent.[12]

Possibly the most crucial reason for high interest rates was that
bankers chose to make quick profits from usury rather than attempt to assist in the development of durable farms and businesses. One banker issued 118 notes and charged short-term rates
ranging from 50 to 2,000 percent. He justified his rates by saying
that loans to farmers were risky. The bank commissioner discov-

ered, however, that this particular bank had lost only $6,000 in fifteen years. During the same period the bank's stock had paid dividends of 700 percent.

Oklahomans became aware of the magnitude of the usury problem when an extensive study of the nation's banking procedures was issued. Carl Williams reported the findings of the study:

> We have known for a long time that the banking business in Oklahoma and Texas is a good business but we have never known how good. Now we know. John Skelton, controller of the currency in Washington, speaking at the Kentucky Banking Association, reported that 1,022 National banks out of a total of 7,615 admitted to receiving more than 10% interest.[13]

Williams reported that 317 Texas banks and 300 of the 350 banks in Oklahoma charged interest on loans in excess of 10 percent. A total of 131 Oklahoma banks charged between 15 and 25 percent interest, 67 banks charged between 25 and 60 percent, and 22 banks charged between 100 and 200 percent. Eight banks charged between 200 and 2,000 percent.

Not surprisingly, the worst offenders were in eastern Oklahoma. In the west only the banks in El Reno, which charged 35 percent interest, and Oklahoma City, which charged 48 percent, were on Williams' list of banks that charged an average interest in excess of 30 percent. In the former Indian Territory, however, the following towns and interest rates were listed: Shawnee (30 percent), Nowata (31 percent), Pryor (32 percent), Claremore (37 percent), Vinita (36 percent), and Tulsa (one bank, 32 percent; another, 42 percent).[14]

Oklahoma farmers were willing to pay exorbitant rates to bankers because local merchants charged even higher interest. One banker wrote to Williams protesting proposed usury legislation and telling about a young man who wanted to borrow $285 from his bank for a team of mules. He knew that the man "was a good risk but that he could not pay $285 plus our 'exorbitant' rate of $30. Consequently, he bought it for $330 from a short-term merchant." The banker knew of four similar incidents.[15]

Another banker offered a self-serving but accurate description of the merchant finance system:

For many years it has been the custom of the western farmer to
go to his bank in the spring and make arrangements to buy his
year's supplies on full-time. . . .
   [The] farmer transacts nearly all of his other business with his
merchant even going to him for cash loans and he has very little
occasion to do business with the bank. As the result he knows
nothing of banking methods, . . and he misses many opportunities that would help him in many ways.[16]

The banker further bemoaned that the banks received the blame
for the merchants' exorbitant prices because the merchants said
that the bankers were pressing them.

   The people who suffered the most from the lack of investment
money and stable banks were the farmers. Farmers with the resources to raise vegetables, poultry, livestock, and broomcorn
could make profits. Unfortunately, however, it cost a large amount
of money to diversify. First the farmer would have to finance the
building of a barn, a henhouse, a silo, and fences. Then the community would have to finance roads to bring his produce to town
and buildings for storage and selling the crops. The task was so
enormous that businessmen and farmers usually did not even attempt it.

   In Marshall County little effort was expended in modernizing
agriculture; the 25 percent of the county residents who lived in
town owned $2,122,580 of the $2,859,546 of real property in the
county. As the result nearly all Oklahoma farms on the eve of
World War I participated in the same single-crop sharecropper
system which had impoverished the Reconstruction South.[17]

   Before 1912, Williams saw ignorance as the prime reason why
Oklahoma was impoverished by single-crop tenancy. He continually admonished landlords to teach their tenants how to diversify.
Williams would constantly "preach the gospel of raising a dairy
cow, brood sows, and hens."[18] In an editorial entitled "Forcing
Farmers to Make Money," Williams revealed his paternalistic attitude. He wrote about Fred Delancy, cashier of the First National Bank of Tulsa, who had 1,000 acres to rent. Delancy advertised for tenants and found out that, of those who replied,
"most wanted to gamble." Delancy, however, wisely decided to

accept "only those who would raise kaffir," and they made a substantial profit for all concerned.[19]

As the result of an exceptionally stimulating exchange, however, Williams eventually changed his mind. Williams' *Farmer-
Stockman* ran a popular series in which farmers wrote about their
worst blunders. Most of the letters were from landowners who had
lost profits by plowing too late or planting too much cotton or
because of recalcitrant tenants. However, the *Farmer-Stockman*
published a letter from a tenant whose worst blunder had been to
select the wrong landlord, who made him plant only cotton.
This letter sparked a two-year exchange in which the concerns of
both landlords and the most isolated tenants were revealed with
remarkable clarity.

Another tenant who chose the wrong landlord wrote as follows:

> The bankers, the commercial clubs and the farm papers tell us
> to raise livestock, build silos and don't sell our grain. . . . [The
> facts were] that we can't pasture our stock. Should we buy expen-
> sive wire and build silos when we can stay but a year? Shall we
> build a silo for 3 or 4 cows? . . .
>
> I know there is money in cows and poultry. If it had not been
> for 3 cows and a hundred hens we would have been mighty poor
> last year. I have always tried to make something for the landlord,
> as well as for myself. . . . I worked from 4 o'clock in the morning
> to 9 o'clock at night.[20]

Immediately after the letter was published, the *Farmer-
Stockman* received many letters from tenant farmers with the
same problem. The tenants were clearly uneducated and uneasy
at the prospect of writing a letter. At first Williams was uncomfortable about publishing the crude correspondence, and he
explained that he would not print any unsigned or unduly inflammatory letters. Williams wrote, however, that landowners needed
to listen to the tenants and then encouraged tenants to speak
their minds.

Three letters were especially illustrative. A tenant from Kingfisher, who was later attacked by corresponding tenants for being
too sympathetic to the landlord, detailed his experience. The

Kingfisher tenant was apparently more affluent than the average tenant; when he started in 1910, he had just been married, and he already owned two cows, four horses, a hog, and a few tools. The first year he raised a "good crop," and he was able to buy two more cows and more tools. The landlord sold the farm, however, and he had to move. The next year's crop was destroyed by drought, and he "lost everything except 180 bushels of kaffir." Again, he had to move. Fortunately he was able to keep the cows and the sow. In 1912, however, he "went broke and lost everything."[21]

A tenant from Okfuskee who had experienced equally bad luck blamed landlords and high interest rates for the single-crop tenantry system: "I am a small farmer and a renter in Okfuskee County where you can hardly rent enough land to plant feed stock. . . . Everything is cotton. I would like to know how a farmer is going to raise stock when the whole county is cotton?"[22]

Another tenant illustrated the process by which renters were forced to grow cotton: "Out of five leases I have had, I have dictated one clause in a contract. . . . My present landlord's exact words were "I have the contract written out over at the office. You can read it and sign it or leave it alone."[23] The tenant also complained that he was required to have "a limit of 10 head of stock" and that he was required to "move out one day after harvest."

The tenants recognized that the single-crop system was wasteful, but they claimed that they were powerless to change things. One tenant wrote that he "hauls manure, repairs fences and stops all washes" but that the land continued to decline. Another wrote that he wanted to improve his land but that he lacked the money. He argued that "if the landlord would spend $250 he would get his money back and the tenants could make out."[24]

Through the months a few more successful tenants and one landlord wrote that it was the slovenliness of tenants which produced the wasteful situation. They argued that tenants refused to take five-year leases because they preferred to live in squalor for a year and then move to a new shack.[25] Other tenants replied that landlords and successful tenants were greedy. At that the tone of the exchange temporarily degenerated. A landlord wrote that incompetent tenants had put him on the verge of insolvency. A tenant replied by calling the landlord a "sorehead."[26]

The debate became humorous when a tenant blamed poverty on a lack of Christian morality. He explained that "contracts are for rascals and for slothful men. No law hurts an honest man. What we need more than any other thing is more real religion in our papers, on our farms, and in the hearts of men."[27] His letter was answered by a witty tenant who attributed poverty to an excess of "Christian morality."

The largest number of tenants blamed the landlords for the problems, and several of them offered suggestions. A tenant from Kiowa County said that "the tenant owns the land. The landlord only skins the tenant." He argued that no man should be allowed to own more than 320 acres. A tenant from McIntosh County suggested a one-dollar tax for every acre over 160 acres and a two-dollar tax for every acre over 320 acres.[28]

The tenant from Kingfisher who went broke after two years concluded his letter by asserting that someday he would get back on his feet. His attitude prompted a couple of exceptionally vitriolic attacks on landlords. One tenant wrote:

> The renter from Kingfisher seems to have great sympathy for the landlord. Let me say here and now that most of the renters have no use for the landlords and they want to own a home. . . .
> Landlords create poverty, crime and tyranny. . . .
> . . . little old shack, no screens on their doors, flies and filth everywhere. Not one in ten have a cow and very few had a pig.
> Children can't go to school. The teacher in this area has only two long-term students. . . .
> Now I don't believe in the total depravity of the human race. . . . I believe it is better to build a home than to erect a church.
> A. S. Bryan says that the landlords are not responsible for our being renters. If they are not, who is? I know one who owns 916 sections of land.[29]

A second tenant wrote:

> No man can make money except through robbery.
> Statistics show us that no man can become rich by honest labor.

They [the poor farmers and their families] work while daylight
lasts in a never ending struggle to build a farm. . . . reasonable
work yes but you tell me why a man should pay rent for land when
the air is free. The same Maker made them both.[30]

Two more prosperous and less angry tenants also blamed landlords. They argued, however, that if landlords would allow minor
adjustments in the system poverty would disappear. J. K. Henry,
of Hughes county, said that cash rental was the solution. He was
a renter for twenty years. Then he "got a chance to rent for
cash." Finally he owned land and was able to negotiate as an
equal with his merchant. "Most of my neighbors buy at 18% to
40% interest," said Henry, "but I get 10%."[31]

Another farmer from Seminole counseled, "Don't undercut
ambition" but take steps to "end speculation." The solution, he
said, was long-term leases: "I know several men who were not
worth a cent when they took such leases [five-year leases] but
after 5 years they owned 3 or 4 farms of their own and went right
on and up financially."[32]

After nearly eighteen months of such exchanges the situation
was clarified by an exceptionally helpful letter from a landlord
who wished to remain anonymous. The landlord addressed the
main issues that had baffled Williams and his contributors:

We are land poor and we want to make a profit and taxes are
increasing. . . . it is true land has increased in value but that
doesn't help us unless we sell it and we do sell it when we get a
good offer, so we can't tie up land in long leases.

My contract says that in event of sale the tenant must vacate
immediately in return for just payment.

I don't try to excuse that condition. It is bad for the tenant and
bad for the land. But we must protect our investment, which
means we must sell when we can. . . .

In other words—and here I get to the discussion of another
point—the average tenant does not produce enough income for
the landlord or himself to justify us in keeping him on the land.
We lease to tenants in many cases, merely because we want to get
something from the land to help us pay the expenses of keeping it
until we sell it.

We are not always this arbitrary. For instance, if I find a tenant who is a really good farmer and who shows that he can produce a real profit from his farm I usually meet him more than half way.

But we don't often find such tenants, which is one reason why most of us are obliged to sell when we can. I have had more than 200 tenants on my farms in the last 10 years and I can count on the fingers of my both hands all of the really good farmers among them.

I have tried the five year lease on new men and I found that it doesn't pay. The average farmer is a "skinner of the land." I have known a tenant to sign a lease and a mortgage on a prospective cotton crop and then move out between days before ever turning a farrow.

Then there are the incapables. . . . One man successfully turned 80 acres so I leased him 200. I bought him livestock and a house but he spread himself over the whole 200 acres, neglected the livestock and his crop failed entirely. He is an 80 acre man. . . .

. . . five times last year I have bought tenants animals and had to take them away because they didn't care for them.[33]

The landlord's letter demonstrated that the problems with cotton agriculture were more fundamental than poor farming methods. The problem was that, as the tenants said, the most profitable industry in eastern Oklahoma was not "farming the soil" but "farming the farmers." The problem was that the real estate business was not a spin-off from agriculture but that farming was a subsidiary to the real estate business. The effort toward diversification was aimed at a symptom of the ailment. The central problem was that the region lacked the money and the expertise to create a durable agricultural economy and as a result local entrepreneurs concentrated on making money and ignored the possibility of making money from the production and sale of agricultural products.[34]

Even if improved methods of agricultural production were adopted, Oklahoma farmers also needed to be better integrated into the market system. Especially in the southeast small farmers and tenants were both psychologically and physically isolated from the market. After facing a difficult journey to town, the farmer was forced to sell in a fixed market. Even though a cotton center might have several cotton buyers, there was no competition between buyers for the farmers' goods.

Carl Williams wrote an exposé on one county in south-central Oklahoma which he said was typical of most cotton centers. He found that despite the existence of twenty-seven gins there was no competition for the farmers' cotton. The citizens had once tried to form a cooperative, but it collapsed when private buyers would not purchase its cotton and bankers would not loan it money. Consequently, farmers were completely at the mercy of the ginners.[35]

The farmer did not even have a sure way of gaining information on prices and market opportunities. For instance, in 1914, Grady County buyers told farmers that they could pay only $10 for cottonseed because it sold for only $22 in Europe. Later the state corporation commission reported that it actually sold for $32 in Europe and that the farmers should have received $20.[36]

Even when farmers were aware that they were being cheated, they had no alternative but to take what was offered. The lack of roads made it impossible for a farmer to try to take his crop to another buyer. The farmers were so vulnerable that they could not even expect their produce to be accurately weighed. The *Farmer-Stockman* reported that the state's cotton farmers lost one to five dollars a year per bale on an estimated million bales of cotton owing to inaccurate scales.[37]

In retrospect it is clear that Williams's faith in diversification was naïve. Southeastern Oklahoma lacked both the transportation system and the marketing institutions necessary for a diversified agricultural system. In 1910 the lack of roads was described by Campbell Russell, a conservative member of the Oklahoma Corporation Commission, as a severe hindrance to the growth of a rational economy. Russell said that one logical solution to the problems of a cotton region which had the potential to produce vegetables also was to attract vegetable canning plants and mattress factories. This was impossible, however, until a system of roads was built. He argued that unless a farmer lived within eight to ten miles of a road or railroad the only practical crop was cotton. Unfortunately, however, he added, "The average farmer in the Indian Territory is fifteen miles from a railroad."[38]

Some Oklahomans took the advice of experts and experimented with diversification, but their results were usually disastrous. In a country without roads, storage facilities, and a reliable market the closest thing to a safe crop was cotton. It was better to take ten cents a pound and then move to another farm than to risk complete failure. Henry Everidge remembers when "those Chamber of Commerce fellows" called a meeting and encouraged tenants in Choctaw County to plant tomatoes. Henry's father spoke against the proposal. Mr. Everidge said that he could grow anything they wanted but first he wanted to know if there would be a market. Everidge remained skeptical and planted cotton. Most tenants, however, followed the urging of the townspeople. They produced a great crop but the "market" did not materialize, and the tomatoes rotted in the fields.[39]

George Milburn portrayed the pitfalls of diversification in the hilarious short story "Garlic." Tom Proctor was an ambitious farmer who accepted the advice of the farm agents. The rest of the farmers resented Tom's initiative and his success. He had come to Oklahoma as a poor tenant "without a pan to wash in or a window to throw the water out," but he had diversified, saved, and bought sixty acres of bottomland. One year he decided to plant garlic. "I've been reading the market quotations," said Tom, "where garlic brings twenty-five cents a pound. . . . You watch me. I'll make plenty. I ain't like these ignorant Arkansawyers around here. I'm a diversified farmer." When asked where he would sell the garlic, Tom replied, "All these chili joints use garlic. They sell lots of garlic to dagos in big places like Kansas City and Chicago. I've done looked into that."

Tom produced an excellent crop. A month before harvest he began writing to commission houses. Tom was able to sell only five hundred pounds of garlic, however, and he had to store the rest. In a hilarious ending to the story Milburn explained that Tom stored the rest in the barn but it was ruined by the weather. Townspeople five miles away could smell his crop. In the end neighbors taunted him, saying that the sound of gas gurgling from the rotting garlic could be heard for a quarter of a mile.[40]

By the eve of World War I almost all the renters were desperate. The region showed little sign of modernization, and the cruelty of the tenantry system had not lessened. In fact, difficult economic conditions tended to force landlords and merchants into expropriating progressively larger sums. Consequently the itinerant farmers of southeastern Oklahoma began abandoning their homes at an accelerated rate. Most of their treks were still moves from one farm to another within the same county. During the second decade of the century, however, larger areas of over-worked and eroded land were rendered completely useless, and many more farmers were forced to abandon the entire region.[41]

6

Northern and Western Oklahoma

As we have seen, the frontier experience of the northern and western prairie differed sharply from that of the southern and eastern hill country. The agriculture of the plains soon grew into a modern, productive, and fairly stable business. The mineral resources in the west and north were developed in a manner that allowed Oklahomans, not just eastern corporations, to benefit from the wealth. Finally, the success of the prairie farms and oil-related businesses attracted to the towns and cities talented entrepreneurs who assisted in the growth of a diversified economy.

The experience of the western frontier followed the outlines of the Great Frontier paradigm more closely than did the experience in southeastern Oklahoma. Although the destitution and the hopelessness that characterized the east and south contrasted with the dominant themes of the frontier myth—that pioneers were aggressive, innovative, optimistic, and successful contestants—the experience of the plainsmen to a large degree conformed to the Great Frontier. Small farmers and townspeople endured great hardships as they homesteaded the prairie. Those who survived the pioneer experience adjusted to their new conditions and developed stability. Most remained poor, but they were not hopelessly destitute, and by expanding the size of their farms, building roads, and marketing, they met with a degree of success.[1]

From 1907 to 1910 wheat agriculture grew at a steady rate. The development of the wheat economy required a degree of social and political reorganization. One example of economic planning was the solution of the harvest labor problems. More labor was required to grow wheat than could be supported on the land year round. The most reliable solution to farm labor shortages was the use of migratory harvest workers. Migratory workers began on the southern border of the Oklahoma wheatlands and followed the ripening wheat north to Canada. This system required a good deal of coordination and communication among counties and states. If the harvesters arrived late, the crop would be damaged, and if they arrived early, the wheat community could not afford to feed and house them.[2]

As the wheat crop and the number of harvest hands increased, the timing became more critical and more difficult. In 1912 and 1913 the surpluses of workers prompted rioting in several communities. Fortunately for the wheat economy, the state government proved to be responsive to the needs of small landowners. The state government encouraged the railroads to provide a better-organized system of transporting workers. It also established a communication network which publicized the numbers of harvesters available in Louisiana, Texas, and Oklahoma and the size of the crops in different areas of Oklahoma. Moreover, the International Workers of the World (IWW) became active among harvest workers, and this motivated state officials to assist harvesters by giving them a precise schedule of the ripening of the wheat.[3]

In contrast to the premarket south, where coal and timber companies conducted their business without the assistance of local residents, government officials and railroad men recognized the need for a stable farm population. Since the west did not have enough natural resources to support the railroads, they had to assist the growth of wheat agriculture if their lines were to make a profit. Consequently, when drought or market conditions threatened settlers, the railroads offered assistance. During 1908 and 1909 railroads offered low-interest loans to farmers threatened by the depression. Evidently the program was successful because an estimated 95 percent repaid their debts. Then in 1911 the west suffered a serious drought that foreshadowed the dust bowl of the 1930s. The state provided relief supplies that enabled the farmers to survive. For several weeks proud farmers went hungry rather than take charity. Eventually, however, families began collecting supplies in the middle of the night to avoid the humiliation.[4]

It should be noted that much of the suffering that accompanied the closing of the frontier was unnecessary. The pioneer capitalists who guided the development of the plains were in too much of a hurry to worry about the public's welfare. The result was frequent disasters such as the collapse of the railroad bridge over the Cimarron River at Dover. More than a hundred persons were killed in that tragedy (the total number of victims was never established). Subsequent investigation determined that the bridge rested on the shifting sands of the river. The railroad had not bothered to lay a foundation.[5]

Perhaps the best illustration of the dynamics of the Great Frontier was the opening and closing of the oilman's frontier. The economy of the Western world appeared to demand production of large quantities of petroleum as quickly as possible, and oilmen responded enthusiastically. Oklahoma's reserves could not have been exploited in such a few years except by daring, resourceful, and often ruthless frontiersmen.[6] The brutal, individualistic, unrestrained oil frontier survived for only a few years. Oilmen also had to deal with less dramatic economic obstacles. For example, the singleminded determination that impelled a wildcatter to gamble everything on a promising hole was useless when he was forced to deal with Standard Oil or J. P. Morgan. The oil pioneers may have needed an independent spirit and an intuitive grasp of geology and mechanics, but it took a willingness to conform and a knowledge of finance to establish a petroleum industry. Consequently the influence of the flamboyant gambler quickly diminished, to be replaced by that of businessmen capable of conforming to the demands of the corporate system, adjusting to the new situation, deferring to the wishes of eastern and European powers, and yet guiding the development of a fairly independent domestic oil industry.

The economic development of western Oklahoma shows that the conquest of the frontier depended on the development of rational business procedures as well as sturdy pioneers. The development of the frontier required private strength of character necessary to survive on the lonely prairie and entrepreneurs to coordinate the plains economy. The settlement of western Oklahoma was successful because it attracted both pioneer farmers, ranchers, and businessmen with the expertise necessary to attract resources from outside power centers. Fortunately, western commercial enterprises were able to attract capital and technology.[7] Moreover, political and social leaders were able to obtain assistance for farmers facing marketing difficulties and bad harvests. The result was that western farming and industrial efforts quickly cohered into a fairly diversified and complex set of institutionalized economic processes.

Oklahoma entered into its second major oil boom in 1911 with strikes near Cushing, in northern Oklahoma, and Healdton, in the south-central portion of the state. The Cushing field was the larger and more profitable of the two. During the first year production from the field reached 174,000 barrels a day, while Healdton peaked at 80,000 barrels a day. Since Cushing was near the center of the state's oil industry, its producers had easy access to pipelines, refineries, and financial institutions. Moreover, Cushing was developed by some of the most powerful and talented oilmen in Oklahoma, men such as Tom Slick and Harry Sinclair. Consequently, its production was assisted by excellent financing and the finest petroleum expertise in the world.[8]

The Healdton field, however, was known as a "poor man's oil field." It was isolated from conventional transportation systems— roads and railroads—and from the pipeline system. Moreover, Healdton's oil was a heavy crude, which was more difficult to refine and brought a lower price. Healdton thus attracted smaller independents who were in precarious economic circumstances. Consequently, the history of the Healdton field was similar to that of the Glenn field, or even of coal mining, rather than that of the Cushing field. In contrast to the bonanza in the northern field, Healdton was developed by vulnerable wildcatters who made profits in good times but were at the mercy of large corporate powers in the East and in Tulsa, Bartlesville, and Ponca City.[9]

When oil was first discovered in 1914, the price was $1.15 a barrel, but within a few weeks it had dropped to $0.75 a barrel. Large Cushing producers made a profit at that price, but the independents at Healdton found themselves losing a million dollars a month. Within a year a million barrels were in storage in Cushing, and prices had dropped to $0.25, and yet production still did not slow. By 1915 pipelines could accommodate only 14 percent of the oil being produced.[10]

R. W. McClintock, former press secretary to Oklahoma's Governor Raymond Gary, wrote a history of the Oklahoma oil fields. He described the problems face by independents and producers in small and isolated fields:

> It was, as usual, the small producer, rather than the big corporations in the Healdton and Cushing fields, who were the chief sufferers from low prices. The bigger the wells, of course, the less the cost of production per barrel and the cheaper the producer could afford to sell. Moreover, the decision to take only 50% of the oil often hurt the small man more than the big producer.[11]

Small producers throughout the state and independents in Healdton tried to organize a program to restrict production and prevent coercion by the large companies. In 1914 a gentlemen's agreement was reached. Attorney General Charles West agreed to cooperate by not enforcing antitrust laws, and the Oklahoma Corporation Commission banned the drilling of any new wells except offsets (wells drilled next to an existing hole to relieve pressure). It was also agreed that pipelines were to accept only one-half of the oil offered by each drilling company.[12]

The program initially had some success, but mistrust, greed, disorganization, and shortsightedness soon defeated it. In the fall of 1914, 156 wells were drilled, "all offsets, of course," and production returned to normal. Prices dropped again, and frustrated oilmen responded with a futile demand that the militia be called out to curtail production.[13]

The Corporation Commission proved as impotent as the producers' association. McClintock explained that theoretically the commission had power to control production but that the Corporation Commission did nothing. It was in a hot spot. It would be damned if it sought to restrict oil just as it was by small producers for failing to do so. It was quite likely the public generally would object to restriction for the 3% oil tax was becoming a large item in the state revenue. And finally, there was a grave doubt as to whether the new regulatory powers granted the Commission were constitutional; and the Commissioner wished to delay a court test until public sentiment was more friendly.

McClintock explained that the commission could not even depend on the support of the Oklahoma oilmen:

> But though oilmen wanted this measure made effective, there was fear lest state regulation might extend too far. Sellers of equipment, naturally, did not want to lend aid to a plan that would have reduced the amount of equipment sold. Landowners generally feared that if there were a decrease in drilling then royalties would be hurt.[14]

Much of the blame, however, must be attributed to Standard Oil and its subsidiary, Prairie Oil and Gas. For instance, it was Standard that first breached the Corporation Commission's prorated program. Local companies welcomed the plan, and Gulf Oil agreed to abide by it. Prairie, however, refused to purchase crude from drillers at the agreed price and continued to buy at low prices in a glutted market. Prairie then held its oil in storage until a shortage was created, when Prairie sold at artificially high prices.[15]

The biggest confrontation between Prairie and the Corporation Commission occurred in 1916. The commission set a $0.75 minimum price, and Prairie responded by setting a $0.65 price. Then the Corporation Commission set a $0.65 minimum. On the same day, however, Prairie lowered its price to $0.55. A few days later it stopped buying oil at any price. Prairie then resumed buying when producers accepted a low price of $.50. The result was that Prairie stored 200,000 barrels that were worth $100,000. A month later the price war ended, and the same oil tripled in value.[16]

McClintock summarized the dynamics of the cycle:

There was of course no excuse whatsoever for a price of 40¢ in February and of $1.20 in December of the same year. There seems no questions that the big interests in the North, the oil and pipe-line industries, and on Wall Street, had held prices artificially low as long as they could possibly do so, in order to secure at low prices as much oil and as many oil properties as they could extort from distressed owners. And then, with a large proportion of the nation's visible supply in their possession, it was in their interest to boost prices.[17]

Although regulations failed to deter Prairie, the more successful Oklahoma oilmen copied Standard's methods and managed to break its monopoly by establishing a domestic oil industry. In 1912 Prairie's control of the pipelines was weakened when the state legislature declared all oil-and-gas lines to be a public utility and a common carrier. Moreover, in 1915, Gulf Oil agreed to build a pipeline to the Gulf of Mexico. Then E. W. Marland built a refinery in Kay County, and Josh Cosden, another Oklahoman, built a refinery in Cushing. The big victory for Oklahoma wildcatters came in 1916, when Harry Sinclair defeated Standard in a price war. Sinclair copied Prairie's tactics and accumulated a large amount of oil when prices were low. He held it in storage until an oil shortage tripled its value. Sinclair then invested his earnings in refineries, pipelines, and banks and thus established a competitive set of marketing and processing systems.[18]

Once Oklahomans broke Standard's monopoly and built their own pipelines, refineries, and marketing centers, a system evolved in which small independents and the major oil companies could coexist. Small wildcatters continued to compete with larger companies in big fields. If a smaller company found oil in a big field, it would usually sell its lease and either buy into an operation in a less congested area or use the proceeds to search for more oil. The arrangement created a democratic and flexible system which benefited all kinds of operations. It meant that the small businessman and even the talented oil-field worker were not excluded. It also meant that larger companies gained from the skills of small entrepreneurs who proved to be the most effective prospectors.[19]

Wildcatters financed their wells in one of three ways. The first method was the use of "dry-hole money," loans advanced by big companies to small drillers. For example, Marland got his start on loans from Standard and the Kay County Gas Company. Large companies realized that, even if the driller went bankrupt, the geological knowledge gained from his drilling was easily worth a few thousand dollars and that if he struck oil everyone would prosper. A wildcatter could also gain financing by selling a certain percentage of his operation to one of the large companies. The third method was to turn to foreign help and obtain a loan from Dutch Shell.[20]

The economic effect of a domestic oil industry was profound. The economy of the northern plains from Osage County to Enid and the southwestern plains from Ardmore to Burkburnett, Texas, was stimulated by the influx of lease money; oil sales; wages for oil-field workers and teamsters; construction of drilling rigs, pipelines, refineries, housing, roads and offices; and oil proceeds, which were invested in farms and businesses.

The biggest effect of petroleum-generated capital was that it allowed the establishment of a banking system in northern Oklahoma. The most prosperous oilmen, Harry Sinclair, William Skelly, the Phillips brothers, and Lew Wentz, invested heavily in banks.

It is problematical whether or not the wealth from petroleum directly benefited the poorest farmers and laborers. Most oilmen's profits were invested in urban areas. The oil-inspired growth of cities, however, gave jobs to farmers who were abandoning overpopulated land for the cities. Moreover, the growth of towns created a market for small produce and thus allowed the diversification of agriculture.[21]

The dynamics of the successful development of the prairie were revealed in miniature in Osage County. The county was first used solely for cattle grazing. The blizzard of 1878, however, killed tens of thousands of cattle and bankrupted the region's economy. George Miller, the owner of the now famous 101 Ranch, refused to abandon his land. Miller thoroughly considered both the natural potential of the land and financial and market conditions, and then he developed a strategy which proved to be successful for both the county and the rest of the state's prairie. Miller recruited dozens of the best farmers, cowhands, and agricultural experts and a "gambling" petroleum engineer to help establish a diversified ranch. His farmers and agricultural experts discovered the best methods for growing wheat, and they also introduced kafir, corn, alfalfa, and fruit trees. His cowhands improved stock-handling methods and rebuilt the herd to a manageable level. Miller's petroleum engineer discovered oil and established an integrated drilling, refining, and marketing company. The result was that Osage County developed a mixed agricultural and mineral economy which could outlast both natural disasters and market difficulties.[22]

There were two keys to the success of the 101 Ranch. The first was the talents of its operators. The oldest son, Joe Miller, was an outstanding farmer who introduced the most recent scientific agricultural methods to the ranch. The second son, Zack, was a cattleman who brought similar innovations to beef raising and dairy farming. The third son, George L., was a financier who attracted the eastern capital necessary to pay for the modernization of the ranch.[23]

The 101 Ranch demonstrated the economic potential of the dry wheat belt when it was managed by knowledgeable, skilled, well-financed farmers. An unwary farmer had no chance of surviving in these marginal lands. Even the enormous oil reserves were of questionable value to a person who did not understand promotion, marketing, and investment procedures. The skills of the Miller brothers, their willingness to attract outside expertise, and the area's mineral resources allowed the area to prosper and modernize.[24]

The second key was the discovery of oil on the ranch. The brothers recognized the potential of oil production and helped

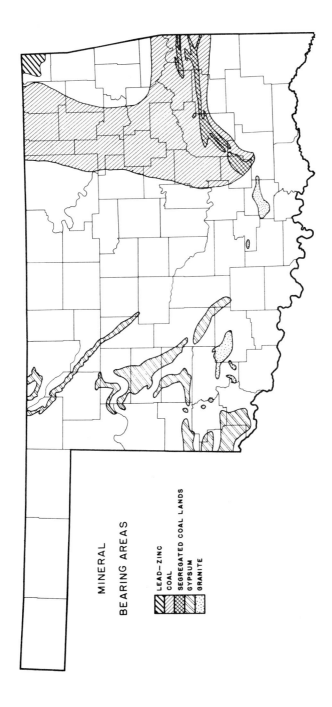

MINERAL
BEARING AREAS

LEAD—ZINC
COAL
SEGREGATED COAL LANDS
GYPSUM
GRANITE

Mineral-bearing regions of Oklahoma. From Burrill, *A Socio-Economic Atlas of Oklahoma.*

E. W. Marland to come from Pennsylvania to search for oil. The oil profits were then used to accelerate research into agricultural methods and to develop better markets.[25]

The experiment which was soon to bring wealth to Osage County eventually provided the formula that was to allow Oklahomans to survive and occasionally prosper on the plains. It should not be forgotten, however, that even during the last years of the territorial period the Oklahoma prairie was essentially a poor and underdeveloped frontier. The hardships which settlers faced often seemed more bearable because the economic potential of the territory was evident. Moreover, the region's social structure was, at least temporarily, flexible, and talented pioneers often had the opportunity to succeed financially or to reform the political system. Life in northern and western Oklahoma, then, was an ordeal, but it was also a challenge which was to allow the growth of a great deal of entrepreneurial energy and a potent antibusiness agrarian ideology.

The conquest of the western frontier was made possible by both the development of a strong agricultural economy and of petroleum reserves. The success of wheat farming enabled settlers to survive on the frontier, but the oil industry brought a measure of prosperity. It was the oilman, especially the wildcatter, who enabled the Great Frontier process of expansion to succeed. If oil had not been discovered, settlers could have gradually learned to tap their land's resources, and the plains would eventually have become as valuable an asset for the settlers' descendants as it was an obstacle for the first pioneers. Oil was discovered, however, and it set in motion a process by which Oklahomans were able to exploit their natural resources in the course of a generation.

The individual settlers, however, had no desire to engage in a heroic though excessively brutal battle with nature. The power of natural forces was too obvious for a settler to relish the idea of a romantic struggle with the elements. An example of nature's ability to remind the frontiersman of his vulnerability was described by an oil-field geologist who watched a farmer from Iowa as he built a dike to protect his fields from the South Canadian

River. The midwesterner explained to a skeptical cowboy that the procedure which he had used in Iowa would allow him to increase his crop production. The cowboy said nothing, looked up and down the bank, spit into the water, and then drawled, "Did you ask the river?" The next rain took the farmer's dike and his field.[26]

The success of the wildcatters in producing oil and in advertising their role as pioneers helped disseminate an unduly romantic myth of the heroic frontiersman. Their success in promotion encouraged similar descriptions of cowboys, ranchers, and farmers as brave and daring characters in the great drama of the winning of the West. An exceptional few may have been bold gamblers who enjoyed the high-stakes struggle with nature, but the typical farmer had no such pretensions. The farmer or rancher who actually made a living on the soil had no illusions about the thrill of the life-and-death battle with nature: nature repeatedly made its power abundantly obvious.

Nature thus weeded out the farmers who believed the rhetoric of the aggressive entrepreneurs. Thomas Frederick Saarinen surveyed the attitudes of the Panhandle farmers and discovered that they were not tempted to try to dominate nature. He asked farmers whether they agreed with highly confident statements such as, "If a man takes chances when things look good the future will take care of him," or "The man who plans ahead will succeed." He then asked for their reaction to more cautious statements, such as, "A man should be cautious, but be able to take advantage of opportunities." Saarinen found that 8 percent of Cimarron County farmers agreed with statements asserting man's power over nature, 15 percent saw man in harmony with nature, and 77 percent saw man as being under the power of nature.[27]

Ironically, it was the "daring" investment practices of bankers, speculators, railroaders, and oilmen that accelerated the rate at which Oklahoma was settled. Their fearlessly aggressive exploitation of the region helped cause the development of the state at a frantic rate which eventually decimated its resources and produced undue suffering for the settlers. The stoicism of the typical farmers, ranchers, and laborers was thus a legacy of the reckless manner in which the state was developed. The contrast between the heroic rhetoric about man's struggle with the frontier, based on a few incidents involving entrepreneurs who gambled their money, and the burden of the persons who had to survive on the soil and whose ordeal was made worse by the frontier businessman's daring investment practices brings to mind an ahistorical commentary. After Sonny Liston, the onetime heavyweight champion boxer, finished a merciless pummeling of the persistent Chuck Wepner, Liston was asked whether Wepner was the bravest man he had ever seen. Liston replied, "No, but his manager is." The same principle applies to the Oklahoma dirt farmers and laborers whose grim and painful struggle was made possible by the heroism of frontier entrepreneurs.

7

Socialism: the Ideology of the Shrinking Frontier

As Oklahomans witnessed the process by which their state outgrew the frontier, as well as its failure to outgrow the pioneer phase, they began to consider a comprehensive radical program Many Oklahomans were appalled by the ruthlessness by which the capitalistic system came to dominate the prairie. Others were angered as they realized that corporate powers sought merely to extract the wealth of the hill country without making an effort to modernize the region. The victims of both the brutality and the stagnation in the south and east and the rapid settlement of the north and west were tempted to conclude that capitalism was inherently evil. The result was that Oklahoma produced one of the strongest Socialist movements in America.

Immediately after the Farmers' Union ceased to represent the more radical ideals of poor farmers and laborers, the Socialist party began to grow. The Oklahoma party won 798 votes in the election for representative in 1900, 1,963 votes in 1902, and 4,443 votes in 1904. In 1906 the party received 12.6 percent of the votes for delegates to the Oklahoma Constitutional Convention. During this period party membership increased to more than 2,000. By 1908, Oklahoma had the largest membership in the United States. The young party boasted 839 local organizations and four newspapers.[1]

At first Oklahoma socialism was merely an extension of the defunct People's party. The key Socialist newspaper, the *Okla-*

homa Socialist, had previously been the *Newkirk Populist*. The party's strength was centered in north-central Oklahoma, which had been the stronghold of the People's party. The first Socialists were former Kansans, usually former Republicans, who had homesteaded the Cherokee Outlet. One such activist described his political life, saying that he was "a republican, then a greenbacker, then a greenback laborer, then a populist and now a socialist."[2]

The first Socialist party platform was almost indistinguishable from the early Populist program. In 1902 the party demanded universal suffrage, election of senators by direct vote, referendum and initiative, a graduated income tax, compulsory education, free schools, and an eight-hour working day. In 1903, however, Socialists formed a statewide program and made contact with the national party headquarters. The national party sent George Goebel from New Jersey to help organize and guide the writing of a set of political principles. From 1904 to 1906 the party developed a program that was distinguished from populism by its position on land, which said: "No person may own real estate. Every acre is owned by whole people through the national government—taxes are simply rent."[3]

As the party became more radical and as the north-central region became more stable, the power base of Oklahoma socialism shifted. In 1902, Socialists received more than 3 percent of the vote in six north-central counties. This region, however, was quickly outgrowing its frontier origins and was less radical. The *Oklahoma Socialist* never renounced socialism, but it gradually lost its stridency. By 1906 no county in the north-central region had a Socialist vote of over 1 percent, and in 1908 the region voted overwhelmingly for William Howard Taft for president.[4]

The arid western portion of Oklahoma had not outgrown its frontier roots, however, and it became the new base for the party. In 1906, Socialist support collapsed in counties in which annual rainfall averaged over thirty inches and where the land had been settled for over a decade. The Socialists received over 6 percent of the vote in only two counties: Kingfisher, 7.6 percent, and Pawnee, 6.1 percent. In those counties rainfall usually approached thirty inches, and farmers had had time to adjust to the conditions. The Socialists gained most of their support in Dewey County (11 percent of the vote), Roger Mills County (6.1 percent), Woods County (6.6 percent), and Woodward County (6 percent), where sparse rainfall (averaging around twenty-five inches a year) had challenged the settlement process.[5]

The Socialist party was also strong in Indian Territory. Its strength there cannot be measured as precisely as in the Oklahoma Territory, but in 1906, Jules Wayland wrote in the *Appeal to Reason*, a Socialist paper published in Girard, Kansas, that "the coal mining region of the Indian Territory is aflame with socialism and the farmers of the Territory are not far behind the movement." Wayland reported that the Indian Territory had 150 locals and 1,500 members, and he estimated that two-thirds of the registered Socialists were members "in good standing."[6] Wayland's estimate was evidently accurate because the first time Socialists in southeast Oklahoma had an opportunity to vote, in the Fourth Congressional District election in 1907, 4.75 percent of the region voted for Tad Cambie, one of the fiercest radicals in the party.[7]

In retrospect, such totals seem modest, but Socialists and their opponents were greatly impressed with their potential. Oscar Ameringer later described the confidence of Oklahoma Socialists:

> The outstanding characteristics of that early movement were burning idealism, unlimited cocksureness, and a naïve faith in the potency of political action.
>
> Some of us saw Socialism in 1908. Less optimistic comrades thought 1912 was the day. And there were the pessimists, "impossibilists" we called them, who insisted that 1916 was as early as socialism would carry the day.[8]

This political strength allowed the Socialists to influence the Oklahoma Constitutional Convention. For the most part they accepted the twenty-six demands of the Farmers' Union, although some conflict occurred over labor's demand that state lands be sold to provide taxable industry and jobs. According to the Socialist program the state should develop its lands by renting to tenants at a reasonable rate. They also advocated an "orderly transfer of banks and public utilities, natural resources and key industries to social ownership and democratic management." Finally, the party asserted that the social-welfare legislation which it and other reformers advocated should be seen not as a method of providing charity but as a "just retribution" for crimes committed against the working classes.[9]

Oklahoma Socialists were strongest from 1912 to 1916. In 1912, Eugene V. Debs received over 42,000 votes (16.6 percent) for president. Despite a very poor showing in the cities (where the voter turnout was twice as high as in the countryside) Debs received at least 25 percent of the vote in twenty-three counties. Socialists were especially impressive in the southeast and the southwest. Fred Holt, the Socialist candidate for the Fourth District's congressional seat, received 24 percent of the vote, while his counterpart in the Fifth District, H. H. Stallard, received 21 percent.[10]

Two years later, in 1914, Holt ran for governor and received 52,703 votes (21 percent) in comparison to the vote for Robert L. Williams, the winning Democrat (40 percent). Holt's greatest strength continued to be in Little Dixie. He received 34 percent of the vote in the area that had formerly been the Choctaw and Chickasaw nations, and he received 41 percent in his opponent's home county, Marshall County. At the same time Stallard again ran for Congress and increased his percentage of the vote to 33 percent (the winning Democrat received only 43 percent). Moreover, in the southwest, Socialists elected six of their members to the state legislature.[11]

Socialist candidates were disappointed, however, by the election of 1916. Although Oklahoma was the only state in which Socialists received a higher percentage of the vote than candidates had received in 1914, the increase was insubstantial (Debs received 45,557 votes, while Charles Evans Hughes received

97,233, and Woodrow Wilson received 148,113). While the Socialist vote increased in twenty-six counties, the response in leftist strongholds diminished, and Socialists received more than 25
percent of the vote in only seven counties.[12]

Socialists were victorious, however, in the most important
votes of 1916. Socialists, with lukewarm support of Republicans, defeated a Democrat-sponsored literacy test by a margin of
132,000 to 90,000.[13] Next the Socialist proposal for a tripartite
election board, known as the "Nagle Election Law," won by a
margin of 147,000 to 119,600. (The victory was subsequently
overturned by the United States Supreme Court. The Socialist
vote fell 4,000 votes short of the absolute majority required for an
initiative petition. The Court ignored the fact that an absolute
majority would have been easily obtained had it not been for a
"shortage" of 10,000 ballots, a shortage that was almost certainly
engineered.)[14]

By 1915 the Democrats realized the extent of the Socialist
threat to their party and initiated an ambitious carrot-and-stick
counterattack. Although Governor Williams and the legislature
were the most conservative in the state's history, they passed various reforms which they frankly admitted were designed to slow
the growth of socialism. The fourth legislature passed laws regulating the hours of female workers, financing welfare benefits for
widows and orphans, regulating warehouses, categorizing cotton
gins as public utilities, and establishing a bureau of weights and
measures. Moreover, even conservatives like Governor Williams
began to advocate legislation controlling usury and taxation programs designed to break up large estates.[15]

The Democrats also took advantage of the patronage system,
which had previously crippled the state's Republicans. The survival of many small businessmen, including newspaper publishers,
who needed the extra business they received from printing material for government agencies, often depended on receiving favors
from the majority party. Farmers and tenants also frequently re-
lied on help from Democratic leaders in arranging credit.

One example of political patronage was a form letter that had
been sent to local party leaders by Williams while he was serving
on the Oklahoma Supreme Court. The letter read in part:

> If you know of any good farmers that want to get loans from the
> state school land department at 5% . . . you have them write to
> me and I will get the application for them and will push the thing
> through. Get good Democrats . . . .
>   P.S. Of course we can't get over 2 or 3 loans in a precinct. It has
> got to be scattered across the state.[16]

The Democrats also began persecuting the Socialists. Socialism
had grown during a remarkably tolerant period which encouraged
a large voter turnout; Oklahomans voted at a rate double that of
Texans. After the Socialists became a serious threat, however,
they were met by a campaign of economic and political discrimination. *Harlow's Weekly* reported that in Marshall County "an
open boycott against socialists has been conducted by landlords,
bankers and business institutions generally" and that it "undoubtedly resulted in many socialists being driven out of the
county." The paper also reported that an estimated 113 Socialists
and their families had left during 1916 and commented that "this
blows up the Socialist party so far as winning any county offices
this fall."[17]

Socialists did not react passively. They formed an alliance with
the Republicans designed to stop Democratic abuses. The Socialists were abandoned immediately, however, and thus had to
resist the majority party by themselves. Even without the Republicans the Socialists mounted impressive campaigns against the
grandfather clause and literacy tests and for bipartisan election
boards. If successful, these battles could have allowed the Socialists to displace the Republican party as the second-
most-powerful political force in the state and might have allowed
them to defeat the Democrats in much of the state. The Socialists narrowly lost on two of the three issues. Their defeats,
however, were the results of massive electoral fraud.

The first dispute was prompted by the Democrats' attempt to

disenfranchise poor whites and blacks. In 1910, Oklahomans approved a "grandfather clause." Although the clause was approved by 135,443 votes to 106,222, electoral fraud provided the margin of victory. The number of votes for the grandfather clause was 20,364 greater than the total voters in the gubernatorial election. Moreover, 20,000 ballots were blank except for being marked in favor of the clause, indicating that they were fraudulent. In one precinct voters were intimidated by an armed guard, while in another an inspector stepped into the polling booth and marked the ballots for the voters. The most common method of fraud, called "short-potting," was the deliberate engineering of a shortage of Socialist ballots; some precincts were assigned as few as three Socialist ballots.[18]

A Socialist in Pond Creek explained how the procedure worked. When he tried to vote, he was told that the Socialist party had no ticket. He persisted, and the election official agreed to go to a neighboring precinct to borrow some Socialist ballots. The official returned an hour later without any ballots. The inspector at the other polling booth had only two Socialist ballots, and although he did not have any Socialists registered in his area, he would not part with either of them. The Socialist eventually voted for county offices, but he was unable to vote in the Socialist primary or against the grandfather clause. He later visited another polling place and discovered that it did not have any Socialist ballots either. The frustrated voter concluded, "I doubt if there were any Socialist votes cast in the city."[19]

The Socialists were granted a rematch, however, in 1916, after the United States Supreme Court ruled the state's grandfather clause unconstitutional (Guinn v. United States, 1915). Governor Williams reacted to the ruling by calling a special session of the legislature to draft legislation to disenfranchise "undesirable" voters. In a hectic session featuring flying inkwells and fistfights in which a Republican legislator was knocked unconscious, the legislature passed a universal registration law and called for an initiative petition to adopt a literacy test.

Under the universal registration law city dwellers registered in

1914, while the grandfather clause was in effect, would be automatically reregistered. All others had to register within three months. During this period Democrats were free to refuse arbitrarily to register blacks. For instance, all-black town of Boley was disenfranchised when the registrar refused to perform his duty. In Seminole County blacks were denied the vote by the ruse of describing all black voters as "red-haired." In McAlester, when blacks who were denied the chance to register tried to counter the Democrats through the legal system, they were charged with conspiracy to intimidate a state official. As a result of the universal registration law an estimated 50 percent of the state's black voters were disenfranchised.[20]

The Democrats' effort to enact a literacy test was equally ruthless but unsuccessful. Even Democrats were offended by the initiative, which was seen as an effort to disenfranchise whites as well as blacks. The literacy test was defeated by a margin of 133,140 to 90,605.[21]

The Socialists sought to follow up their victory with the initiative petition for electoral reform mentioned above. The public voted on two proposals, one to repeal the universal registration law and another to mandate bipartisan election boards. The Democrats, who had their backs to the wall, utilized all available vote-tabulation tricks including the creation of a shortage of 20,000 ballots. Examples of vote fraud occurred in Eufaula, where only 6 of 400 blacks were able to vote; Rentiesville, where 4 of 180 blacks were able to vote; and Boley, where 4 of 500 blacks voted.[22]

In Okmulgee blacks were forced to enter the polling place by a second door, and then they were given the illegal grandfather test. Democrats in Carter County bought votes for a shot of whiskey apiece. Voters would vote over and over again until they were too drunk to continue. In Adair County the totals in heavily Socialist precincts were "inadvertently" reversed, and others were reported inaccurately owing to errors in addition. In a postelection investigation a Socialist inspector accompanied by an election official toured six counties and found 1,143 errors against the proposition. The state's Democratic attorney general then forbade officials to cooperate with the investigation and thus forestalled a complete survey. [23]

Despite the massive theft of votes both proposals were approved. The Democratic officials then retabulated the vote, using a different formula for figuring the "silent vote" (the number of votes cast for the presidential election who were not cast in either way on the initiative; initiatives must receive a majority of the total vote, rather than a majority of those cast on the proposal). Under the new formula the repeal of the universal registration law failed, but the reform of the election board passed. The Democrats then retabulated the vote a second time, using a method of determining the silent vote which had never been used before (and which has never been used since). They compared the yes votes against the total number of ballots issued, meaning that all damaged or unused ballots counted as a no vote. The beauty of such a formula was clear. Any number of no votes could be created by adding extra spoiled or blank ballots. [24]

It is clear that the theft of the 1916 election destroyed the Socialists' chances of victory at the polls. There is a limit to the numbers of voters who will take serious personal risks to vote in elections in which corruption preordains the outcome. At the time, however, Socialists were confident of electoral victory within a few years. Their confidence was based in part on the success they achieved and the respect they earned when they gained public office (in 1915 six of the thirty-one Socialists elected to state legislatures throughout the United States were Oklahomans).

When they controlled a local government agency, Socialists refused to respond in kind or to compromise with the established system of graft and patronage, which they condemned as a "system of interlocking parasites." In fact, Socialists were so scrupulous that they often reduced the number of government employees and thus cut spending. Instead, they formulated a program known as "Industrial Democracy" in which the benefits of patronage would be shared by all of the public. [25]

Industrial Democracy was described by Oscar Ameringer as "industry of the people, by the people, and for the people." It was based on the argument that capitalists unfairly monopolized the tools of production. If the working class, however, could gain equal access to modern technology, the world could be freed from material want, and the masses of people would naturally exercise the talents that God gave all human beings, and a righteous and cultured world would evolve.[26]

It is unclear whether Oklahoman's vision of Industrial Democracy should be called Marxism. Even the rank-and-file party members commonly called themselves Marxists. Their concept of Karl Marx's philosophy was usually derived from the *Age of Reason* (Girard, Kansas), the *Tenant Farmer* (Kingfisher), or the local papers, not from their own reading of Marx. Oklahoma Socialists, however, typically were very conscientious in their investigations of political thought.

The question of the depth of Oklahoma Socialists' thought was addressed by Sheila Manes. She found that rural socialism in Oklahoma had much in common with rural Socialist movements in Canada, Italy, and France. She rejected the argument that Oklahomans' unusual land program was evidence that they were not true radicals, observing that "even the Russian revolution in 1917 *gave* land to the peasant, rather than took it away." She further noted that "Despite their lack of orthodoxy, Oklahoma Socialists were surprised at the debate whether they were Socialists."[27]

James Green's *Grass-Roots Socialism* and Garin Burbank's *When Farmers Voted Red* provide a basic outline of the nature of Oklahoma socialism. Green paraphrased Lawrence Goodwyn's description of populism, commenting that southwestern Socialists also provided a "culture of self-respect" and a "schoolroom for ideology." Green demonstrated the Socialists' "fusion of nineteenth-century moralism with scientific socialism." They were led by flexible and perceptive veterans of the People's party and labor movements. The Socialist party established an extensive network of local organizations and sponsored lecture tours and encampments.[28]

Eugene V. Debs speaking at a Socialist encampment at Snyder, in western
Oklahoma, ca. 1900. Courtesy of Western History Collections, University
of Oklahoma Library.

At first glance Oklahoma seemed to be a poor breeding ground
for socialism. Poor Oklahomans typically shared a "mentality of
impoverished country people," including belief in "white suprem-
acy, natural rights to use and control the land, and truths that were
revealed in the Bible." Even tenant farmers were inclined to follow the southern traditions of refighting the Civil War rather than
directing their hostility at the elite of their own society.[29]

Oklahoma's Socialist leaders, however, enjoyed remarkable
success in transforming impoverished farmers and tenants into
leftists. Green attributed Oklahoma socialism in part to the talents of leaders like Oscar Ameringer, Patrick Nagle, and Otto
Bransetter. The basic reason for their success, however, was that
the political and economic conditions of the new state made
it obvious to them that something was seriously wrong with
the system.

Oklahoma tenants were initially inclined to ignore or suppress
blacks, but when they found their political future intertwined

with the future of the blacks, they often reconsidered their prejudice. Even the poorest tenants usually hoped that capitalism
would bring them private property, but when they saw the number of landless farmers double in the course of a decade, they
concluded that capitalism, not socialism, was the chief threat to
their way of life. Socialist strength was inflated by a protest vote.
Some who voted Socialist never completely realized that it was
more than a new Populist party. Green, however, demonstrated
that frontier culture was fertile soil for a genuine Socialist ideology. He showed that Oklahomans were literate and that they
were inundated with intelligent political tracts and skillful propaganda. Green described how "the style as much as the exegesis
of frontier religion provided an effective medium for spreading
socialist ideas." Green also showed how labor organizers were
able to contribute a great deal to transform the dissatisfaction of
rural Oklahomans into a sophisticated and powerful Socialist
movement.[30]

Green concluded that the psyche of impoverished Oklahomans
contained elements of "possessive individualism" but that it also
contained many strains of a traditional culture. This traditional
concern for the health of the community made Oklahomans receptive to persuasive radical political methods when they were
faced with almost intolerable economic hardship. Oklahoma
socialism grew into a phenomenon that was more than social
protest.[31]

Garin Burbank's work was similar to Green's in many ways, but
he argued that Socialist ideals were not as thoroughly understood
or as deeply ingrained as Green indicated. Burbank noted that
the Oklahoma frontier was tied up in the modern corporate capitalist market. Its farmers and tenants were not the European
peasants who had been tied to the land for generations. Oklahoma farmers typically were liberal, individualistic members of
the capitalist system. They may have been impoverished, but
they still had faith that they could someday gain property of their
own. Burbank admired the Socialist party leadership as much
as Green did, but he was more skeptical about whether it was

able to transform the suffering of the poor into more than a populist protest.[32]

The basic problem with both Green's and Burbank's analyses is that they did not differentiate between southern and eastern Oklahoma, on the one hand, and northern and western Oklahoma, on the other. The situation is confusing because Green accurately described the isolated "traditional community" of the old Indian Territory, but his description of an intellectual Socialist movement was more appropriate for the plains frontier. Conversely, Burbank's description of a capitalist agricultural society accurately described western and northern Oklahoma. His conclusion, however, that Oklahomans failed to understand the true nature of socialism applied more to the people of southeast Oklahoma than to those of the western prairie.

An analysis of southern and eastern Oklahoma must synthesize much of Green's description of Oklahoma's culture with Burbank's description of Oklahoma's politics. Green romanticized the tenants of eastern Oklahoma, indicating that these isolated, ignorant, and malnourished survivors of a culture of poverty produced an intellectual socialist ideology. Their evangelical spirituality, their hatred of the wealthy, and their heritage of violent reaction to outside influences were channeled into an extremely fervent radical movement. Their great concern, however, was the survival of their own families. An able cadre of organizers was remarkably successful in introducing tenants to socialism, but, as Burbank concluded, the party was destroyed long before the masses gained a profound Marxist consciousness.

A similar approach is necessary for an analysis of the culture and politics of the northern and western region. Burbank was correct when he described wheat farming as essentially a corporate enterprise. He incorrectly concluded, however, that plains farmers were in sympathy with the methods of a capitalist expansion. Moreover, as Green demonstrated, they possessed the awareness necessary to develop a Socialist ideology. Plains farmers, who were usually not starving but who were always threatened by corporate powers, thus had enough freedom from absolute deprivation that they could afford to study alternative political ideas, and yet they were poor enough to hate the present system.

SOCIALISM IN THE SOUTH AND EAST

The history of socialism in the southern and eastern part of the state is an especially confusing subject. Although the number of Socialist voters in Little Dixie was comparable to the number in the southwestern plains, socialism in the hill country remains an obscure subject. The isolated tenants and laborers who comprised the eastern movement were less likely to leave written records. Moreover, political repression ruled out completely open campaigns, which would have left a better record. As a result, one of the most powerful, if not the most powerful, Socialist movement in American history remains fairly inaccessible.

Undoubtedly many leftists in Little Dixie did not understand Marxism. One example of naïve radicalism was the "Jones Family," a secret organization affiliated with the Working Class Union (and perhaps with the International Workers of the World) whose members swore allegiance to the workers in a ritual involving a Bible and a six-shooter. Even James Green, who consistently praised the character of backwoods radicals, acknowledged that the Jones Family possessed little class-conscious ideology. Their radicalism was based "upon the traditionally clannish resistance" to outsiders which was prevalent with southwestern "hillbillies." They were the ancestors of backwoodsmen who had been "notorious for bushwacking federal 'revenoorers' and Confederate draft recruiters." They may have hated capitalist intruders, but they lacked the minimal amount of awareness that is necessary for a Socialist.[33]

Little Dixie also produced a surprisingly sophisticated form of socialism. The tenants of the region apparently turned to Marxist ideas in an effort to obtain basic democratic and human rights. These southerners felt that they had been deprived of their dignity by Yankee capitalists and their agents. Stanley Clark explained that his followers rebelled as they discovered that they had been "psychologized." Socialists, however, were teaching farmers and workers to reject "inbred" false ideas.[34]

Even orthodox members of the party, however, were willing to use violence to protect their political gains. Clark, who was perhaps the most popular Socialist organizer in Little Dixie, chose as his motto "Not mad, but desperately in earnest." As early as 1910, when Democrats threatened to disenfranchise propertyless voters, Clark warned, "Rob the people of their ballot and there remains no other course open to them to restore their rights but organized, determined physical force and further attempts of the election thugs to nullify the will of the people may result in something far worse for them than the penitentiary."[35]

A major reason why Little Dixie was able to produce a creditable socialist movement was the efforts of the party's educators. Two groups of organizers thoroughly canvassed the region "making Socialists." Both groups included talented and effective educators. The official party leadership arranged lecture tours and encampments that introduced thousands of potential converts to Oscar Ameringer, Patrick Nagle, Kate and Richard O'Hare, Kate Barnard, Eugene V. Debs, and Mother Jones. At the same time an equally effective group of leftists, members of the insurgent "Red" faction of the party, introduced the populace to the thought of Ted Camby and Stanley Clark.

The citizens of Little Dixie were less responsive to logical arguments than were settlers on the western plain. Party organizers, however, were adept at translating their messages into a language which ignorant and often semi-literate tenants and laborers could understand. Oscar Ameringer best illustrated the methods which organizers employed while touring the eastern counties. In his autobiography Ameringer described a number of incidents which indicate that even the most talented organizers often failed to educate their converts about the true nature of Marxism. Ameringer also indicated, however, that such efforts were frequently successful and that isolated backwoodsmen commonly developed a meaningful class consciousness.

Ameringer good-naturedly narrated an example of one of his failures, an attempt to organize a local in Frogville. While Ameringer was touring the Choctaw Nation, he attempted to reorganize the once-flourishing Socialist local in Frogville. He discovered that the party had done well until the treasury grew to the considerable sum of three dollars. The local was thrown into disorder, however, when the treasurer embezzled the money. Ameringer quickly took charge and, ignoring the protest of the members, appointed a new treasurer. The Frogville organization again grew until the treasury reached $1.86. At that point Ameringer's appointee ran off with the money and a comrade's wife.[36]

Ameringer's efforts were usually much more productive. He once held a meeting during a flood that washed out all the nearby roads and bridges. Despite the deluge he filled the lecture hall. The chairman of the meeting made it to the lecture by swimming the rain-swollen North Canadian River.[37]

Ameringer enjoyed an equally remarkable success while recruiting in the Choctaw Nation. One afternoon, Ameringer met a couple of drunken Indians who invited him to speak to their friends. Ameringer reluctantly consented and visited their barn in the Kiamichi Mountains. Ameringer was met by a large number of drunken Indians as well as fifty tie-hackers from a lumber camp and some farmers who were also drunk. His audience included large numbers of "earnest, sober, determined people with Winchesters. They were prepared to protect him from Democrats who had sworn to lynch the first Socialist agitator who came into the area. Ameringer then gave a speech during which "every time I took my breath [I was met with] thunderous applause, rebel yells and Indian war whoops that shook the rafters."[38]

Ameringer developed a unique method of presenting his ideas to potential converts. While lecturing in the Winding Stair Mountains, he converted a hypnotist, who explained to him that his logical arguments were not effective with his gullible audiences. The two formed a team which proved to be extremely effective in communicating with backwoodsmen. First, Ameringer would play his clarinet to attract a crowd. Then the hypnotist would take three scraggly volunteers, hypnotize them, and tell them that they were John D. Rockefeller, J. P. Morgan, and Andrew Carnegie. The crowd would then watch its neighbors become robber barons. The three would invariably let the power go to their heads. They would begin selling railroads and oil fields for hundreds of millions and even billions of dollars. The hypnotist would then tell the crowd that the capitalists had it hypnotized just the way he had hypnotized the volunteers. He would proclaim, "Funny, isn't it, to make these poor devils imagine they are rolling in money? But just as I had them hypnotized, so the capitalists have got you hypnotized into believing that all of you can become Rockefellers, Morgans and Carnegies if you work hard and save your money."[39]

Ameringer would then take the stand and explain his land program. He might first build rapport with the audience by addressing them as "my fellow rabble-rousers." Then he would mock the Democrats' claim that tenants could work their way out of poverty. One of this best speeches was a parody of the Horatio Alger ethic:

> The trouble with you tenant farmers of the South is that you spend your money foolishly. Take your table for instance. What's the use to squander money on such luxuries as baking powder biscuits, corn pone and salted swine's bosom?
>
> There are all kinds of mussels in the nearby creek that are mighty good eating when you take them out of their shells. Grasshoppers are plentiful too, . . . and if you bite their heads, they won't kick in your stomach. John the Baptist became a great man on a grasshopper diet.
>
> It's extravagance that's availing you. You raise a crop and give one third to your landlord who is kind enough to furnish you with an opportunity to work. You give out a third to your mules. But you have no right to squander a whole third on yourself. You should save that . . . so your children will have a place to rent when they grow up.
>
> Everyone can have a farm that way if they save hard enough.[40]

The second method by which socialism was introduced to southeast Oklahoma was by newspapers. Socialist papers in the eastern part of the state were in a more precarious situation than that of their counterparts in the west. They were fewer in number and usually smaller. Papers in Little Dixie were edited in a less professional manner, and their local contributors were not as articulate. In contrast to western papers, all of which were engaged in hometown boosting, eastern papers faced attacks by local merchants, landlords, party leaders, and opposition newspapers. As a result, eastern papers rarely survived as long as those on the plains.

Ironically, the socialism which was introduced to the poorest social group in the state was concerned with moral reform. As Garin Burbank demonstrated, the renters of Little Dixie were infused with a nondenominational, fundamentalist Christian millennialism which opened them to radical ideology. Local Socialists recognized this and described Marxism as the vehicle by which the sinful capitalist system could be replaced by a truly just system. The *Johnston County Socialist* informed its readers that their choice was between socialism and hell. Among other things, it promised that socialism would stop white slavery and divorce. It also made a point to mention that one of the monopolies which Socialists planned to destroy was the liquor trust.[41]

The influence of evangelical Christianity was further illustrated in a letter written by a Socialist from eastern Oklahoma who explained that "the principles of socialism stand for justice, equity and the Golden Rule." He emphasized that "Christ's church is the working class church."[42] A similar form of Christian socialism was exhibited by a citizen from Bokoshe, in the eastern part of the state, who wrote, ". . . in our state of Oklahoma the sordid tragedy of 2000 years is re-enacted. The elements entering into the case are the same. A man [a local socialist] dares to speak for the oppressed. The result is the same. Failing their efforts to curb the man, the ruling class crushed him."[43]

Socialist papers in Little Dixie were preoccupied with attacking tenancy. They advocated a program described as "socialism for the farmer who farms the farm." Its basic principle was that the small farmer and renter have a "natural right to the use and occupancy of the land for production but not for exploitation."[44] Two common themes in the region's publications were that the natural right of the individual to land was now denied by capitalism and that the small farmer could survive only if he gained control of the tools necessary for modern agriculture, a goal that was possible only under socialism. According to this analysis the modern corporate power which had recently monopolized American industry and finance was well on the way to doing the same thing in agriculture. The only way farmers could retain their independence was to gain the ability to employ new technology and to control their marketing institutions.[45]

A similar attitude was revealed by H. Grady Milner, a member of the Red Faction of the state's Socialist party, who wrote in the Sulphur-based newspaper *New Century*: "Our land is gone; an industrial giant has robbed us of our subsistence. What matters to us if modern science has relegated the crude horse-powered machinery to the rear, and supplanted it with machinery one hundred times superior in point of efficiency? We are penniless. We cannot buy it."[46]

The anger of the region's radicals was illustrated by a letter to the *Social Economist* (a Socialist paper based across the river in Bonham, Texas) from an Oklahoman, who bluntly wrote: "The renter is a slave. It makes no difference whether he is a subject of the Czar of Russia or an American citizen. His economic position is that of a slave. A large part of his life work is lost to him."[47]

Another letter to the editor of the *New Century* revealed the bitterness that pervaded the region: "Ten years ago you were eager to unfold your plans of acquiring and fitting a snug little farm home for the maintenance of yourself and your family. How did your plans pan out? The fact that you are still renting is deemed sufficient answer."[48]

During the growth years from 1912 to 1916 when electoral victory seemed possible, the region's newspapers often issued confident political predictions. For instance, during the election of

1914 the *Ardmore X-Ray* published an article headlined and sub-
titled "No Money in Banks to Move Cotton Crop but Enough
Cash on Hand to Finance Democrat Campaign for State Office."
The article read:

> These workers that have heretofore voted for the old parties
> may not know the meaning of surplus value or of economic deter-
> minism, but they are certainly learning that the class struggled in
> Oklahoma between the Interlocking Parasites on one hand and
> the renters, farmers and workers on the other hand, can be fought
> to a successful issue on the political field only. . . . With the ad-
> vent of a Socialist administration in the state we will not yet have
> the millennium. But we will have in our hands that weapon
> which is ever and ever used in the interest of the class that con-
> trols the government. Today it is the Interlocking Parasites that
> get the material benefits from the control of the government.
> Under a socialist administration it will be the working class that
> receives the material benefit.
>
> Carl [sic] Engels said "Elections indicate the degree of work-
> ing class intelligence." Let us show our intelligence by casting
> ONE HUNDRED THOUSAND VOTES FOR THE ENTIRE
> SOCIALIST TICKET and thus lay the foundation for a FREE
> OKLAHOMA.[49]

Their apparent optimism, however, was tempered with both
fear and an inability to conceptualize a totally new social reality.
In contrast to the extreme optimism of the plainsmen's ideology,
Socialists from Little Dixie were not overly hopeful that human
beings could create a better world. Their ambivalent confidence
was illustrated by a passage in the *New Century* which capsulized
many of their goals: "Use and occupancy should be the only true
title to the land. With each man secure in his knowledge that the
land he is using remains in his possession while he uses it, he will
then take the necessary steps to erect a decent home, get telephone communication to the outside world and prepare to enjoy
life."[50]

Their modest objectives were further described in the *Okemah
Sledgehammer*, which defined real happiness as a result of "permanence" and the possession of a "sure-enough home" with shade

trees and flowers.[51] The contributors to the *Sledgehammer* were especially suspicious of the efforts of the experts, on either the right or the left, to create a better world. There would be no place for "social scientists" in a Socialist's world. The people did not need the help of "sociologists" who try to "fool around with Mother Nature" or farm experts trying to mechanize agriculture. The skepticism with which these Socialists viewed social engineers was best illustrated in a satiric series which updated the results of the "Better Baby Contest." The *Sledgehammer* periodically reported the size and weight of babies of Iowa farmers who were supposedly rearing a better "crop" through scientific methods.[52]

The best summary of the Socialist ideology of Little Dixie's party members and sympathizers can be found in the *Sledgehammer*. The editor of the paper promoted an exceptionally idealistic and humanitarian philosophy. At times, however, he unintentionally indicated that Socialists simply needed to dismantle the godless capitalist power structure. He sometimes implied that once individuals were freed from corporate oppression individuals would inevitably become honest and loving. The *Sledgehammer* also attempted to analyze Oklahoma's problems within a historical perspective. A modern reader often doubts, however, whether the *Sledgehammer*'s contributors realized that the history of Western civilization was more than a longer version of the history of Hughes County.[53]

The eccentric yet imaginative Socialist ideology of the *Sledgehammer* was introduced in a unique historical analysis. "The class struggle," wrote the editor, "has existed from time immemorial. . . . Labor unions are not of modern origin." He then traced the forerunners of modern Marxism back to the "Solonic socialism" of ancient Athens and Greece and went on to explain that Peter was president of the fisherman's union, and Jesus was a member of the carpenter's union.[54]

The editor indicated that capitalists would attempt to lure the proletariat just as the devil tempted Jesus. "The capitalists say, 'Get in the game—take chances and some will win and some will lose.'" The masses, however, should not be "deluded," because the "cards are stacked against them."[55]

The editor would not be content to remove the economic abuses created by the elites. He wished to eradicate the dehumanizing nature of economic competition. "Even in a fair game some will still be losers." The editor maintained that capitalism was inherently evil because it would inevitably "rob human beings of economic security," and it would "stab every sweet sentiment within [man's] soul." The problem was that "without assurance of food and shelter, the soul of man becomes a desert. Lost is every deeper sense of life. Music and laughter are forgotten, art is unknown and love perishes."[56]

Socialism was dedicated to the creation of a system in which one's children would be assured both material security and an opportunity to live a meaningful life. The editor described his basic motivation in an article entitled "For the Kiddies!":

> The children! It's all for their sake. Babies born and unborn are what we have in mind when we build, plan—fight! Socialism will bring us more bread, socialism will bring our babies more life, more laughter, more love! And that is why our movement is so intense, firm, determined. It is all for the sake of the kiddies. We are building for tomorrow.[57]

The editor was keenly aware of eastern Oklahoma's frontier roots. He elaborated on the manner in which capitalists exploited humanity by tracing the destruction of the pioneer society of his childhood:

> Where is the frontier our fathers knew? Into the hands of the land sharks, just a few. They've got your birthright and mine too. It's a shame, a meazley shame how the old parties have worked the skin game. The workers have been too docile and tame. Arouse ye workers! Make this our motto, "Ye landlords of the earth, give us back our land," and for your rights bravely take a stand.[58]

The editor also predicted that this wasteful process was destined to be repeated as unsuccessful Oklahomans were driven to more inhospitable frontiers:

The exodus to Montana, Idaho and other parts is going to be large. Almost every renter in this part of the state who is financially able to move is talking of emigrating. What chance will the renters who are left here ever have of acquiring homes? There is only one chance. Socialism offers every tenant farmer an opportunity to acquire a home.[59]

This process was explained in more detail when the editor published a letter from a former resident of Pottawatomie County who had migrated to Montana. The immigrant urged his former neighbors to move to a newer frontier. The editor took the correspondence as an opportunity to describe the nature of frontier capitalism. He argued that it was a myth that the "world is overpopulated." The fact was that most of the tillable land in the United States lay idle. For instance, 91 percent of Iowa was arable, but only 57 percent was tilled, and in Wyoming 28 percent was tillable, but only 1 percent was tilled. He then explained why so much land was wasted.

> There are two reasons for so many landless men and so much manless land. One is that much of the land has been gobbled up by speculators, . . . and the other is that much of the land is situated where conditions are such that it is difficult or impossible to make a living on it. Socialism will remove both of the causes and put landless men on manless land.[60]

The *Sledgehammer* was able not only to explain socialism as a teleological process but also to translate the process into concrete terms. For example, the editor illustrated the exploitative nature of the system by measuring in pounds of cotton the benefits a farmer received from a bale. He estimated that the farmer did at least half of the work in providing a 500-pound bale of cotton. The farmer then should receive the benefit of 250 pounds. Instead, the farmer and his family were lucky to own 15 pounds of cotton clothes. He closed his analysis with an admonition: ". . . so take a pencil, figure it out. And then take a good look at your pants, . . . put them on and go out behind the barn (if your landlord owns one) and kick yourself."[61]

The third medium by which socialism was introduced to Little Dixie was the Renters' Union. The Renters' Union was an off-shoot of the Socialist party, organized in 1909 by two renters, Sam and Luke Spencer. It was designed to appeal specifically to tenants in southeast Oklahoma. Although its members and leaders were not necessarily Socialists, the union received guidance and support from orthodox members such as Oscar Ameringer, as well as the more radical "Red Faction." The union, which its leadership defined as "not a political body but a fighting organization," tended to be more sympathetic to the IWW. They also welcomed the assistance of Oscar Ameringer, who wrote the pre-amble to their platform.[62]

The union further described itself as "the economic arm of so-cialism." The renters self-consciously patterned themselves after coal miners. Their first goal was to protect their economic status. Their preamble began with the affirmation "In union there is strength."[63] It continued, "If we renters can stop the competition among ourselves for the land, we can not only keep the rent from rising, we can force it down."[64]

The unionists were clearly preoccupied with concrete eco-nomic problems. Their pragmatism was best illustrated in their official list of demands. The union's first positions were demands that renters be supplied by landlords with two fourteen-foot-square rooms, each with an eight-and-a-half foot ceiling, plaster, wire screens and a lumber floor, as well as a lean-to to serve as a kitchen. They also demanded that contracts require landlords to supply three horses and a chicken coop. Finally, the land-lord would be required to supply a stable 100 feet downwind of the house.[65]

The Renters' Union also had a moral aspect. The renters expressed their long-term desires with their motto, Leviticus 25:23: "This land shall not be sold forever, for this land is mine: and ye are sojourners with me." Unionists vowed not only to re-form the system but also to "abolish rent, interest and profit" and to do so "by revolutionary means if necessary."[66]

The renters further committed themselves to

bind ourselves together in one great army of emancipation from landlordism and all its attendant evils so that the American home may be builded on a rock, that the teaching of the Bible be lived up to in our daily lives, to the end that we shall live under our own vine and fig tree and raise our children so that they may receive a thorough education as befits the sons and daughters of the soil.[67]

The true strength of the Renters' Union was based in its campaign for reforms which were far more substantial than any offered by the Democrats but which did not necessarily constitute a comprehensive Marxist program. The union reforms included a demand for the establishment in each county of an agricultural arbitration court consisting of a tenant, a farmer, and a landlord. The court would be empowered to fix the rates local tenants paid, handle disputes between tenants and landlords, and order rebates when a tenant's crop was completely or partially destroyed by weather. The union also demanded the recognition by law of an association of farmers and an association of renters and the establishment of a state department of agriculture to assure "the protection of the farmer and renter from the exploitation of the capitalistic class."[68]

The union also demanded the construction of state-owned warehouses, elevators, and cotton gins. The state was also to help administer a program of cooperative sales of products. Proceeds from the state's school lands would be used to assist groups of farmers in purchasing and sharing expensive farm machinery. School land revenue would also be used to conduct scientific research into cultivation for the benefit of democratically managed groups of farmers and not for huge corporate farms.[69]

The most important of the Renters' Union's proposals was the "Farmers' Program." The program was a quasi-socialistic arrangement designed to advance the principle that "use and occupancy should be the only true title to the land." Under their system the state would rent plots for one-quarter of the value of the crop.

Then tenants would continue to pay that rate until they covered the value of the land. Afterwards the tenants and their families would live on the land rent free for as long as they chose to cultivate it.[70]

At one point the Renters' Union seemed to have unlimited potential to mobilize the largest group in the state. Its program included extremely popular, as well as obtainable, reforms. Moreover, it successfully appealed to the emotions and the ideals of the proletariat. The union won converts by challenging workers and tenants to stand up for their personal dignity. Finally, the Union was an effective medium for educating farmers in the principles of socialism.

The demands of the Renters' Union prompted a strenuous counterattack by landlords, merchants, and bankers. One reason why socialism had been able to flourish was the tolerance which existed on the Oklahoma frontier. Conditions in the Indian Territory were not much worse than those in east Texas, Arkansas, northern Louisiana, or the Deep South, but only in Oklahoma did the Socialist party seriously challenge the established parties. One reason was that the poor in the rest of the South had been met by more extensive political repression. Unfortunately, once the Renters' Union began to challenge directly the welfare of local elites, Socialists began to encounter fairly systematic retaliation. The subsequent conflict, which is described in Part Three, eventually grew into a violent struggle which the Socialists had no chance of winning.[71]

SOCIALISM IN THE NORTH AND WEST

Socialism in the west occasionally resembled the belligerent reformism of eastern Oklahoma. Undoubtedly some Oklahomans who called themselves Socialists desired no more than to protect their land. They joined the party simply because it was the most strident opponent of the status quo. Other Socialists may have accepted only portions of the party's ideology. Such supporters may have doubted that revolutionary change was necessary, but they joined the party because they had been abandoned by the established parties. Consequently, it must be assumed that many Socialist workers, voters, and sympathizers were not true revolutionaries who wished to make a great leap of faith and create an altogether new society.

It should not be concluded, however, that most of the Socialists in western Oklahoma were moderate reformers. Westerners were keenly aware of the difference between reformism and socialism. Memories of how fusion had destroyed the Farmers' Alliance made western Socialists extremely suspicious of compromise. In fact, leftists were typically more bitter against Democrats and fusionists, whom they considered had betrayed the people, than they were toward Republicans, who at least were candid about their loyalties. The *Stillwater Gazette* wrote:

> The socialist party is composed of the remnants of the old populist party which refused to be swallowed up by the democrats. . . . they are the class of people who refused to sacrifice their principles for self and now while standing out by themselves they are helping to build up a new party in the ruin of the old populist platform. They are exceptionally bitter against the party which swallowed the big end of the organization.[72]

Educated party organizers were pleasantly surprised by the quality of Socialist thought exhibited by the plainsmen. Eugene V. Debs wrote of them that "the most class conscious industrial workers in the cities are not more keenly alive to the social revolution."[73] Ameringer agreed with Debs and added that the westerners were poor enough to be dissatisfied but had not been oppressed to the point that their social structure had been destroyed or their will had been broken. The best description of the kind of westerner who turned to socialism can be found in Ameringer's analysis of his audiences:

> These frontier people constituted the most satisfactory audience of my long experience in "riling up the people." They were grateful for anything that broke the monotony of their lonesome lives. Of more than average intelligence, they followed the main argu-

Oscar Ameringer, the key leader of the Oklahoma Socialist party. Courtesy of Freda Ameringer.

ments easily and caught even more subtle points quickly. Humor appealed to them immensely, for they belonged to the tribe from which America's great humorists from Mark Twain down to Oklahoma's own Will Rogers have derived their inspiration.[74]

In Ameringer's view these pioneers were able to adopt socialism because they were not the sort of people who could be intimidated by corporate powers. They were "a brave folk, courageous, yes, and above the average in intelligence." These "Scotch-Irish white trash were capable of fighting their battles between man and nature if given a Chinaman's chance." He described "Herdlaw" Johnson as an example of their strength. Johnson was a former Populist who had been instrumental in forcing cattlemen to fence their grazing land. As a young child he had watched as his father was lynched for remaining loyal to the Union. While homesteading in Mew Mexico, Herdlaw single-handedly fought off a band of Apaches as his child was born. If he was not intimidated by drought, lynch mobs, Apaches, and cattle companies, he was not likely to be intimidated by small-town bankers and merchants.[75]

Western Socialists were landowners who were not accustomed to enduring much of the psychological abuse that was the norm for tenants in Little Dixie. The plainsmen expected to receive all the democratic rights of an American citizen, and they refused to allow townspeople or businessmen to question their respectability. E. O. Enfield illustrated the confidence that was at the core of prairie socialism when he countered the charge that socialists and war resisters lacked patriotism:

> There is but one thing that prevents workers from rising up in mass and taking affairs into their own hands through the ballot box and that one thing is mental slavery. Men are *Afraid* to *Think*. Renters fear the lord—the landlord I mean. Borrowers fear the bank. Customers fear the merchant. Soldiers fear the superiors— superiors! Ye gods it makes my blood boil at the thot [sic] of some dinky dude of a whipper-snapper officer from West Point to order me about! Superior indeed![76]

Western Socialists typically did not need to be as belligerent as their besieged counterparts in the south and east, but when they were threatened, prairie Socialists could sound as radical as the "Reds" in Little Dixie. For instance, the editor of the *Beckham County Advocate* responded to the arrest of William Haywood with these words:

> William D. Haywood is the leading revolutionist on the American continent . . . . he believes in going to the root of things. He

does not believe in begging the master for crumbs of bread in the form of slight political advantage. He believes that we are in the midst of a fierce class struggle and that the fittest will survive.[77]

Jasper Roberts, the editor of the *Sayre Agitator,* and W. W. Hornbeck, of the *Sentinel Sword of Truth,* occasionally became equally belligerent. One of the first letters published in the *Agitator* was from Al Jennings, the train robber turned gubernatorial candidate and a friend of Roberts, who praised the *Agitator,* saying, "I knew you would be an agitator for you always were one." Jennings then added, "I'm still the same but I am raising hell with a lot of double-crossing thieves."[78]

W. W. Hornbeck, editor of the *Sentinel Sword of Truth,* also welcomed conflict. He published an ad for the IWW under the headline "Guerilla War Against Capitalism. The Sword of Truth must be kept on the Line." Later, when the *Appeal to Reason* announced that it was to take a less moderate approach, Hornbeck happily proclaimed, "Fight the Devil with Fire." He added: "Corrupt officeholders who vilified the editor are now up against the real thing. . . . From this day the *Appeal* is no longer on the defensive." Hornbeck culminated his attack on the system:

Permeate our souls with divine discontent and righteous rebellion. Strengthen within us the spirit of revolt, and may we continue to favor that which is fair and to rise in anger against the wrong until the Great Revolution shall come to free men and women from their fetters and enable them to be good and kind and noble and human.[79]

Consequently, Westerners did not appear defensive about their radicalism. Indeed, they asserted that socialism, not capitalism, was a respectable democratic ideology compatible with American and Christian values. Many plains newspapers introduced their readers to Marxist principles by quoting dictionary definitions of socialism. The most common citation was a dictionary definition of socialism as "Christianity applied to social reform." Another definition was that socialism was "a conscious endeavor to substitute organized cooperation for existence in the place of the present *Anarchical* system."[80] They reported still another dictionary's statement that socialism was an "intelligent explanation of human society [that shows] that as each step in the long course of development from the institution of private property through chattel slavery, serfdom and wagedom was inevitable, so the next step, from capitalism to socialism, is also inevitable."[81]

In contrast to the pragmatism of the declining Farmers' Union and of the Democratic reformers of their day, the plains Socialists held an intensely idealistic, almost millennial faith. Three of the more optimistic papers were the *Ellis County Socialist* (Shattuck), the *Great County Socialist* (Medford), and the *Otter Valley Socialist* (Snyder). The *Ellis County Socialist* based its political opinions on the metaphysical assumption that "man is mind and the action of the mind is in accord or discord of the Divine Mind." It asserted that "goodness" was "like the waters of the earth, there is just so much of it but unequally divided. This leads to the thought that in life there is plenty for every want; yet the trouble is in the distribution."[82]

The editor of the *Otter Valley Socialist* expressed an equally idealistic vision. He challenged his readers to "lend your ear to nature and hear the voices of the earth, air and stream, the powers that are longing to become the tireless servants of mankind, then turn to the useless want of mankind and ask why."[83] A similar article in the *Otter Valley Socialist* denied that the cruelty of the current system was the permanent condition of mankind: "Humanity is incurably good. All it needs is a decent chance. Take care of your children as your hogs and horses, if you want fine human stock. That means all children, none must be neglected."[84]

It must be emphasized that the western Socialists sought to do a great deal more than redress economic grievances. They joined the party with faith that "socialism will remove the unhealthy surroundings. Socialism will remove the struggle for mere animal existence. Socialism will remove the lack of hope."[85] The optimism of the plainsmen may have been somewhat naïve, but it was also the result of a good deal of thought. A more detailed explanation of their faith was presented in the *Otter Valley Socialist*:

> Pure souls can not exist in poverty-eaten bodies, and before purity can be enthroned and intelligence developed, . . . conditions here must be changed so humanity will live pure. . . .
>
> [Today] the masses of people in this land and all other lands are mere machines creating wealth they are not permitted to enjoy. Like idolators they have been trained from childhood to believe in things as they are.[86]

The plainsmen were able to hold such a benign view of the future largely because they placed their situation in a historical perspective. One western Socialist explained: "Socialists regard the present as an outgrowth of the crude and single handed methods of long ago." He added that the modern corporation introduced machinery which increased each worker's productivity tenfold. The worker, however, was not allowed to consume ten times more. Then the owners lost profits by undercutting each other. But they soon saw the folly and waste of such methods and combined to produce more cheaply and to control output.[87]

In the short run these combinations, or monopolies, imposed great hardships. Fortunately, however, the development of trusts laid the path for future evolution. By bringing workers together to labor "collectively" in factories and cities, the capitalists unwittingly aided the growth of unions and a class-conscious proletariat. Moreover, the next step, the development of industrial democracy, was inevitable because "capitalists did not make capitalism, the labor of millions did. Socialists will not make socialism. The working class will."[88]

The *Ellis County Socialist* acknowledged that it was easy to be timid and fear change, but the writer argued that

> a man is not a grower when he expects evolution to trip him. Man must have faith in new life, else he is not ready to enjoy the benefits that come him. He should train himself to be at ease and to be graceful with new environments. . . . Make your mind up to be progressive and boss no one and let no one boss you.[89]

In an article entitled the "Pioneer Farmer" the *Grant County Socialist* put the destruction of the small farmer in a historical perspective:

> It was the pioneer farmer who faced danger from hostile Indians (made hostile by cunning deception practiced upon them by greedy proprietors and the loss of their lands).
>
> The rapid sweep of the agricultural class across the country doubtless is unparalleled in the history of any nation and it is evidence of his desire to free himself from and leave behind that class of wealthy combinations and parasites responsible for his rapid western movement.[90]

He had to continue migrating because "to turn back was to be prey of the greedy, unscrupulous monied class."

The result of the frantic migration was the devastation that Socialists witnessed in Oklahoma. A letter to the editor of the *Woods County Constructive Socialist* (Alva) described the close of the western Oklahoma frontier:

> One hundred years ago, even fifty years ago, there was no scarcity of practically free land. My family, willing to forego the pleasures of an older community, could improve its financial condition by moving west. Less than twenty years ago Oklahoma was opened for settlement but in all this migration the exploiter was close at hand with his high transportation, his tariff taxed goods, and his outrageous interest rates. And as soon as a claim was proved up it took on a death grip of debt. And in young Oklahoma how many free homes are there now?[91]

A similar explanation was reported in the *Otter Valley Socialist.* The writer analyzed the settlement of Texas and concluded: "A few years ago land cost so many cents an acre. Now it has 280,000 renters. Think of it! A population of 1,400,000 lives on rented land in a state where 25 years ago land was as free as the cowboy bunkhouse!"[92]

These Socialists anticipated the arguments of Walter Prescott Webb. They recognized that the Oklahoma frontier had been settled too quickly for its own good. For example, the editor of the *Stillwater Common People* wrote: "We used to think that a rail-road was a benefit to a community but we are not so sure as we were before the road was built. On a visit to Pawnee a few days ago we were shown some more effects of the railroad." Pawnee, he wrote, had two railroads, but it was less prosperous than it was before they arrived: "The disposition of many people to rush to a town which is reported to be prosperous has a tendency to produce the very things which they were trying to escape from, that is, a great influx of laborers overstock the labor market. . . . we would advise everyone to avoid booming towns for permanent homes unless you get in on the ground floor."[93]

A debate in the letters-to-the-editor column of the *Common People* had the unintended effect of revealing the attitudes of a sample of the paper's readers. Their philosophy of nature and their attitude toward the frontier did not, however, resemble the portrait of a pioneer as one who enjoyed the challenge of sub-duing nature. On the contrary, the correspondents without ex-ception had an abiding respect for, if not fear of, the power of nature. While arguing that the state should sell its school lands to its tenants, one Socialist farmer revealed his belief that "land is a tool of production" but that it is more: "It is mother of all and while we may dispense with other tools we cannot with land." Another letter writer described land as human "heritage" which human beings had a responsibility to protect for future generations.[94]

The correspondents typically did not seem reluctant to try to improve the land, especially if the alterations were administered by Socialists. Several wrote about the need for irrigation and ex-plained how the arid west could support large numbers of Amer-ica's poor in a cooperative commonwealth which provided mod-ern irrigation and transportation facilities and machinery. One Socialist wrote that the commonwealth should adopt the meth-ods of the bonanza farms and mass-produce wheat at a minimal price. Another wrote:

> I sit in my little hovel and look forward to the near future and
> picture in my mind irrigation ditches and railroads, owned and

controlled by the public, cutting through these hills and valleys past nice houses and barns built under socialism, and hearing the irrigation gates squeaking and car-wheels humming "socialism is here to stay."[95]

The letters also reveal anxiety. A Beaver County Socialist wrote to support another resident in the county's call for public irrigation projects. He wrote: "This country as everyone knows was settled once before but people could not live here without irrigation and had to give up their land." Then he quoted a poem:

Once there was a desert where sun shone night and day and farmers combed their whiskers, swore a streak and moved away. For they said they'd be jimdasted if they'd live in such a land where the dew would boil the herbage and the creeks as dry as sand; and they said that they'd be jottwosted if they'd linger where the sun stayed up nights to roast and sizzle just as though it thought it fun. And they hitched their poor old horses to their sad old jaunting cars much as men in other countries hitched their wagons to the stars; and left this country to the skunks, coyotes and cattlemen.

He concluded: "And I fear that unless we can get some irrigation we will follow in their steps." He signed the letter "Hoping we will be successful."[96]

Not everyone, of course, stood in awe of nature. One correspondent believed that "land is simply a tool of production. It gives a man a steady, though sweatshop job." He added, however, "A man had rather be a railroad paddy if he can get it."[97] His testimony yields no support to a romantic view of the frontiersmen captivated by his dramatic struggle with the wilderness. On the contrary, it stands as a refutation of the theory that the pioneer relished a dramatic conflict with nature.

Most Socialists greatly respected nature even if they did not revere it. Some of them, however, retained an idealistic view of the land equal to or greater than the latter-day back-to-the-earth movement. The editor of the *World Wide War* (Pawhuska), for example, had a love of nature which could be considered the antithesis of the Great Frontier ethic. He fervently condemned wastefulness, saying, "What a travesty our political and social economics is upon the word of him who fed the multitude on a few loaves and then commanded 'Take up the fragments that nothing be lost.' National and individual waste puts Heaven's economics to shame."[98]

The editor argued that "man has only a right to occupy so much of the world created for all animal life." When Pawhuska was crippled by a record-breaking flood, he wrote: "This is an incident in the World Wide War between man and nature. We must fight one continuous battle for existence and he that is best prepared suffers least." He urged man to learn to "submit" to nature.[99]

Mankind, however, because of people's desire to "get rich quick," was inviting calamities. The editor listed recent disasters, including the Pawhuska flood, the Galveston hurricane, mine accidents, shipwrecks, and an oil-tank explosion at Ardmore and concluded: "All indicate criminal carelessness by somebody. Commercial grafting entices man to locate his home on a mere sand bar of sea shore. Land grafting often causes poorer classes to build their homes on the low bottoms, nooks and corners of water courses."[100]

The editor argued that "were it not for political and individual grafting in the resources of His handiwork, all would be reserved, except for present needs, for all the people of future generations." The editor's method of preserving nature's bounty was particularly farsighted. His proposal was to "take up this slogan: A farmer on each section of land in Osage County, a quarter for cultivation and three quarters for better bred stock and shelters from winter's storms. This alone will bring permanent prosperity. Oil and gas soon exhaust. Intensive farming is earth's Eden."[101]

Apparently the editor's socialism was inextricably intertwined with his prescient ecological philosophy. He wrote: "We dwell in a latitude of nature's extremes and only a cooperative community can save the renter-farmer from perpetual and lean poverty. They can barely live while occupying such land in their own right much less can the producer hope to live decently on leased land."[102] His alternative was to realize that "if nature is helping to crush us under the present system we must cooperate in gathering from

nature the greatest possible rewards by cultivating less land which
we must irrigate. . . . the cooperative use of the best machinery
and conserving all nature's moisture are remedies necessary to
counteract the farmers' gambling conflicts with nature."[103]

In their concern for nature western Socialists were not, of
course, Oklahoma versions of Henry David Thoreau. Nor should
it be assumed that the western Oklahomans were humane, idealistic intellectuals while Socialists in the eastern part of the state
were backward and narrow rubes. The differences between the
Socialists in the two regions were subtle outgrowths of their re-
spective economic, cultural, and political heritages. Western Socialists exhibited the confidence of the proud democratic culture
of the yeoman farmer, while eastern radicals hoped to gain for
the first time fundamental material and political rights. Nowhere
is the difference between the analytical and farsighted radicalism
of the prairie and the moralistic and immediate socialism of the
east more evident than in their views of nature. The easterners'
respect for the land was expressed in an effort to stop the "mining
of the soil." Westerners, however, had the opportunity to dream,
and they envisioned a cooperative commonwealth which revered
both humanity and nature.

Western socialism was thus characterized by a thoughtful yet
steadfast antagonism toward the methods used in subduing the
Oklahoma frontier. Prairie Socialists were deeply aware of the relationship between the destruction of their homes and fundamental dynamics of the expanding capitalist system. Western
Oklahoma Socialists recognized that the growth of a competitive system based on the careless exploitation of virgin land was
destined to produce comparable suffering wherever it intruded.
Moreover, they doubted that the corporate system, whose representatives had been so contemptuous of the welfare of the inhabitants and the natural resources of Oklahoma, could ever be
reformed. Consequently, they demanded the institution of an entirely new system, Industrial Democracy, in which those who actually farmed and labored both controlled the tools used to
develop nature's resources and decided how wealth would be cre-

ated without damaging nature or traditional social bonds, such as the family and the community.

It could thus be argued that Oklahoma's Socialists, who were veterans of the United States' last great frontier, recognized the nature of the Great Frontier. They saw that Oklahoma's sad history illustrated the crucial dynamics of capitalism's conquest of nature, and they rejected that process as barbaric. Instead, they formulated an ideology which was the antithesis of the Great Frontier. Rather than an individualistic, materialistic, frantic, and often brutal competition for wealth, Oklahoma Socialists advocated a patient, evolutionary political program designed to create a cooperative commonwealth consistent with the principles of Christian charity.

PART THREE

Postfrontier Oklahoma, 1916–1923

The soil is the nation's greatest resource. It is the basis of all life. When the soil is wasted, the people perish and the nation is destroyed. The soil is precious to us, for by it we live. We have not lived well because we have not been at liberty to care for the soil as we desire; because we have not been free men. Take this earth as a symbol of the new day of freedom which is about to dawn for all men who till the soil. Take it as a symbol of our united struggle for freedom, peace, and plenty on the land throughout the world, among all the sons and daughters of men.

—Ceremony of the Land

8

Prosperity and Poverty

DURING and after World War I a combination of fortuitous economic and natural forces helped northern and western Oklahoma outgrow its frontier conditions. During the war demand for wheat and oil rose as prices remained steady. At the same time a wet cycle of weather enabled prairie farmers to increase production significantly. Plainsmen took full advantage of their opportunities by expanding their acreage and adopting new technology. In the same period, however, southeastern Oklahoma failed to outgrow its premarket frontier status. The value of Little Dixie's cotton and coal briefly surged and then collapsed. No effort was made to modernize production, and the steady destruction of the region's soil and natural resources continued. Consequently, southeastern Oklahoma remained in the 1920s the impoverished region it had been at the turn of the century.

The crisis produced by the closing of the frontier in southeastern Oklahoma virtually paralyzed the region from 1914 to 1923. The most isolated areas of the old Indian Territory remained an almost completely underdeveloped premarket economy. During the late 1910s and early 1920s even the region's oil fields lacked the road system that characterized the wheat and petroleum-producing regions in the north and west. It took about five hours to drive the twenty miles from the Healdton oil fields to Ardmore.[1]

William Cunningham best illustrated the physical and also the psychological isolation of the southeast in his novel *The Green Corn Rebellion*, published in 1935. At one point in the story two Socialist tenants were given rides to Oklahoma City. The auto-

mobile was driven "on the ruts so that one wheel was in the center of the road and the other was in the sandburs." When they
met another car, the occupants of both vehicles had to fill the
ruts with weeds and push their cars out and around each other.[2]

When the tenants reached Oklahoma City, they were terrified
by a world with electric lights, "loose women," and tall buildings.
Not unpredictably, these men, who spent a great proportion of
their lives in the hot sun, were particularly perplexed by ice water.
They were even more shocked by elevators. Neither tenant could
understand why the elevator operator was not as terrified by the
elevator ride as they were. The tenants encountered an almost
completely incomprehensible phenomenon when they went to
the motion-picture theatre.[3]

Many incidents which Cunningham described were amusing,
but such ignorance helped produce serious social problems. In
1932, Frederick Ryan had lamented the backwardness of voters
and leaders in southeast Oklahoma. "Until a few years ago," he
wrote, "many portions of the state were isolated because of bad
roads, a condition which resulted in a lack of knowledge in
one region of industrial conditions in another section of the
state." Ryan asserted that these Oklahomans "should be able to
learn from the experience of older communities. Unfortunately,
though, much of this failure to make intelligent use of the rich
social and political experience of other communities is due to
sheer ignorance."[4]

Ryan claimed that one result of the lack of knowledge of economic principles was the failure to reform child-labor laws. He
noted that many representatives from Little Dixie who voted
against the prohibition of child labor did so merely because they
did not know that a serious problem existed. Their only concept
of child labor was the sons and daughters of farmers doing their
chores. Their opposition to reform simply proved that they had
little or no appreciation of the modern industrial world.[5]

Despite its isolation the southeastern section of Oklahoma enjoyed a brief period from 1916 to 1919 when coal and cotton
brought good prices. Moreover, several counties in the south-

central and east-central portions of the state experienced an oil boom. Unfortunately, however, the profits from coal and cotton where largely nullified by wartime inflation.

Even the discovery of oil near Healdton did not lead to prosperity as similar finds did for the northern portion of the state. The Healdton field turned out to be a "poor man's oil field." It produced "heavy oil," a much thicker, asphaltlike substance which was costly to refine. Moreover, only smaller independents and wildcatters chose to take a risk on the Healdton field, whose less valuable oil was isolated from the pipeline and marketing system. Consequently, low oil prices, which were only a temporary setback to the oil industry in the Cushing field and the Glenn Pool in the northeast destroyed the industry in south-central Oklahoma.[6]

The key segment of the economy of southeastern Oklahoma, cotton farming, remained as weak in the early 1920s as it had been two generations before. The dominant method of production in southern and eastern Oklahoma, single-crop tenancy, remained essentially unchanged. Although it was possible to make a living through diversified farming, few farmers attempted to do so.

During the war years it appeared that cotton farming might finally yield a profit. The war prompted a gradual increase in prices from $0.08 a pound in 1914 to $0.39 a pound in 1919. It was hoped that the higher prices would attract outside capital and stimulate modernization of the region's agricultural system. Farmers would be able to finance the implementation of scientific cultivation techniques. Then, it was hoped, a domestic cotton and cloth industry could be developed.[7]

Wartime prosperity, however, was extremely uneven. In 1916 cotton production increased by 26 percent over that of the previous year, and prices increased from $0.11 to $0.16 a pound. In 1918 production rose 10 percent over that of the previous year, and the price remained almost stable. The crops of 1915 and 1917, however, produced mixed results. In 1915 prices rose from $0.08 a pound to $0.11 a pound, and in 1917 prices rose to almost $0.30 a pound. The crops of both years, however, were almost 20 percent smaller than those of the previous years.[8]

When the war ended, the dream of prosperity in the cotton lands of Little Dixie was shattered. In 1919 prices at first soared, but cotton production decreased by almost 20 percent, and then prices collapsed to $0.15 a pound. Moreover, the financial panic of 1919 wrecked the plans of local developers and recreated the shortage of capital which had produced the tenancy system in the first place.

Conditions in the coalfields were even worse. From a peak of 197 working days in 1918, the average number of days worked by Oklahoma miners dropped to 184 in 1919, to 141 in 1921, and to 114 in 1922. In the Henryetta fields miners worked only 80 days a year for three years until 1924, when their company went bankrupt. When the mine closed, the miners lost altogether $6,500 in back pay. Throughout the rest of the decade the average number of days worked fluctuated between 124 and 150. The result, said one miner, was that the mines were so full of miners that "their feet were sticking out of the top." Moreover, surplus miners had difficulty supporting themselves because the surrounding land was "so poor you couldn't raise a fuss on it."[9]

Burton Rascoe, the Oklahoma-reared literary critic for the *Atlantic*, lived in southeastern Oklahoma during the postwar years and described the collapse of its agricultural economy. Rascoe blamed the ignorance of the tenants for much of the disaster. During the war, Rascoe recalled, a tenant would be offered an inflated price of $300 for his only mule. The farmer would not consider that he could not replace his mule once it was sold. Moreover, tenants attracted by a price of $0.39 a pound for cotton would plant it from "fence post to fence post" and then be forced to buy corn for $20 a bushel.[10]

In his autobiography Rascoe presented the following portrait of small farmers in southeastern Oklahoma:

> I have learned to have no sentimental illusions about the average farmer in Oklahoma in 1920, be he small landowner, tenant farmer, or sharecropper. Individually, all those—or nearly all

those I met—were kindly, hospitable, generous with what they
had, compassionate and eager to help one another out at harvesting or in times of trouble from childbirth to prairie fires.

But the average farmer of the Southwest, at least, is woefully
ignorant, clannishly mistrustful of townsfolks, independent to the
point of brutish pigheadedness and unenlightened selfishness. He
is narrow and bigoted. Field workers from the Department of Agriculture stand ready to help him, instruct him in scientific farming, in the conservation of resources; but most farmers will have
none of this, even though it is free of charge; they refuse to
change their wasteful ways of doing things, saying "no city dude or
college kid is going to tell me how to farm my land." [11]

Such farmers planted their entire arable acreage in cotton for
sale and neglected to plant corn and vegetables for their own
needs: ". . . being so cash-greedy they had no vegetable gardens;
they planted their cotton right up to the doors. They then would
have to buy corn in town, usually on a rising market and in a
falling market for their one crop." [12]

Rascoe, the son of a diversified farmer in Seminole County,
chided his neighbors for refusing to diversify. In 1919 he accompanied his father to a farmers' meeting and listened as his father
urged the tenants to cut back on their cotton acreage. The tenants agreed and pledged that they would grow less cotton. Rascoe's father, however, knew that his message had been ignored.
Rascoe recalled:

"But," my father told me, "something in the way that they acted
told me that every farmer there except me said to himself as he
drove away from the meeting 'all these other sons a bitches will cut
down their acreage and produce a short crop. The price will go up.
I'll play it smart and plant my whole damn farm in cotton and
clean up.'" And as it turned out that is just what every one of
them did at planting time. I have been all over the county and
seen their farms. Every inch of arable land is cotton and cotton
prices are down so low that they can't pick and sell it without
a loss. [13]

The accuracy of Rascoe's analysis of the farmers' psychological
motivation is problematical. That their options were limited by

an exploitative system may be sufficient explanation for the over-production of cotton. The existence of exploitation, however, does not preclude the possibility that the tenants were greedy. Perhaps the overproduction was a result of both the dynamics in-herent in the tenantry system and the avarice of tenants.

Regardless of the causes, the effect of overproduction on south-east Oklahoma was devastating. In June, 1920, farmers were re-ceiving $0.24 a pound for a crop that cost $0.25 a pound to produce. By December the price had dropped to $0.09 a pound. Consequently, tenants abandoned their crops and "lost their horses, mules and implements and survived the winter on sow-belly and black-eyed peas and corn pone." "Their kids," wrote Rascoe, "will get rickets and pellegra and next year the family will be hiring out at farmhand wages, if they can get work."[14]

Charles Bush was another writer who had firsthand experience with the farms in the southeast and was critical of the tenants. Bush explained his credentials in a footnote in his thesis: "This writer was, for six years, an officer in a bank at Prague, just north of Seminole County. Statements concerning conditions are from personal observation and actual business contacts."[15] Oklahoma tenants, wrote Bush, were superstitious and bigoted. He called them "Holy Rollers" and said that in their religious services "every human emotion was shown except pity." Oklahoma ten-ants were

> little more than serfs or peons, slaves to a "cash crop" demanded by their landlords. Yet they did but little to help themselves. When they did have money they spent it freely and often foolishly. The practice of savings was generally neglected, and they lived from crop to crop, year to year, vaguely dissatisfied, always dream-ing of a new country somewhere.[16]

Bush and Rascoe recognized that the political and economic structure, as well as ignorance, were at bottom the causes of rural poverty. Bush explained that the basic reason the land was ruined was that "most of the land was held for speculation, and the own-ers were not interested in anything but an income." they lived in a system in which even landed farmers were powerless because "much of the best land had been allotted to Indians or purchased by urban capitalists and investors."[17]

Bush also offered a forthright description of the role of bankers and merchants:

> The more responsible tenants were financed by the banks, who secured their loans by chattel mortgages on property and crops and charged from 20 to 40% or even higher for their money. Less desirable risks were financed by the general merchandise store. These firms not only exacted mortgages and high interest rates but added to the cost of the merchandise they forced their clients to purchase from their store.[18]

Rascoe also illustrated the destructive nature of the region's backward financial system. He knew that the greed and backwardness of the small farmer was in large part a consequence of the banking system:

> A small town bank in Oklahoma and in the South and Southwest generally, was properly speaking, not a bank at all. It was primarily a firm engaged in real estate speculation, horse trading, and mortgage foreclosing on notes bearing usurious rates of interest. The farmers were not depositers, they had nothing to deposit, most of them, they were borrowers at the banks in which the officers put their own money or working capital.
>
> But this is the way it worked in 1920. Farmer Brown, say, has a pair of mules worth $350 in the 1919 market and farm implements worth a couple of hundred more. He needs $200 for food and for salary of farm hands until he had finished bringing in his crop. Early in the season he has already mortgaged his crop at the bank for the money necessary to live on while he is planting his crop. He applies for a loan of $200 giving as security a mortgage on his mules and implements. He receives $175 in cash and signs a note promising to pay $200 at 7%.
>
> In other words $25 in interest is collected before he gets his money. The amount subtracted from the loan varied in 1920 according to the urgency of the farmer's need and the readily liquidating value of the collateral. Sometimes the amount deducted from a $100 loan was as much as $30. If the farmer invoked the usury law (as some poor devils did to their sorrow) he would be blacklisted by every bank in the state.[19]

The cotton economy of southeastern Oklahoma thus was un-able to pull out of the postwar depression. Land prices, which had been rising for twenty years in the hope that the region's vast potential would be realized, began to stabilize. At that point landowners had little reason to keep cotton-growing tenants. They began evicting their tenants, abandoned cotton, and began using the land for cattle grazing.[20]

The western and northern sections of Oklahoma were better able to cope with the closing of the frontier. By the time the United States entered World War I, almost all the wheatlands of northern and central Oklahoma were at least a generation re-moved from the pioneer period. Even in the Panhandle and the far-western corners of the state farmers had plenty of time to es-tablish a modest wheat economy as well as ranching and broom-corn and cotton cultivation. Moreover, by the early 1920s there was hardly an area in western Oklahoma that was not being stim-ulated by an oil boom. Consequently, many postfrontier western Oklahomans were able to achieve an unprecedented level of prosperity.

The successful close of the frontier in the west and north was characterized by two developments: the increase in farmland and the increase in the average size of farms. Large amounts of land had previously remained unclaimed for as long as a generation because they could not support a family. In Woodward County alone 100,000 acres went unclaimed during the first decade of the twentieth century. Many farms were abandoned by unsuc-cessful owners. Such marginal lands, however, could be incorpo-rated into large farms. A farmer who owned enough land that he need not depend upon receiving a good crop from each of his fields could make a living from a combination of wheat, alfalfa, and corn crops and cattle raising. He could rotate his crops and avoid soil depletion.[21]

From 1910 to 1920, as the arid northwest outgrew its pioneer phase, the percentage of land under cultivation increased to nearly 100 percent. In Grant and Garfield counties, which were among the first counties with large numbers of settlers, the proportion of land under cultivation rose from 97.1 to 105.6 percent in Grant County and from 95.6 to 104 percent in Garfield County. In the more arid counties of Ellis and Woodward and in Woods County, the percentage of land under cultivation also increased. The proportion in Woods County increased from 81.7 to 92.1 percent; the proportion in Ellis County increased from 78.8 to 96.7 percent.[22]

From 1910 to 1920 the average size of farms in the least arid counties increased at rates ranging from 3.5 to 47 percent, while the average size in the most arid counties increased at rates ranging from 78 percent to 104 percent. In such counties as Alfalfa, Grant, Garfield, and Major, where the less inhospitable longgrass prairie bordered on the more formidable shortgrass prairie, the average size increased as farms that were already fairly profitable expanded to their optimal size. The average size in Garfield County increased from 196.3 acres to 204.2 acres, and the average size in Alfalfa County increased from 194.5 acres to 223 acres. During the same period the average size in Grant County grew from 207.9 acres to 242.2 acres and in Major County from 213.1 acres to 268 acres.[23]

On the high plains the increase in the sizes of farms was much more significant, as previously worthless land was incorporated into profitable farms. A farmer in the extreme northwest could not plan on any acre producing more than two bushels of wheat a year or supporting more than a single head of cattle over a long period of time. His only protection against drought, storms, disease, and fire was to own extremely large amounts of land. Consequently, the average size of farms in Woods County increased from 246.6 acres in 1910 to 364.4 acres in 1920, the average size in Woodward County increased from 227.1 acres during the same decade to 404.7 acres and the average size in Ellis County increased from 219.6 acres to 447.7 acres.[24]

The reorganization of the economy helped, but the real reason for the prosperity was that the plains entered into a wet cycle. During the twentieth century the typical rainfall in the far-western plains has averaged between 16 and 22 inches. During the first two decades of the area's settlement rainfall in the far west averaged around 14 inches a year. From 1916 to 1927, however, in even the driest areas, rainfall averaged 26 inches a year.[25]

The combination of favorable weather and reorganization of farmland in the northwest helped spur a wheat boom that was far more profitable than the settlers could have anticipated. Oklahoma's hard, dry red-clay soil defied the conventional wisdom of experts and farmers and produced crops equal to those of any other wheatlands in the world. By 1919, Oklahoma was second only to Kansas in wheat production. The state's grain acreage increased from 1,940,000 acres in 1913 to 4,718,000 acres in 1919. During the same time annual production increased from 16,490,000 bushels to 66,052,000 bushels.[26]

The wheat boom was most spectacular in the far northwest, which had previously been thought to be too dry for wheat. During the 1920s, Texas County, in the Panhandle, became the leading producing county in Oklahoma. By 1927 the county was producing one-eighth of the wheat grown in Oklahoma. Moreover, during four years in the 1920s (1921, 1926, 1918, and 1929), Texas County produced more winter wheat than any other county in the United States.[27]

The combination of bumper crops and good prices enabled farmers to invest in farm technology. The number of tractors in Oklahoma increased from 5,789 in 1920 to 10,039 in 1925. Moreover, the use of combines steadily increased until 1926, when half of the wheat was harvested by combines.[28]

The good fortune of cotton, the second-most-important crop in western Oklahoma, was equally unexpected. Ironically, while cotton farmers in the humid black-soil regions of Oklahoma and the southern states were being impoverished by cotton, farmers on the dry, red-clay shortgrass prairies of west Texas and southwest Oklahoma were prospering. The spread of Texas stormproof cotton made it possible to produce bumper corps of cotton on land that was barely fit for cattle. The soil of the plains was fragile, but it had not suffered decades of abuse. Moreover, the flatness of the region made it easier to plow new fields and introduce farm machinery. Consequently, southwestern cotton crops were comparable to those of farmers in the Indian Nations in the 1830s and 1840s.[29]

The size of the average cotton field in southwestern Oklahoma was sixty to one hundred acres. A farmer could expect to grow one and a half bales per acre (the typical plot in the east was three to twenty acres, and it yielded from one-third to one-half bale per acre). Prices for western cotton were the same as those for eastern cotton, and a return of $25 to $50 a bale could be expected. Moreover, interest rates and marketing costs were usually much lower in the west, where a system of co-ops kept bankers, merchants, landlords, and agents from gaining a stranglehold on the farmers.[30]

Southwestern cotton farmers had another major advantage in their ability to use farm machinery. Some cotton growers in Tillman and Kiowa counties successfully utilized tractors. Most producers, though, benefited from one or two more modest cotton-harvesting technologies, "sledding" and "snapping." Sledding was a process by which a slotted blade was mounted on a sled and pulled across a field. Using this process on a large field, one man could harvest nine acres a day. The second method, snapping, was the system in which harvest hands pulled both bolls and burrs. Gins charged higher prices for snapped cotton, but it greatly reduced harvest cost. One study made in 1933 said that snapping saved $1.66 a bale.[31]

Southwestern cotton farmers also benefited from improvements in processing and marketing facilities. In 1920 the Oklahoma Corporation Commission began exerting pressure on ginners who used old, inefficient equipment, thereby accumulating "excessive profits," to render better service. Also during the 1920s plains farmers began establishing cooperative gins (50 percent of the state's co-op gins were in Tillman, Jackson, Kiowa, Carter, and Garvin counties). As a result ginning rates paid by westerners dropped from $0.60 to $0.20 per hundredweight. By comparison, few cooperatives were established in the southeast. Moreover, because of lack of capital, the cooperatives in eastern

Oklahoma had to charge roughly the same rate as the privately owned gins in the west.[32]

This period was perhaps the era when oil brought the largest profits to Oklahoma. By 1920 the United States was producing 65 percent of the world's oil, and Oklahoma's Mid-Continent field supplied half that total. The system of pipelines and refineries had been completed, and Oklahomans were involved in the entire petroleum industry from the initial drilling to the final marketing. Moreover, the war and the automobile increased demand with the result that prices remained stable.[33]

The best example of the benefits that could come from a mature petroleum industry was the Tonkawa field. Victor Harlow wrote that while Tonkawa may not have been the most productive Oklahoma oil field it produced the most wealth. Its entire production was 100,000 barrels a day, but little of that amount was wasted, because the field had access to twenty-six pipelines and storage for a million barrels. Tonkawa prospered. Wrote Harlow, "Tonkawa had known for a long time what was happening and got ready for it."[34]

The economic effects on Tonkawa were dramatic. Before oil was discovered, the county seat had three banks with a combined capital of $1 million. By 1927 the three banks had capital of $13 million. By 1923 more than five hundred farmers were receiving $100 to $5,000 a month from oil royalties. The county's roads were upgraded because one-third of the 3 percent gross tax on oil production was reserved for road construction in the home county.[35]

The orderliness of the Tonkawa field also benefited the workers, who had previously endured a housing shortage and a rash of petty crimes. Violence was surprisingly rare: only ten murders were committed. Workers jokingly complained that the field was "boring" and that unrepentent sinners would be forced to spend eternity there.[36]

Tonkawa's prosperity was shared by farmers and laborers. Drilling operations provided 5,000 jobs for teamsters. Local farmers received regular incomes from pulling cars out of the mud at a price of $5 to $10 a car. The field also employed 8,000 oil-field workers at high wages. A roustabout received $125 a month, a tool dresser received $10 a day, and a driller received $12 a day. Hundreds of carpenters had jobs as rig builders at a base pay of $13 a day.[37]

The petroleum industry eventually transformed the economy of much of the western plains in a manner similar to the growth of the 101 Ranch. As explained in Part One, the adventurism that characterized the oil booms helped diminish their economic benefits, as did the influence of Standard Oil. The vastness of the oil reserves, however, ensured that, regardless of the drawbacks, the economy of oil-producing regions would be greatly enhanced. Oklahoma's petroleum reserves were so enormous that even when oil sold at $0.25 a barrel the influx of money helped the prairie outgrow its frontier conditions.[38]

Fortunately, during the second decade of the oil boom Oklahomans began to avoid the worst excesses of unrestrained drilling. Oilmen never successfully regulated production, but they slowly imposed a degree of rationality on the industry. The more successful wildcatters established a domestic oil industry through which Oklahomans were able to transport, refine, and market oil as well as drill for it. As a result Standard's monopoly was broken. This meant that the money from Oklahoma's oil, in contrast to the profits from its coal, was not extracted by eastern corporations. Much of the state's oil profits remained in the region and helped finance a diverse agricultural and commercial economy.[39]

In retrospect, it is clear that the prairie was settled in a reckless manner that led to the devastation of the Dust Bowl and the oil bust of the 1930s. Moreover, the Panic of 1919, the erratic oil market, and the corruption that remained common even in western Oklahoma gave contemporary Oklahomans cause for alarm. Many destructive characteristics of the Great Frontier were not obvious, however, on the postwar Oklahoma plains. Consequently, the loyalty of many of its citizens to class-conscious radical political efforts is all the more noteworthy.

9

Class Conflict

JAMES Scales and Danney Goble have persuasively argued that Oklahomans have typically engaged in "politics of personality." Political behavior has usually been a result of "temporary emotions and fleeting preferences."[1] From 1914 to 1917, however, the most important social, economic, and cultural phenomenon in the state was the emergence of a class-conscious political struggle. During this brief era hostilities between tenants, laborers, and landlords became the state's overriding political concern. Consequently, the public subordinated its interest in pork-barrel appropriations and personalities and challenged the state's power structure through antiusury legislation and efforts to break up monopolies and huge farms.[2]

The period from 1910 to 1917 also saw the rise of "social banditry," or the perception of robbery as an expression of class conflict. For example, in 1912, Oklahoma led the nation in bank robberies. Conservatives and bankers angrily declared that these ostensibly criminal acts were actually political deeds. Many poor people, however, admired the robbers as successful businessmen. Victor Harlow, reporting in 1916, commented that many of the numerous recent robberies in eastern Oklahoma were probably carried out with the active cooperation of local residents. "There is no doubt of the existence of a most dangerous sentiment among a large element of people that there is little crime in robbing a bank."[3]

It became fashionable to describe any criminal act as a political protest. The career of Al Jennings, a former train robber who ran a strong primary race for Democratic candidate for governor in 1914, was the most notorious example of the trend. Jennings claimed that train robbers were more honest than the Democratic establishment.[4]

At first the Jennings campaign was seen as a joke. He undercut his already dubious credibility by interrupting his campaign with a trip to New Jersey, where he starred in a motion picture. When he resumed his campaign, however, both voters and party leaders proved receptive to his rebellious message. At the end of a ludicrous primary campaign Jennings placed a strong third with 21,732 votes, or 24 percent of the total.[5]

Political disagreements in Marshall County led to the first widespread conflict. Marshall, a cotton-growing county on the southern border of the state, was the home district of Robert L. Williams. Williams used patronage and personal favors in a successful effort to gain dominance over the Democratic party. By 1910, however, 79 percent of the county's farmers were tenants, and Socialists began gaining the support of that voting bloc. In 1912, 35 percent of the county voted Socialist. Williams and his colleagues responded in a manner that resembled the repression of Populists and Socialists in Texas but was unprecedented in Oklahoma. Bankers and landlords "passed discreet letters among themselves to facilitate discrimination against Socialist voters." They strenuously enforced the Universal Voter Registration Act, requiring voters to reveal their political preferences. Many landlords refused to rent to Socialists, and merchants refused them credit.[6]

Similar incidents occurred in Johnston County. Socialists imposed a boycott on Tishomingo businessmen who refused to contribute to a party encampment. The town's merchants and landlords responded with a retaliatory measure to rid Johnston County of Socialists. According to Harlow, Democrats threatened that the official list of Socialists would be used as a "blacklist for renters." In the course of the conflict the editor of the *Tishomingo Capital-Democrat* obtained a copy of the voters' register and threatened to publish the name of every "varmint" who registered Socialist. The editor then received several threats on

his life. He persisted, however, and published the names of a few
party members.[7]

In 1916 the next open conflict began in the southeast. For
years Oklahoma cattle had been vulnerable to tick-borne Texas
fever. In 1915 cattlemen in the northern and central areas of the
state inaugurated a new method of combating ticks by dipping
cattle. Results were not accurately recorded, but cattlemen were
generally pleased.

When the program was introduced into the class-conscious
south, however, violence arose. The owners of larger herds of
cattle almost always approved of the program. It was claimed that
treatment increased the weight of cattle by 20 percent. It was
also estimated, however, that perhaps 1 percent of the stock died
from the treatment. Large owners willingly accepted the risk, but
a tenant who might own only one cow and did not care what the
animal weighed was unwilling to risk the compulsory treatment.

Tenants and small farmers also balked at the program for economic and political reasons. The burden of paying for the program rested on the owner. He had no choice about whether to
cooperate, and then he was assessed to pay for it. Moreover, if he
refused to participate, the sheriff could take the cow and sell it to
pay the fee. Advocates of the program explained away the tenants' opposition as ignorance or native intransigence. Perhaps
some of the resistance was due to "instinctive rebelliousness," but
a key motivation was that tenants saw sheriffs and state officials
as representatives of their political enemies who would arrogantly
assert their will over them.[8]

At first most citizens were amused by the situation. Few feared
for their cattle because there was little evidence that the treatment
destroyed ticks, not to mention cows. The cattlemen tended to ignore the regulations, and at first local officials were lax in enforcing the seemingly silly rules. In 1916, however, state officials began enforcing the law rigorously. Sheriff's deputies seized the
cattle of several resistant owners, had the stock dipped, and then
sold some of the animals to pay for the treatment. Farmers retaliated by dynamiting cattle-dipping troughs.

One sheriff who tried to investigate the saboteurs was the target of a murder attempt, and other officials' barns were burned. The violent resistance temporarily halted the program, but in 1919 authorities resumed their efforts. Again night riders dynamited troughs, and a protracted guerrilla war resulted. By 1926 all but twelve of the eighty cattle-dipping troughs in Choctaw County had been destroyed or abandoned as the state conceded defeat and gave up the program.[9]

The third major crisis erupted in 1915 in Seminole and Hughes counties and lasted for two years. L. C. McNabb, an attorney, founded a secret leftist-oriented organization known as the Working Class Union. The WCU, which had large numbers of IWW members, was far more radical than the state Socialist party. McNabb began by filing usury suits against the state banks. Although he won most of the cases, interest rates remained high. McNabb was then elected to the county court, but he was prevented from taking his seat on the court. McNabb's publicity helped the WCU grow to 1,800 members in Seminole County. McNabb preferred peaceful resistance, but when that failed, his followers began a night-riding campaign.[10] The barns of exploitative landlords were burned, and tenants who cooperated with them were beaten. By the winter of 1916–17, the region was close to civil war. Then when the United States entered World War I and the draft was instituted, a group of renters initiated a revolt that came to be known as the Green Corn Rebellion. It was a brief skirmish fought by farmers who hoped to march on Washington D.C., and force the United States government to abandon the war effort.

Historians disagree about the nature of the Green Corn Rebellion. Oklahoma-reared historians have usually dismissed the rebellion as mob action. Even more recent Oklahoma historians such as James Meredith, Sherry Warwick, and John Womack, Jr., have seen the rebels as backward peasants. Leftists such as William Cunningham and Oscar Ameringer, as well as James Green and Garin Burbank, however, have offered a more sympathetic treatment. They acknowledge that the rebellion was a misguided and

futile effort but have not regarded it as a farce. Instead, they have
sought to empathize with the rebels and to reconstruct their view
of the world first and then to understand the historical importance of their uprising.

Charles Bush presented the orthodox interpretation of the
rebellion. He demonstrated that it was not merely an antidraft
revolt. The typical rebel was middle-aged, and many rebels were
in their fifties and sixties. They were fighting not against the war
and the draft but against capitalism, which produced wars and
conscription.[11] Bush did not see the rebellion as a Socialist campaign. "The finer tenets of Socialism were undoubtedly but faintly
understood by these people," he wrote, adding:

> A few decades before these same people, illiterate, patient,
> dumbly enduring, would have been among the pioneers of the
> West. [But the frontier closed, and] . . . the restless, periodic stir-
> rings of those people were limited to their annual moves from one
> poor farm to another.
> The lack of an outlet—an escape to a new country some-
> where—was a loss they translated into agrarian discontent.[12]

Bush, as well as Womack (in an undergraduate thesis), Warwick, and Meredith, all of whom were critical of the rebels,
extensively quoted WCU political pamphlets and posters as illustrations of the attitudes of the rebels. They used WCU liter-
ature first to show that the rebels were motivated by class hatred
that antedated the war and by "fervent" opposition to the war
and the draft. The documents also show that the rebels were
motivated by a propaganda campaign which spread misinforma-
tion and paranoia throughout the area. They demonstrate that,
unlike the official Socialist party member, the WCU agitator
cared more about stirring up the populace than educating potential Socialists.

For instance, Rube Munson, an IWW agitator who helped
organize the rebellion, capitalized on the fears of tenants that
they would have to leave their land and be forced to labor on
corporate farms. One rebel explained that he was attracted to the
movement when Munson said that

we had to protect ourselves and our families; that if we did not,
our young men would be sent to Germany to fight, our old men
put on ten-thousand acre farms to raise food to feed the young
men and that college and school boys would live with our wives
and daughters. [Munson] said that we had our wives harnessed to
cottonsacks, our babies lying on the ground in the shade and their
eyes being eaten out by ants and other insects, and we ought not
to stand it any longer.[13]

Bush's deprecatory analysis was based in large part on the fact
that the rebellion quickly degenerated into a farce. He showed
that the rebels behaved in a panicky, confused, and even comic
manner. He indicated that only those incapable of appreciating a
serious political ideology would have engaged in such ludicrous
riots. Scholars who sought to treat the rebellion in a more professional manner, however, have blamed the rebels' failure on their
isolation. The rebels were assured that they would be supported
by 35,000 WCU members in other parts of Oklahoma as well as
by 50,000 in Texas and 3 million throughout the nation. They
also could expect financial support from the 6 million German-
Americans.[14] Such an estimate did not seem implausible to dirt
farmers who had never been outside their home counties.

For example, a rebel named Homer Long had been a resident
of Seminole County for sixteen years, but he had never been to
the county seat until he was arrested. The sheriff who guarded
Long commented: "Many of those men never travel and don't
know anything except for what occurs in their own community.
Long, for instance. Everyone around him talked socialism and he
thought everybody in the world except a few rich men belonged
to the union."[15]

The rebels' isolation helped prompt skepticism about the need
for the war. The account of another rebel, who had been one of a
group of WCU members captured by a posse, provided an insight
into the reasons for the revolt: "The papers said we were cowards
but we weren't. Some of the men in the posse were neighbors of
ours and we couldn't shoot 'em down in cold blood. That's the
way we felt 'bout Germans and all the rest of 'em; we didn't have

no quarrel with them a-tall." The rebel explained why he and his companions rebelled:

> . . . we decided we wasn't gonna fight somebody else's war for 'em, and we refused to go. We didn't volunteer and we didn't wanta leave them here to do all the work of harvestin' and us have to go over there in France and fight people we didn't have anything against. . . . We didn't have any bands and uniforms and that stuff down here in these sand hills so that crap about the Germans comin' over here when they finished up the English and French didn't go over with us.[16]

An objective analysis of the rebellion was offered by Burbank. He rejected assertions that the rebels were stupid or irrational or illiterate. Instead, Burbank argued, the rebellion represented an essentially parochial, defensive action. He argued that the rebels understood a "generalized program." They also possessed a "fundamental" understanding of exploitation and imperialism, which encouraged the rebels to gravitate toward the southern IWW form of syndicalism.[17]

A slightly different interpretation was offered by James Green, who argued that the farmers who joined the rebellion were more than "syndicalists" or "primitive rebels." They were members of a traditional community with longstanding methods of protecting their society, and their institutionalized methods of self-protection proved to be compatible with socialism. In Green's view the rebels probably did not understand the "finer tenets" of socialism, but they were not ignorant night riders or religious fanatics, and their rebellion was certainly not "apolitical." They followed Eugene Debs, Kate O'Hare, Ameringer, and others because these popular propagandists talked about politics and economics in a simple concrete way that tenants and workers could understand. The rebels understood and accepted the Socialist party's analysis of the causes of World War I and its reasons for opposing interventions; they simply rejected its nonviolent tactics.[18]

Perhaps the most interesting description of the rebels was

offered by Oscar Ameringer, the "Yellow Socialist," or moderate, whose advice was scorned by the radicals. Ameringer copied verbatim Bush's description and then responded to it:

> Illiterate, poorly schooled, doped with all the mental poison their "betters" could pour into them, yes; but ignorant, no. There is a great deal of native intelligence among these people. Their state of illiteracy protected them, partially at least, against the flood of lying propaganda with which their "betters" of press, pulpit and rostrum deluged the country. . . .
>
> . . . Why should they get excited over menaced democracy across the sea? What had democracy ever done for them over here except to rob them of the first requirements of democracy, the opportunity to make a living without paying tribute to others? . . .
>
> Why should they get excited over the poor Belgian children three thousand miles away while their own rickety, hookworm-infested children shivered in the cotton field sucking their bleeding fingers, cut by cotton burrs in the cruel November and December winds? . . .
>
> To me, the grimness of that situation was not that these people were so naïve as to think they could stop the great madness by means of a few rifles, belts of cartridges, and a few hundred sticks of dynamite in their possession. . . .
>
> No, the most appalling aspect of the Green Corn Rebellion was not the naïveté of these people, but the effrontery of the rabble on top, so ignorant and conceited as to believe that these simple-minded folk would swallow their blah.[19]

Regardless of whether the rebels had a profound political awareness, their outburst sparked a massive reaction. Soon after the insurgency was crushed, fifty participants were arrested. The initial reaction of many of their captors was to punish the offenders ruthlessly. William H. Murray said that they should be marched to a hillside and shot. The government official who took the most severe action was Judge John H. Cotteral, who presided over the trial of eight former members of the Jones family. Cotteral allowed the defendants to be questioned until one of them became confused and contradicted himself during cross-examination. Then he charged the bewildered defendant with perjury. Cotteral intimidated another defendant to the point that he attempted suicide. All of Cotteral's defendants were convicted and received the maximum sentence, six years in prison.[20]

The rest of the rebels were treated in a much more selective manner. According to Bush, the authorities adopted a carrot-and-stick approach. The rank-and-file who repented were treated leniently, receiving sixty-day sentences, while the leaders received sentences ranging from six to ten years. Bush further noted that during the trial the judge addressed the defendants as "sir," a title they were unaccustomed to hearing. The judge then taught the rebels political lessons that "they should have learned in elementary school." One rebel, Spearman Dolby, was even praised as a hero when he agreed to join the army.[21]

The state's press took an ambivalent editorial attitude toward the rebellion. The newspapers that covered the revolt typically condemned it in the harshest terms. On the other hand, they also tried to dismiss the rebellion as insignificant. Other papers tried to ignore the event entirely. For instance, the *McCurtain Gazette* never mentioned the Green Corn Rebellion because "there were too many Socialists in that community." The *Capitol Democrat* (Wewoka), on the other hand, was too close to the action to avoid the subject. Luther Harrison, its editor, condemned the rebels as traitors and threats to the American way of life. He followed up his criticism by characterizing the rebels as a cowardly mob that could have been dispersed by boy scouts and by claiming that reports on the revolution were "greatly exagerrative."[22]

The authorities were not content to crush the WCU. They also set out to destroy the IWW, the Socialist party, and reform-minded Democrats. During 1917 and 1918 the Oklahoma Council of Defense, charged with overseeing Oklahoma's contribution to the war, all but destroyed all forms of political radicalism as well as much of the state's cultural diversity. The membership of the councils of the seventy-seven counties, which included sixty-eight bankers, thirty-nine editors, twenty-three merchants, twenty-one farmers, twenty-one businessmen, four clerks, four doctors, two army majors, a priest, a worker, and a "clubwoman," were veterans of numerous boostering campaigns, and they recognized the economic threat to Oklahoma if the state should be tainted as disloyal. Since the state legislature did not meet during the war, this voluntary group served as a quasi-official state government institution. Very frequently in the eastern part of the state and often in the west the county councils degenerated into mobs. They were mobs led by members of chambers of commerce and community leaders, but mobs nonetheless.[23]

Members of the state council believed that prompt and forceful action was necessary to protect the state's reputation from being tarnished. In the elections of 1916 the defeat of prowar Murray and the reelection in 1918 of the fervently antiwar U.S. Senator Thomas P. Gore indicated that Oklahomans were decidedly unenthusiastic about intervening in Europe's troubles. Enlistments in the national guard were extremely slow, especially in the eastern part of the state. Moreover, few counties were coming close to their Liberty Bond sales quotas. Beckham County reached only 17 percent of its assigned quota. John Simpson estimated that nine out of ten farmers were opposed to the war. He probably exaggerated, but the recalcitrance of rural Oklahomans was noticed by the Council. The final report of the State Council of Defense explained that at the beginning of the war "barely fifty percent of the people were of the attitude to give their whole-hearted cooperation." It attributed the intransigence of Oklahomans to having been "flooded systematically" with pro-German and Socialist propaganda.[24]

The county councils and the press worked diligently to overcome Oklahomans' reluctance to contribute. The *Daily Oklahoman* warned in a headline "Buy bonds Lest Slacker Wagon Will Get You" and explained that those who refused to buy bonds would be "subpoenaed" by a "strong arm" committee. The council implemented a policy on the purchasing of liberty bonds known as "Buy or Fight." Several farmers who refused to buy bonds had their crops expropriated and the proceeds used to buy bonds.[25]

Walter M. Harrison, an editorial writer for the *Daily Okla-homan*, later commented with some bitterness on his role in helping win the war:

> Big type and sensationalism was my meat. Under the impact of war enthusiasm our circulation jumped by thousands. . . .
> Our papers backed the County Council of Defense and never, by the remotest suggestion, indicated that our zealous patriots were going beyond the bounds of intelligent enthusiasm in blud-geoning the German sympathizers in our community.
> I saw a dentist's office kicked to pieces when he refused his quota of Liberty Bonds set by our local Fascists. I never went out on a night mission with the rough squad but I was pretty well satis-fied that the brawny platoon, led by great sons of Democracy, . . . ganged up on the stubborn holdouts with pretty rough fists, meth-ods frowned upon horribly a few years later when the Ku Klux Klan pursued its dizzy way to destruction.[26]

Other examples of wartime repression included the tarring and feathering of a Bessie farmer who protested when John Simpson was prevented from speaking, the same treatment of a Socialist lecturer in Elk City, and the repeated near-fatal hangings of a Mennonite preacher in Collinsville. The speaking of German was prohibited in many towns. A note was placed on the door of a German church that said: "God Almighty only understands English. Speak to him in that language. Do not remove this card." (A town across the border in Texas advertised that cus-tomers were free to speak German, and encouraged German-Oklahomans to shop there.)[27]

The worst outrages were committed in the northeast part of the state, in and around Tulsa. The *Drumright Daily News* printed an article headlined "Frisco Flyer Speeds into IWW Trap of Death. Three Killed." The article reported that steel bars clamped to the rails had caused the fatal accident. When it was learned that the wreck had been caused by a metal toy left on the track, the paper refused to apologize, saying that such sabotage would have been in harmony with IWW practices.[28]

The Tulsa County Defense Council proudly described its contributions to the war effort. It proclaimed that it had investigated 319 cases that required full written reports and many other petty cases. It reported that it had solved "eighty-four cases of disloyalty. Many of the persons investigated were sent to an insane asylum." It also dealt with "twenty Liberty Bond slackers. These were made to see the light."[29] The council and its cousin the home guard also helped deal with the wartime labor shortage. In its final report the council boasted:

> The Home Guard also rendered efficient service in the slacker raid conducted throughout the county on August 17, 1918 when more than two thousand men were rounded up and a large number of slackers caught. Again in October, the Home Guard organization was the backbone of the drive resulting in over a hundred men signing up for work in war factories.[30]

One of the more remarkable and effective official outrages was committed in Tulsa by a group of the city's leading businessmen who called themselves the Knights of Liberty. At the encouragement of the Tulsa County Council the local press reported that the IWW had sent a group of agitators to destroy the city's waterworks and explode incendiary bombs in vulnerable places like oil refineries. In October, 1917, the home of oilman Edgar Pew was bombed. Although there was no evidence, it was reported that the bombing and a subsequent explosion in a local refinery were supposed to be the signals for a violent general strike, Both local newspapers reported the council's analysis and called for citizens to lynch Wobblies. A week later Tulsa's IWW headquarters was raided by local police headed by one or more federal agents.

Eleven Wobblies were arrested for vagrancy and jailed for three days. It was agreed that one of the accused would be tried and that the verdict would apply to all. During the trial the Wobbly was reprimanded for not owning a Liberty Bond. He was convicted and fined one hundred dollars. The verdict was applied not only to the other ten defendants but also to six defense witnesses.[31]

On the day of the trial the *Tulsa World* printed an inflammatory editorial entitled "Get Out the Hemp." The editorial urged:

If the IWW, or its twin the Oil Workers Union, gets busy in your neighborhood kindly take occasion to decrease the supply of hemp. A knowledge of how to tie a knot that will stick will come in handy in a few days. . . . The first step in the whipping of Germany is to strangle the IWWs. Kill them just as you would any other kind of snake. Don't scotch 'em; kill 'em. And kill 'em dead. It is no time to waste money on trials and continuances and things like that. All that is necessary is evidence and a firing squad. Probably the carpenter's union will contribute the timber for the coffins.[32]

After the trial, while they were being escorted by the police, the seventeen prisoners were intercepted by a group of 200 vigilantes. They were stripped, beaten, tarred and feathered, and run out of town as shots were fired over their heads.[33]

Although the vigilante group included the chief of police and community leaders, their methods were not unanimously endorsed. The secretary of the chamber of commerce refused to participate, as did a lieutenant in the home guard. The lieutenant acknowledged, however, that the vigilantes had used weapons from the guard's arsenal. Many of the Tulsa police and a deputy United States marshal did not participate. The deputy explained "I tried to get them not to do it." He added, "You would be surprised by the prominent men in town who were in this mob."[34]

In a fitting epilogue to the event, a month later an IWW member was arrested for the Pew bombing, and was acquitted in May, 1920. The witnesses at the trial consisted of oil-company detectives and "stoolies" who were incarcerated at Leavenworth Federal Prison. One witness broke down during the trial and admitted that he had agreed to perjure himself in return for a pardon. Two other witnesses testified that they had turned down similar offers.[35]

After the Armistice came a rebirth of the Ku Klux Klan, which performed many of the functions of the council of defense. The Oklahoma Klan was not preoccupied with racial matters. One historian has estimated that only three of the 147 Klan incidents between 1919 and 1923 were primarily racial disputes. The Klan was basically an agent of punishment of socially disreputable behavior, such as bootlegging, sexual immorality, or advocating radical political positions. The Klan, like the council, dominated the prosperous urban areas of the northeast. Seventy of the Klan's 102 violent raids occurred in Tulsa County, and another 25 occurred in neighboring Okmulgee and Creek counties.[36]

The Green Corn Rebellion and the political repression during and after the war were dramatic illustrations of a more general, and perhaps more tragic, phenomenon. Oklahoma, like and other frontier, had had an exceptionally open and tolerant atmosphere in which personal eccentricity, as well as divergent political and religious opinions, was welcome. As the state matured, pressure to conform was greatly intensified. Local leaders and ambitious farmers and workers feared that Oklahoma's reputation for turbulence would discourage outside investment and thus prevent the state from outgrowing its "colonial" status.

A new concern for appearances was the central theme of George Milburn's short-story cycle *Oklahoma Town*. Oklahomans were portrayed as being torn between the simpler, impoverished, yet less inhibited life of the frontier and the pressure to conform to modern realities. Milburn perceptively described how the attempt to improve the state's image as a safe place for economic growth altered the social atmosphere of a small town. Milburn introduced one of his better stories as follows:

> It used to be that a stranger in our town was never asked why he had left the place he had been before or how he happened to come to Oklahoma. That was in the early days. After a while it got so that it was just the other way around. A new man was expected to get about introducing himself to people. Then they could talk over local conditions and where he had been located before and how much better he liked our town.[37]

Neopopulism: the Radical Postfrontier Ideology

As the frontier closed, radical Oklahomans were forced to rethink their ideologies. Idealistic pioneers in the north and west
had believed that if they were intelligent and strong enough to
pioneer a new land they were also capable of building a new social order. By the end of the war, however, it had become clear
to the most visionary plainsmen that the only way their vulnerable region could prosper was through cooperation with the
established corporate system. In the southeast Oklahomans reconsidered their radicalism for a different reason. They had attempted to rebel, and they had been crushed. The frontier's radical ideologies were durable, however, and both regions produced
a last effort to restructure the social and economic world.

The social conflict from 1915 to 1918 prompted Oklahomans
to reconsider their attitudes toward socialism. A majority of the
voters were sympathetic to key planks in the Socialist party program, such as land reform, control of big business, and protection of the rights of the public. They did not consider the Socialist alternative to be subversive or inappropriate. The violence
that accompanied the rise of the Renters' Union, the IWW, and
the Working Class Union, however, caused many to begin to
question whether the Socialist party should be welcomed or even
admitted to the political system.[1]

Oklahoma Socialists had hoped to sidestep a controversy over
whether their approach was alien to the spirit of representative
democracy. Party members were political rebels, but they were

not social rebels. They had no desire to alienate their neighbors unnecessarily or to create unneeded social conflict. The party members realized that their political base was precarious; they represented the most vulnerable class in one of the weakest states in the union. Socialists were often confident that the state's workers and farmers could take control of the state government, but they hoped to avoid social upheaval that would invite a counterattack.[2]

The film *Northern Lights* brilliantly illustrates the fearful dilemma that faced exploited farmers. The film is based on a narrative by Henry Martinson, a Socialist organizer in North Dakota. *Northern Lights* illustrates the complex process by which Ray Sorenson, a troubled wheat farmer, comes to be an organizer for the Non-Partisan League. Ray, his brother, and his neighbors are reluctant to discuss radical ideas because they know that if they commit themselves to a popular movement they and their families could be destroyed. After the father of Ray's fiancée loses his farm, however, Ray overcomes his fears and begins to promote the Non-Partisan League. In the course of his political campaigns he loses his farm, and his marriage is nearly destroyed. His efforts are rewarded when the league wins power, but the fact remains that the decision to embrace political ideology is a risky and difficult decision.[3]

During World War I the vulnerability of Oklahomans who sought to spearhead social revolution became even more obvious. The Green Corn Rebels discovered the hazards involved in radicalism. The opponents of the war and the German-Americans were harassed, and Socialists participating in legal political activity were intimidated.[4] The participant in the Green Corn Rebellion quoted in chapter 9 recalled:

> I got a 2-year suspended sentence, some of 'em got nothing at all to 5 years suspended, and the leaders got from a year-and-a-day on up to 10 years in the Federal pen. They went off laughin' and singin', but they came back old men. They really gave 'em the works. I had a friend used to live up there in the woods east of my shack; they slapped him and beat him till he went nuts. . . .

I was a "slacker" too, but I didn't get my brains beat out and didn't have to fight somebody I never had seen and wasn't mad at. But it was plenty tough. I couldn't get a job here and I had to report to the judge ever' week, so there wasn't much chance of gettin a job someplace else. My wife divorced me in 1918; she got tired of starvin' and havin' to face all the wimmen in town. . . . I couldn't get credit for seed and no work to speak of. . . .

I wasn't anything but a punchin'-bag for a couple of years. Ever'time the Klu [sic] Kluxers had a meetin' or when the town boys got drunk and didn't have anything else to do they'd come out and beat up on me.[5]

During the postwar era one piece of legislation, the Criminal Syndicalization Law, which had been passed during the conflict, was enforced with telling effect. The Oklahoma act, like similar laws in other states, was patterned after the Oregon law. It outlawed any "doctrine which advocates crime, physical violence, arson, destruction of property, sabotage or other unlawful acts as a means of accomplishing or effecting industrial or political revolution." The maximum penalty for violation was ten years in prison and a $5,000 fine plus court costs. Although he later denied that he had said it, the author of the law, Luther Harrison, who had been outspoken in his condemnation of the Green Corn Rebellion and the WCU, was quoted by the *Daily Oklahoman* as promising that the bill "will bar the IWW from Oklahoma forever."[6]

The law was first invoked in December, 1922, when Arthur Berg was arrested outside Haileyville, near McAlester. Halfway through his thirty-day jail term Berg was charged with "syndicalism and sabotage." His offense was carrying an IWW union card on which was printed the preamble to the organization's constitution. In February, 1923, he was convicted and given the maximum sentence. The judge then admonished Berg: "We don't want any IWW's in this land and no red flags and when you do get out of prison I would advise you to leave these parts as you have the mark of Cain on you."[7]

In June of that year another IWW member, Homer Wear, was

arrested in Vinita and charged with vagrancy. When he was arrested, Wear, a resident of Picher, thirty miles from Vinita, was distributing an article supporting Californians charged with violating that state's Criminal Syndicalization Act. Wear was convicted under the terms of the Oklahoma act, sentenced to six years in prison, and fined $750. The convictions of both Berg and Wear were reversed early in 1925. Although they were freed, their experience of serving three years in prison was not lost on other Oklahomans.[8]

Intimidation was not limited to leftists. In 1921 a black youth was charged with molesting a white elevator operator in a crowded downtown Tulsa building. A crowd of armed blacks who feared for the safety of the accused (two Tulsa blacks had recently been lynched for less serious charges) placed themselves between the jailhouse and a group of armed whites. Shots were fired, and a battle erupted in which the black community was razed. During the conflict whites reportedly bombed the black section from a biplane. The most reliable estimate of the death toll was around seventy-five; other estimates have been as high as three hundred. White businessmen were able to buy large sections of burned-out property and thus prevent the rebuilding of what had been a thriving community celebrated in song by white musician Bob Wills as well as by proud blacks.[9]

In case the message that differing political, ethnic, and racial cultures were unwelcome in postwar Oklahoma was not yet clear, the *Daily Oklahoman* spelled it out during its first annual "Americanization Day" parade and celebration, on April 27, 1921. The *Oklahoman* announced the holiday on a front page decorated with twenty-seven miniature American flags. Inscribed across the masthead were the words "Americanization day is to remind you that this is a grand old country regardless of late frosts and those who don't like it can find Russia on the map." An article by the parade marshal warned that there should be no more than a handful of observers on the sidewalks. The entire community belonged in the march. He warned that anyone on the sidelines might be taken for a hyphenate, that is, a German-American.[10]

The force with which the minorities were crushed was also noted by non-Socialist Oklahomans. Both conservatives and reformers feared that if Oklahoma were to be seen as a "Red" state it might be destroyed by an antisubversive campaign. Oklahomans were exceptionally aware of their economic weakness, and they attributed much of their poverty to the failure of two previous alignments, the Confederacy and the Farmers' Alliance, and they showed little desire to be martyred for a third time.[11]

As has been mentioned earlier, bankers and businessmen feared radicalism because they believed that it spurred bank robberies; thus business leaders were horrified by the national publicity that quasi-political crimes in the old Indian Territory received. They worried that eastern investors would assume that the entire state was as backward and as tumultuous as the hills of Little Dixie.[12]

The violence of 1914–1916 thus forced moderate reformers, as well as Socialists and conservatives, to rethink their attitudes about the nature of the social and political system. During the territorial days and the first decade of statehood, liberal-minded Democrats had little reason to doubt that their eclectic approach would improve conditions. They attributed the state's extreme poverty to its youth and its subservience to the eastern corporate establishment. A combination of patience and reform legislation promised to be the cure for the new state's frontier crisis. At the close of World War I, however, after a generation of reform, postfrontier Oklahomans suffered greater poverty than before.[13]

Reformers such as publisher Victor Harlow, former Attorney General Charles West, publisher John Fields, U.S. Senator Robert L. Owen, U.S. Senator Thomas P. Gore, and philanthropist-oilman E. W. Marland were appalled by postfrontier poverty. They attributed the suffering to capitalist exploitation and recognized that fairly radical methods were required to redistribute the wealth. At the same time they were realists who saw that socialism had sparked class conflict that threatened to depress Oklahoma's economy further and thus impoverish the tenants more severely.[14]

During the middle and late years of the second decade, an ideology that came to be known as "neopopulism" grew to be the dominant political orientation in the state. Neopopulism was a looser coalition than the Populist or the Socialist movements. There was no discrete party or program; indeed the term "neopopulism" was imposed by historians after the fact. The term, however, accurately reflects the outlook of various reformers who sympathized with many of the goals of the Socialists. They wished to redistribute the state's wealth and to hamstring corporate power. Neopopulists, however, were skeptical about whether socialism had a chance of succeeding, and they believed that, if Oklahomans attempted radical solutions and failed, the effect would be disastrous. Consequently, they tried to reorganize the state's economy and to humanize its society without encouraging class conflict.[15]

Neopopulism included dissimilar persons who were unexpectedly brought together by economic and political events. Consequently, an analysis of the nuances of neopopulism ideology requires a narrative of Oklahoma political history from 1915, when Harlow began formulating the intellectual basis for reformism in Oklahoma, to 1923, when Governor Jack Walton, the most successful exponent of belligerent reformism, was finally defeated. During the decade various coalitions of activists ranging from Socialists to born-again Populists to efficiency-minded intellectual progressives to eccentric oilmen dominated Oklahoma's political system. Neopopulism was an amorphous, often self-contradictory movement, as well as one of the most colorful and curious reform movements in American history. In retrospect, however, it is apparent that neopopulism was not simply a series of unrelated protest movements but an ideological response to the crisis of postfrontier Oklahoma.[16]

A study of the origins of neopopulism must begin with Harlow, owner and editor of *Harlow's Weekly*. Harlow took many of the key positions that recent scholars have listed as the hallmarks of the progressive. He was an intellectual who wrote a rationalist biography of Jesus. He had faith in evolutionary progress. The

key to economic growth, he believed, was the adoption of an efficient technological system and conservation practices and education. Harlow believed, however, that the potential benefits of
science could not be realized as long as an arbitrary corporate
business class and aristocratic landowners oppressed the common
people. Thus, for both pragmatic and humanitarian reasons, a
modest redistribution of the wealth was necessary.[17]

On the whole Harlow was an attractive person. He was competent, thoughtful, and even-handed. When his vision of Oklahoma's social and political problems is considered, it is clear that
there have been few shrewder analysts of Oklahoma's politics.
Moreover, *Harlow's Weekly* was by far the best non-Socialist
paper in the state until Frosty Troy began the *Oklahoma Observer*
in the 1960s. Harlow's paper was nearly the intellectual equal of
other great Oklahoma newspapers, Oscar Ameringer's Socialist
Oklahoma Leader and *Oklahoma Pioneer*, and its vision of the
state economic and political reality was equally profound.

From 1911 to 1916, *Harlow's Weekly* was the most influential
political journal in the state and guided the development of the
neo-Populist ideology. Harlow's paper addressed social problems
ranging from penal injustices, oppression of Indians, the waste of
natural resources, unsafe labor practices, and the disenfranchisement of blacks and poor whites to the increase of tenancy.[18]

Harlow provided thorough and fair-minded coverage of the
growing Socialist party. He took socialism very seriously, and he
encouraged his readers to consider its program carefully. He extensively covered Socialist social experiments such as Milton, a
cooperative mining community, and party-owned cooperative
cotton farms. He also concentrated on the effectiveness of Socialists elected to county offices in the western part of the state.
In each instance Harlow began his coverage with a statement
that the results of the Socialist experiments were extremely important because they would indicate whether or not Socialist ideas
were practicable in Oklahoma. In succeeding articles Harlow reported that Socialists were enjoying surprisingly good success and
were proving themselves worthy of Oklahomans' consideration.[19]

There was a genuinely humanitarian component in the reformers' ideology. They acknowledged the dominance of corporate capitalism, but they never minimized or justified the human
costs of its accession to power. Non-Socialist reformers occasionally issued stern statements attacking Socialists as ideologues, but
the vehement tone of such statements was largely rhetorical. For
example, as the Socialist party gained strength, Harlow reported
on the "menace of socialism." Harlow's articles, however, made it
clear that he was much more concerned about poverty than
about radicalism.[20] He barely concealed his glee that his predictions that capitalism must reform or face revolt were being
proven correct. Harlow welcomed the growth of radicalism because it gave reformers leverage in their struggles with the power
structure.[21]

Harlow attacked any group, including Socialists, whose behavior did not correspond with the spirit of representative democracy. He mistrusted Socialist officeholders because their chief
loyalty was to the party and not the electorate. He was convinced, however, that capitalism, not its opponents, was the
greatest threat to democracy.[22]

During the turbulent years 1915 to 1918, when many Democrats who called themselves Populists tried to crush socialism,
Harlow continued to offer critical support to radicals. In an article entitled "One Way of Dealing with Socialism," he reported
on efforts of Democrats in Johnston and McIntosh counties to
chase radical tenants from the area. Harlow commented that the
defect of such a plan "is that the Socialist is not a foreign element
who can be sent away and replaced with a different kind of tenant. The Socialist in Oklahoma is the normal product of the tenant system which prevails in this state." In a subsequent issue
Harlow reported at length from Pat Nagle's Socialist newspaper,
the *Tenant Farmer*, and concluded that "Pat Nagle is doing the
state a service in bringing the problem to the public."[23]

Later, when most non-Socialist political leaders, including
Harlow, were shocked by the Green Corn Rebellion, Harlow reminded his readers that the revolt was a symptom of deep social

unrest and not simply an antiwar riot. Harlow was much less harsh with the rebels than with the power structure that made their actions inevitable. In an article entitled "Lack of State-menship Responsible," Harlow wrote:

> The late R. G. Ingersoll, whose patriotism was above question, asserted that few men are patriotic enough to take up arms in defense of a boarding house. Had he studied the tenant system and all its ramifications as existing in Oklahoma he might have said "Few tenants are patriotic enough to take up arms in defense of the tenant system." Conditions among these people have for some time been unendurable. . . .
>
> When the legislature has been asked to relieve conditions that produce working class Unions, it has hastily passed an impotent graduated land tax, puerile antiusury, and ineffective "home-ownership" laws.[24]

Another proponent of neopopulism was E. W. Marland, an independent oilman who later became a New Deal governor of the state. Marland was a benevolent aristocrat concerned about the welfare of the people. Marland had been educated by Sir Thomas Hughes, the author of *Tom Brown's School Days*, who taught him a paternalistic form of goodwill. Marland brought this paternalism to the prairie and sought to build frontier Oklahoma into a civilized environment.

Many of Marland's charitable contributions were of little substance. His efforts, for example, to build polo fields for his workers had little lasting effect on the quality of life in Oklahoma. Other examples of Marland's generosity, however, significantly contributed to the state's fragile economy. For instance, Marland paid "not a living wage but a saving wage." He was also the first Oklahoma businessman to institute life-insurance, hospitalization, and dental-care programs for his employees for both on-the-job and nonoccupational illnesses.[25]

Marland's beneficence was best illustrated by his labor policy, known as the "Marland Golden Rule." It was an arbitration system instituted following a labor dispute that occurred when Marland was out of the state. A conflict arose between his foreman and laborers who refused to work with an open-shop crew from Kansas. When Marland returned, he solved the problem by praising the union and assuring his workers that all laborers should be organized. He set up a permanent arbitration panel through which representatives of employers, employees, and the public could discuss labor disputes.[26]

A third key reformer was Ernest Bynum, the state banking commissioner of the Walton administration. The career of Bynum, a thoughtful politician who was not shy about sharing his wisdom, gives a valuable glimpse of the neopopulist response to Oklahoma's problems. Bynum entered reform politics after his farmers' loan business was bankrupted by the deflation of 1919. Bynum was the archtypical minor businessman who resented the powers of the huge corporations. A glance at the writing style of his memoirs reveals that Bynum did not see himself as a member of the proletariat. He worked closely with small farmers, however, and he understood their world-view and their problems. Moreover, his concern for their welfare was genuine, and it led Bynum, the gentleman progressive, to join the campaign of "Our Jack" Walton, one of the earthiest political rebels in American history.[27]

In his history of the Walton administration Bynum explained how the actions of eastern banks and corporations had thrown Oklahoma into a depression. Bynum did not know whether the crisis was caused by honest mistakes or by group decision. He argued, however, that it was useless to debate whether the suffering was produced by error or by conscious exploitation. Such discussion wasted energy and undermined compromise between different types of social activists.[28]

Bynum, however, often pondered the relationship between the power of big money and the social welfare. He did not see small-town bankers as the kinds of people who could be agents of an exploitative system. Bynum noted that the typical banker was a stable member of the community and that bank failures were seen as personal humiliations and drove many bankers to suicide. When Bynum served as bank commissioner, New York bankers were cordial, hopeful, and proper. On the other hand, Bynum's experience as finance manager for the Walton campaign taught him that the power of big money in influencing political leaders was the "greatest peril facing our nation." Bynum said that "they knew what they wanted and how to get it." Although Bynum was never pressured or bribed by representatives of corporate powers, he knew that many of the more powerful lobbies chose "to do business with the Big Chief alone."[29]

Bynum's attitude toward socialism was as ambivalent as his attitude toward the exploitative behavior of big business. Bynum thought that there was a place for Wilson Democrats, oilmen, and Socialists in the Walton movement and sought to temper the more extreme demands of all factions. He often fought bitterly with Pat Nagle, the top Socialist in the administration, but he admired Nagle and respected his political insight. Bynum would have been more amenable to Socialist arguments if he could have become convinced that the system was hopelessly corrupt. He knew, however, that Oklahoma was a young state, and he concluded that there were less ambitious options that had not yet been tried.[30]

Until the election year of 1914 reformers such as Harlow were in an enviable position in that they could communicate with both reformers and radicals. The years from 1914 to 1916, however, were more difficult for reformers who chose to remain within the two-party system. The populace demanded radical changes in the established systems. But the statehouse and the legislature were firmly controlled by conservative Democrats, who proved to be exceptionally adept at sabotaging even moderate reforms. Liberal-minded Democrats could not conscientiously support the reactionary policies of Governor Robert L. Williams. Yet if they attempted to offer real solutions, they would find themselves in a situation as vulnerable as that of the Socialists.[31]

The war and social and economic developments stimulated by the war brought new opportunities to neopopulism. During the war the Socialists had to slow their highly successful campaign for land reform and concentrate on surviving attacks on their right to exist. At the same time the Williams administration became preoccupied with promotion of the war effort. The voters, however, were less concerned about patriotism than about bread-and-butter issues. Consequently, reformers who claimed to be ideologically neutral, as did neopopulists, found themselves in strong positions. They could leave ideological issues to the embattled Socialists and their conservative antagonists and concentrate on always popular economic reforms.[32]

Neopopulists were also fortunate in growing in power at the time that the state was finally becoming financially capable of initiating reforms. The austerity programs of Governors Cruce and Williams had nearly dismantled the state's modest road-building programs. During the war years, however, Oklahoma received federal help in the construction of a highway system. Such reformers as James B. Robertson, a pragmatic and free-spending liberal who was elected governor in 1918, could launch an ambitious construction program and not worry about bankrupting the state.[33]

The administration of governor Robertson can be seen as embodying some of the basic spirit of neopopulism. Robertson was not as reflective as Harlow, he probably would have denied that he had a political ideology, and he did not attempt to arrive at a theoretical basis for his actions. He did, however, work to implement neopopulist programs. Next to the construction of 1,300 miles of highways, Robertson considered his most important program to be the Free Homes Law. Arguing that home ownership was the sure antidote for "anarchy," Robertson achieved passage of a system to provide low-interest state-regulated co-ops and by regulating large corporations and utilities.[34]

Governor Robertson proved to be less tolerant of radical ideas than Harlow, and he lacked an understanding of the state's most serious social and economic problems. Robertson was a westerner who understood the need to control railroads, wheat merchants, and bankers, but he had little idea of the extreme poverty of tenants and laborers in the east. Consequently, the rhetoric of Socialists seemed to him to be excessively shrill. Then when Socialists questioned whether the American system was worth fighting for, Robertson lost all patience and joined with the superpatriots who wanted to crush dissent.[35]

Robertson's program was attractive because it did not offend any political constituency except the Socialists. Other reformers were satisfied because his reforms were intended to benefit the small farmers and many tenants, as well as the wealthier classes. He proved to be less sensitive to the plight of tenants, however.[36]

After the war Harlow, Fields, Robertson, Marland and other reformers began to abandon their radicalism and replace it with an orthodox reformism or even an outspokenly conservative ideology. Faced with the prospect of being drawn into another round of unrestrained conflict, the more timid reformers abandoned the movement. Harlow gradually stopped writing social and political exposés and began publishing inane articles about high society in Oklahoma City.[37] In 1922, Fields surprised political analysts who remembered his progressive campaign of 1916 by running as a conservative against Jack Walton. Marland continued to support the Democratic reformers, and he helped finance the Walton campaign, but he did so reluctantly.[38]

Postwar economic turmoil also renewed the more militant version of neopopulism, and within four years of the financial panic Oklahomans had rebuilt the radical movement of the prewar era, captured the democratic party, and elected a governor. During this period the North Dakota–based Non-Partisan league was introduced to western Oklahoma; the state's labor unions were revitalized; and cotton tenants, wheat farmers, and workers joined together in the Farmer-Labor Reconstruction League.[39]

The Non-Partisan League was briefly the most important radical organization in the state. Oklahoma wheat farmers had become used to good crops that brought high prices. When the panic threatened to reduce them to their prewar poverty level, wheat farmers revolted. In 1917, when the North Dakota headquarters decided to expand into Oklahoma, it sent L. N. Sheldon to travel incognito throughout the state to review the prospects for an Oklahoma league. Sheldon reported that conditions were right, and the league decided to hire twenty organizers. Evidently Sheldon was correct because by 1918 the league had between three thousand and five thousand members in Oklahoma.[40]

The league demanded a tax exemption on farm improvements and tools, a graduated land tax, a rural credit bank operated at cost, state inspection of grain docks, state regulation of grain grading, and state-owned elevators, warehouses, flour mills, packing plants, coal mines, and printing plants. It summarized its purpose by saying that its goal was to take the government out of the hands of special privilege and return it to the people.[41]

The league gained the support of many members of the Farmer's Union and other agricultural leaders. Its most valuable ally was John Simpson, the former head of the Farmers' Union. Three members of the union board tried to oust John Simpson from the organization in an effort to keep the union nonpolitical. They failed, however, and many unionists accepted positions in the league as salaried organizers. In 1918 the league was bolstered when it received the cautious endorsement of Carl Williams, the most prominent moderate spokesman of the farmers, who wrote, "Oklahomans could well afford to sit quietly by and watch this North Dakota movement with tremendous interest as an experiment in government which if successful will be worth adopting everywhere."[42]

The league, however, was unable to live up to its promises. The first problem was that by 1918 the social, economic, political, and cultural gap between eastern and western Oklahoma was so great that the wheat farmers of the league had little in common with the cotton farmers of the east. One organizer who tried to recruit in the east wrote in despair that he could not "talk the cotton farmers' language." Moreover, opponents attacked the league as being "disloyal." The league received a letter from George Creel, chairman of the Committee on Public Information, confirming their patriotism, but even so the league gained the antiwar stigma that was attached to any radical farm organization.[43]

The Non-Partisan League was unable to achieve electoral success, but its brief progress encouraged others, and in 1922 dozens of former members of the league met with representatives of labor, reform Democrats, and Socialists and formed the Farmer-Labor Reconstruction League. The farmers formed a united co-alition of cotton tenants, wheat farmers, and laborers. The new organization met in Shawnee and adopted a platform that one historian referred to as a "modernization of the 1906 Farmers' Union platform with socialist refinements."[44] The Reconstruc-tion League demanded a political bank to provide low-cost loans to farmers; state management of elevators, warehouses, and cotton gins; and a state department of agriculture. It also in-cluded the Oklahoma Plum Plan, which provided for the state to issue bonds to buy the railroads and then give a half interest in the state-controlled rail line to the railway union.[45]

The Farmer-Labor Reconstruction League was not a Marxist organization. It was a reformist movement that briefly captured the Democratic party and implemented moderately socialistic and populistic programs through the electoral system. Marxist elements in the Reconstruction League should not be discounted, however. Its official newspaper, the *Reconstructionist*, was fi-nanced by Victor Berger's Socialist organization in Milwaukee and edited by Oscar Ameringer. Its leaders included such impec-cable Socialists as Dan Hogan; J. Luther Langston; "Red" Boyle, of the United Mine Workers; George Wilson, a Socialist from the Non-Partisan League, and Patrick Nagle. Nagle summarized the attitude of former Socialists when he wrote of the seven hundred delegates at the Shawnee convention: ". . . more than a hun-dred were socialists at the meeting for it was practically impos-sible to reorganize the party under the present conditions."[46]

The Reconstruction League chose Jack Walton, the mayor of Oklahoma City, as its candidate. The choice of Walton was a gamble for he was uneducated and erratic. He was a former civil engineer who came to Oklahoma City in 1911 and was soon elected mayor. During his term he was best known for his strong support of unions. Walton proved himself an effective agent for the working class, especially during a packinghouse strike. Walton was not a Socialist, but he was a charismatic leader whom Socialists were willing to follow.[47]

Ernest Bynum, the man who best understood Jack Walton, illustrated Walton's lack of ideological orientation with an anecdote of how Walton became a Jeffersonian. One day before giving a prepared speech, Walton asked, "Who in the hell is this Thomas Jefferson?" Walton's ignorance did not, however, prevent him from delivering a beautiful, passionate oration in praise of Jeffersonian Democracy.[48]

Walton was ignorant, but he was a political opportunist. During the winter of 1921 he demonstrated a talent for taking advantage of unexpected circumstances that won him the league's nomination. At the height of the packinghouse strike a crank bookseller named Reverend West placed an ad in the newspaper urging the unemployed to meet at a certain place in Oklahoma City. Evidently West had wanted to hire some book salesmen, but he inadvertently attracted a restless mob of five thousand persons. The mob was growing disorderly when the quick-thinking Walton arrived and took advantage of the situation to establish a soup line.[49]

Walton used the same flexibility in his campaign. He would hire a jazz band to attract crowds and then launch into a vicious attack on the corporate system. Walton's methods were extremely expensive, but he was able to extract huge sums from both oil companies and Socialists without letting either completely realize the extent of the other group's contribution. Largely on the basis of his personality and the skills of his extremely talented staff, Walton was able to put together a coalition of landowning Democrats, oilmen, veterans, wheat farmers, union members, and cotton farmers, and he was elected governor by 280,206 votes to 230,459 for his Republican opponent, John Fields.[50]

The success of the coalition was due in large part to the skill with which Socialist campaign managers like Oscar Ameringer and Pat Nagle appealed to the various sectors of the working class. An example of their resourcefulness was a widely circulated cartoon of a capitalist beating a worker. The caption cautioned a businessman and a farmer who were witnessing the incident, "Stop him! He's clubbing your best customer!" An equally effective cartoon appealed to disgruntled World War I veterans. It showed a legless veteran watering a tree he had just planted in hopes that someday it would provide wood for a set of crutches. The caption read, "Slow, but so is waiting for the government."

With the election of "Our Jack," radical Oklahomans came to believe that they were on the verge of a new age. Some Oklahomans felt that they had elected another William Jennings Bryan, while others saw Walton as an Oklahoma Eugene V. Debs. The enthusiastic citizens celebrated their victory with a great barbecue and an inaugural celebration similar to the one that had greeted Andrew Jackson at the White House. The state fairgrounds was opened to the people, and three miles of barbecue trenches were dug on the lawn. An estimated 200,000 Oklahomans ate beef, pork, and mutton and greeted their new governor.[51]

Ameringer described the popular response to the election of "Our Jack":

> In spite of the most violent barrages from Wall Street stooges, from the state press, and from all "right-thinking people," the uprising of peasants, workers and ex-service men swept Our Jack into the governor's chair with the healthy plurality of sixty thousand votes. His inaugural was celebrated with a barbecue such as a wondering world had never seen. . . . The heady odors of that Gargantuan feast were wafted throughout the nation by the press stories of amazed correspondents. . . . [The press] became lyric about the "last of the frontiers." They described cow-punchers, Indians, share croppers and miners tottering through the streets of Oklahoma City gorged with slabs of whole steers, cross-sections of titanic hogs, Paul Bunyan helpings of sizzling mutton. . . .
>
> Childish as the wild enthusiasm of the barbecue may appear to the sophisticated denizens of the Atlantic brain belt, to me it signified the dawn of a new epoch in American history. . . . we had triumphantly elected Our Jack, destined to become the Andrew Jackson of the Nineteen-twenties.[52]

At first it appeared that, despite Walton's personal and political limitations, the Reconstruction League might revolutionize the state. A "Committee of Twenty-One" legislators was established to oversee legislative efforts. In the first session they expanded the power and role of farm cooperatives and passed warehouse regulations and marketing inspection laws. They also appropriated nearly a million dollars for school systems, provided money for free textbooks, and authorized three million dollars for the construction of highways. They were unable to establish a state bank, but on the whole their first session was fairly successful.[53]

Walton's personal traits, however, overshadowed the league's accomplishment. Within weeks Walton had pardoned 253 prison inmates without bothering to study their case histories, and he appointed scores of cronies to do-nothing positions. In one humorous incident he authorized ten thousand dollars for his two personal policemen to search for a fugitive in Mexico, although the fugitive was hiding on his ranch in northwestern Oklahoma.[54]

Immediately after his election Walton inexplicably began to forget his Socialist support. First, he chose only a single leftist for his staff. Then he shocked his allies by briefly joining the KKK in an apparent effort to gain more personal power. This ill-advised flirtation with the right was soon abandoned, but it created a split in his administration that was to prove fatal.[55]

Ernest Bynum, a member of Walton's administration, tried without success to make sense of Walton's behavior. Bynum said that it was unfortunate that Pat Nagle, who was suffering from ill health, was not around the capitol because Nagle was the only person whose advice Walton always respected.[56]

After the disaster of the first weeks Walton's Socialist supporters began to reassert themselves. Ameringer and his coworkers at the *Leader* launched a campaign to have Socialists appointed as presidents of the two state institutions of higher education. They persuaded Walton to appoint two talented but anti-intellectual Socialists, George Wilson and "Battle-Axe" Glover, as presidents of Oklahoma A&M College and the University of Oklahoma. Their appointments brought crowds of students into the streets

to oppose the Socialists and their plans to democratize higher education. The intensity of the students' reaction gave the conservative State Board of Regents confidence, and they rejected the
appointment of Glover and opposed the nomination of Wilson.[57]

The conflict surrounding Wilson probably did more than any
other issue to destroy Walton. Wilson was a tactless and stubborn
radical. During the campaign he had scandalized the league by
saying that every time he saw an American Legion pin he had the
almost uncontrollable urge to shoot if off the wearer. Wilson
brought the same belligerence to his post at Oklahoma A&M.
Wilson was determined to rid higher education of all forms of
elitism. He was going to open the system to the sons and daughters of tenants and laborers, and he did not mind antagoniz-
ing the pampered children of the middle and upper classes in
the process.[58]

The battle to protect Wilson's position quickly became the
most significant issue of the Walton administration. The Wilson
controversy symbolized the essence of the struggle for Industrial
Democracy. Socialists and radical reformers realized that their
political advances were worthless if they could not gain control
of the state's economic and educational institutions. Moreover,
the control of A&M was doubly important because it was an institution with the power to guide the implementation of new
farm technology.

Oscar Ameringer explained why the battle for control of A&M
was pivotal:

> There was one state institution in particular which we were de-
> termined to capture and hold, come what may. That was the
> Oklahoma Agricultural and Mechanical College. A pitifully small
> number of its graduates returned to the shops and farms from
> which they had come. Instead, this institution of learning had
> been turning out, to the vast disgust of our farmers and miners,
> a pedigreed collection of potential life-insurance, lightning-rod,
> patent-fence-gate, and oil-burner salesmen. . . . Older heads
> among our crowd figured that it might be a good idea to give the

youngsters some idea of the economic time of day. Nothing wild, mind you, but merely a look at how we got this way and where we're going, in the nature of what the Eastern professors call "orientation courses."[59]

Ameringer steadfastly backed George Wilson as the key to the success of their attempt to restructure the education system. He praised Wilson as a teacher and as a democrat. Although Wilson had no Ph.D., he would teach a much more valuable curriculum. "There would be no worshipping at the Shrine of Mammon while George was there," wrote Ameringer. "If we could bring up a cross-section of the next generation of Oklahoma farmers and workers to a real understanding of the world about them, we could let the political ward heelers wallow in the troughs."[60]

Within a matter of weeks the Socialists lost the battle for Walton's soul, and Wilson was fired. Ameringer attributed Wilson's defeat to a well-financed campaign organized by the petroleum industry. These "oil-smeared libels," as Ameringer called the anti-Wilson coalition, were able to have Wilson fired as a "stirrer up of the people, and a dangerous Red."[61]

For Ameringer and most of the other Socialists, the defeat of Wilson signified the destruction of their movement. The radicals became disillusioned. Ameringer wrote:

> To what avail this sacrifice and suffering . . . to elect a man like Walton who could so treacherously betray us and the cause for which he had stood? If there had been a real Red agitator anywhere in the state in those dark days he would have found willing converts in our disillusioned ranks. But as it was, the most bitterly disillusioned turned to cynicism as an escape. Never again would they answer the summons of any rank-and-file movement.[62]

By the summer of 1923, Walton's administration was in shambles. He had been implicated in scandals. He had lost his Socialist support. He was involved in disputes with the State Highway Commission, and he had no contact with the legislature. Then, in an apparent effort to divert attention from his failures, Walton declared war on the Klan, which had become very active across the state. A Klansman murdered three persons in Okmulgee County, and Walton placed the county under martial law. He did not stop at that point. Ten days later he declared martial law in Tulsa. In the fall Walton placed the entire state under martial law.[63]

Even though the legislature had to pass through barbed wire and machine guns to reach the capitol, they overwhelmingly voted to impeach and convict Walton. For a brief period the Klan was perhaps the dominant political force in the state, but within three years its power had collapsed. Afterward no political party espoused a significant ideology, and politics was reduced to a noisy method of distributing patronage.

During the Great Depression the state experienced what James Green called the "Indian Summer" of Oklahoma socialism. In 1933 unemployed workers in Le Flore County organized the Workingman's Union of the World, "whose preamble was a blend of hill country religion and IWW doctrines." In the same year communists and other leftists organized a series of Unemployed Councils, which conducted a series of large and often violent demonstrations (the membership of the councils grew to 7,000 in Oklahoma City and to 30,000 in the state). After the councils were disrupted by the arrest of their leaders, Ira Finley, a Socialist legislator from Oklahoma City's Capitol Hill, organized the Veterans of Industry, a 40,000-member "pressure group for the propertyless." From 1935 to 1939 the Southern Tenant Farmers' Union represented sharecroppers and migrants in eastern Oklahoma. By 1940, however, no radical political alternative remained for the state's farmers or workers. They either left politics altogether or returned to the Democratic party.[64]

Speed now the day when the plains, the hills and all the wealth thereof shall be the people's own, and free men shall not live as tenants of men on the earth which Thou has given to all. Enable us humbly and reverently, with clean hands and hearts to prepare ourselves for the day when we shall be Thy tenants alone and help us become faithful keepers of one another and of Thy good earth—our home. Amen.

—Ceremony of the Land

11

Conclusion

By the mid-1920s the Oklahoma frontier had closed, and the last of its radical frontier ideologies had been defeated. Neither development, however, seemed to discourage citizens of northern and western Oklahoma. During World War I and into the 1920s good prices and technological innovations encouraged Oklahomans to farm west of the dry line. During this period even the most inhospitable areas, such as Cimarron County, prospered. From 1925 to 1930 the driest county in the state averaged more than nineteen inches of rain a year. Wheat farmers took advantage of their good fortune by acquiring new technology and expanding their holdings (in 1920 a single dealer in Boise City sold an unprecedented total of sixty-five tractors). The result was that for a brief period the Panhandle became one of the wealthiest regions in the United States.

Then in the late 1920s and the early 1930s the rains stopped, and the region was inundated by dust. By 1931, Cimarron County farmers were receiving only 0.9 bushel of wheat per acre. By introducing modern agriculture to the semiarid plains, Americans had severely damaged a fragile environment. In less than two decades Oklahomans had created a phenomenon that has been labeled one of the three worst ecological disasters in the world's history.[1]

A different set of dynamics produced a comparable ecological disaster in eastern Oklahoma. According to Carry McWilliams, even after the frontier in the southern and eastern portion of Oklahoma had closed, the region remained an impoverished,

216

overpopulated, and underdeveloped territory. Little or no effort was made to build an industrial base, to improve roads and marketing centers, or even to establish a diversified agricultural economy. The area's farmers continued to cultivate subsistence tracts of ten to fifteen acres of nearly worthless land. Tenants remained uneducated, malnourished, and perpetually indebted to their local merchants. Moreover, they continued to be a highly transient population that continually moved from one set of eroded plots to another. The only difference between their situation and that of their fathers and grandfathers was that by the late 1920s and 1930s larger numbers of tenants were unable to find even a tiny piece of ravished land and were forced to leave their overcrowded region.[2]

In 1935, 62 percent of Oklahoma's farmers were tenants. Moreover, 40 percent of them moved each year. As in previous years, a much higher percentage of Little Dixie's farmers were dispossessed. It was also the most overcrowded region of the state. It was estimated that in southeast Oklahoma there were 30 percent more farm families than the land could support.[3]

By the time of the Great Depression the best farmland of the last of America's frontiers, the former Indian Territory, had lost up to five feet of topsoil. In 1942, Carry McWilliams wrote that 62 percent of the state's farmland had lost at least 25 percent of its topsoil and thus required "curative treatment" (another 13.9 percent required "preventive treatment").[4] According to McWilliams, the situation caused the greatest suffering in the eastern part of the state, where the following cycle prevailed:

> The worst eroded lands are, of course, the cheapest lands. Like magnets, therefore, they attract ex-oil workers, ex-miners and dispossessed farmers and tenants who cannot get a foothold, through lack of capital, in better farming areas. Population reservoirs are created in areas of greatest erosion. The constant pressure of population upon depleted acres results in ever-smaller units of farm operation, which lead to bad soil practices which in turn accelerate the process of erosion.[5]

The result of the state's twin disasters was that from 1930 to 1945 Oklahoma lost 440,000 persons, or 18.4 percent of its 1930 population (the population of Kansas, the state that lost the second-largest number, declined by 224,000). During the same period the state also lost 15.6 percent of its farms. The out-migration total would have been much larger if more Oklahomans had had access to transportation. Untold numbers of displaced persons were unable to afford the ten dollars needed for gas to drive to California, so they "doubled up" or tried to support two families on a plot of land that had previously been inadequate to support one.[6]

Despite the common misconception that Oklahomans were "dusted out and tractored out," an estimated 97 percent of the net population loss occurred in the eastern half of the state, which was not crippled by dust and underwent almost no farm mechanization. These migrants were instead dislocated by landlords, merchants, and bankers.[7] Woody Guthrie claimed: "For every farmer who was dusted out or tractored out another ten were chased out by bankers. That's just an estimate but I bet it's not far wrong."

Subsequent research has confirmed Guthrie's estimate. Oklahomans were the victims of a process comparable to the enclosures in England. Oklahomans, however, were "eaten" by cattle, not by sheep. The cotton tenants were displaced by a shift from single-crop cotton to cattle grazing. The shift began in the 1920s, when the price of land ceased to rise and landlords could no longer support themselves by speculation. Rather than improve cotton agricultural methods so that farming was profitable, landlords ejected their tenants and began stocking cattle. They saved themselves an estimated $600 a farm that would have been necessary to reclaim the typical cotton plot. Moreover, the land's new occupants did not join Socialist movements.[8]

Landlords thus began consolidating their small farms into cattle ranches of 1,800 to 3,000 acres. They refused to renew renters' leases and then burned their shacks to discourage squatters. The homeless renters relocated on almost worthless farms, moved to a city, or left the state.⁹

Various migration patterns resulted during this period. Some Oklahomans journeyed to the California lumber mills in the spring, spent the winter in south Texas, and then tried to find summer work back in Oklahoma. Many displaced farmers periodically traveled between the automobile factories in Detroit or the cotton, wheat, and broomcorn harvests in western Oklahoma and Kansas.¹⁰

The persons who probably suffered the most were those who lost their homes and went to the city but were unable to find work or leave for California. Many of the refugees who moved to Oklahoma City settled in a sixty-five-acre "community camp" on the North Canadian River on the outskirts of town. In the mid-1930s the camp, which came to be known as Elk Grove, had a population ranging from 1,500 to 2,000 persons. They were mostly displaced renters who survived in shacks made of sheet metal, cardboard boxes, and discarded lumber in spaces that they rented for one to five dollars a month.¹¹ In 1934 graduate students from the University of Oklahoma surveyed one hundred families at Elk Grove and discovered that fifty-nine owned no property at all and the other fifty-one owned between them one squirrel, one wagon, one goat, two rabbits, eight hogs, twelve chickens, and forty broken-down cars and trucks.¹²

The study further revealed that more than half the adults had never gone beyond the fifth grade in school. Of the families then living in the camp, seventy-five had five or more persons living at home. Most of the homes had dirt floors; there were almost no chairs, stoves, or furnishings, and five or more persons often slept in the same bed. Among the one hundred families investigated, there had been fifty-four cases of pneumonia, forty-three of typhoid, twelve of syphilis, sixteen of insanity, thirteen of epilepsy, four of tuberculosis, three of pellagra, and several of gonorrhea (including six girls under the age of ten).¹³

In the 1940s, McWilliams visited the camp and recorded his

impressions in words similar to those used by Oscar Ameringer when he described the conditions that their parents and grand-parents faced in 1907:

> The last day I was in Oklahoma . . . I visited the Elk Grove camp. On one of the crooked dirt roads running through the camp I came upon the Union Gospel Tabernacle: a long, narrow low-ceiling hovel. . . . On the benches near the rear of the hall were 10 or 20 young girls, kicking their toes in the dust, swatting flies and chewing gum. Immediately in front of them was a boy, about 12 years of age. With tears streaming down his face, and an old Bible clasped to his breast, he was groveling about in the dust and dirt. The aggregation of girls paid not the slightest attention to his sobbing anguish. Further forward in the hall, the younger children were seated on a row of benches. They were all blonds, all dirty and bedraggled. On a side wall near the platform were 15 or 20 complacent and toothless old drones. Intent upon knitting and whispered gossip, they ignored the proceedings except to shout an occasional "Amen, Brother!" On the platform were 3 mourners on a noisy emotional binge—a woman and 2 men shouting and crying, they crawled on the dirt floor and now and then beat their heads on the platform. Their sinful penitence was expressed in a shrill, unceasing and completely unintelligible wail. The only words I caught, after much patient listening, were: "Look what they got for their souls, O Lord!"
>
> Outside, strolling through the camp, you could see former sharecroppers and tenants asleep on their collapsing porches, standing in the doorways of their huts, tinkering with jalopies in the streets, feeding crumbs to a few stray chickens. But the placid sunlight did not efface the recollection of the dismal tabernacle. It haunted me for days; it became an obscene and depressing symbol. Nor could I think of the people in the camp without a sense of shame and horror. Here, indeed, were the "stragglers of routed armies," living in an unforgettable rural ghetto.[14]

Once the state outgrew its frontier status, Oklahomans abandoned radical political ideology. With the defeat of Walton the revolutionary ideals of the Farmers' Alliance, the Socialists, and the neo-Populists were repudiated. The populist wing of the Democratic party was replaced by supporters of the Ku Klux

Klan, as well as representatives of large landowners, business-men, and oilmen. Socialists lost not only their influence but also their reputation as a legitimate political force. They were branded Bolsheviks, subversives, and malcontents who had no place in the democratic system.

The decline of the Socialist party was perplexingly abrupt. The party leadership was quickly dispersed. Preacher Clark and Tad Cumby were sentenced to prison, Pat Nagle died in 1924, and Oscar Ameringer left to organize coal miners in Illinois. Large numbers of the rank and file left the state as their farms were absorbed by large landowners. Those who stayed behind may or may not have retained their political faith. They had no opportunity, however, to recruit new members, for the social and political structure of rural Oklahoma was disrupted by the out-migration.[15]

Various useful interpretations have been offered to explain why Oklahomans abandoned revolutionary ideology. One theory is that socialism, populism, and even reformism were aberrations and that few Oklahomans completely understood the radical ide-ologies. A more subtle and helpful hypothesis is that the Socialist party briefly flourished because it was able to adjust Marxist prin-ciples to the economic conditions and the culture of frontier Oklahoma. The result was a powerful radical coalition of both Socialists and radicals who did not completely understand Marx-ism. After the Bolshevik revolution, however, leftists tried to im-pose a program that did not conform to the needs and values of Oklahomans. The flexibility that had been the strength of the old Socialist party was replaced by the dogmatism of the new Communist party. The result was that hope for a coalition be-tween Socialists and reformers was destroyed.[16]

Both theories have merit, but neither hypothesis is adequate. A satisfactory explanation of the decline of radical ideology must be grounded in an analysis of Oklahoma's frontier history. So-cialism, as well as populism and belligerent reformism, prospered in a frontier environment of which merchants, landlords, and businessmen had not yet gained control. On the frontier social, economic, and political institutions were malleable, and pioneers were confident of their ability to create a new world. Socialism was especially attractive in the most primitive frontier areas, where economic and political behavior had not been institutionalized. Moreover, the personalized nature of the system encouraged radical thought. The economic order in much of Oklahoma was so primitive that there often seemed to be no difference between a small businessman and a common criminal. Consequently, pioneer farmers and laborers often rejected reformism and considered revolutionary proposals.

The more prosperous areas of Oklahoma, the oil fields, the cities, and the plains, quickly outgrew their frontier conditions. They soon became integrated into the national and international systems. At that point Oklahomans working within the flawed but functional national wheat and petroleum market system gained the option of reforming the existing economic structures instead of creating entirely new ones. Large segments of Oklahoma's society, however, most notably cotton tenants, remained excluded and remained without hope that minor alterations in the capitalist system could benefit them. The result of this uneven development was a fatal division in the fragile coalition of diverse segments of the Oklahoma working class. Revolutionaries and reformers in the western half remained sympathetic to socialism, yet they were also lured by less risky political and economic solutions.

If this theory is correct and the decline of frontier socialism was due in part to the realization of postfrontier Oklahomans that with the defeat of their revolutionary ideals their only option was orthodox and inoffensive political programs, then the decline of other forms of radicalism may have been the result of the same dynamic. With the close of the frontier both agrarian and right-wing ideologies declined as rapidly as did socialism. One example of modern Oklahoma's distrust of radicalism occurred when Farmers' Unionist Alfalfa Bill Murray was defeated at the polls because modern voters were embarrassed and offended by his unkempt appearance and idiosyncratic behavior. Similarly, within months of their greatest victories Ku Klux Klan members were ostracized and rejected. The reason was that Oklahomans had decided that both left- and right-wing radicalism was bad for the state's image.

The story of the close of the Oklahoma frontier and the growth and collapse of one of America's most powerful radical movements illustrates two basic yet contradictory dynamics of the history of the United States. The closing of the frontier on the Oklahoma prairie was a tragedy in which the hubris that pervaded the American frontier experience led to economic depression, class conflict, and ecological disaster in the course of subduing the West. In this epic the plains were conquered and wealth was created, but at a great cost. The settling of eastern Oklahoma, however, was not a tragedy; it was simply a failure. It did not include heroic protagonists who defeated material obstacles but succumbed to their tragic flaw, pride in their power to manipulate nature. Instead, their story was one of a forgotten American frontier experience in which pioneers failed to cope with the economic, political, and natural hardships of their new home. The result was ignorance, bitterness, starvation, disease, brutality, and oppression. It was not a struggle between prideful humans and recalcitrant nature in which victorious frontiersmen lost their respect for nature and thus abused it. Instead, eastern Oklahoma was settled by losers in the battle between precapitalist, preindustrial farmers and the modern corporate system. It was inhabited by displaced Indians, disenfranchised blacks hoping to escape the Deep South, and the poor whites of the Reconstruction South.

Unlike the settlers on the Great Plains, pioneers in the hill country did not attempt to create a capitalistic system. Eastern Oklahoma never attracted entrepreneurs with the expertise or the inclination to guide the development of an agricultural economy or a mining industry. Oklahomans simply supplied cheap cotton and coal to eastern markets. No effort was made to build a rational system through which both Oklahoma and its customers could benefit from its soil and minerals. Both eastern corporate powers and local businessmen were content to remove the easily extracted resources without making any effort to institutionalize the state's commercial relationships. In fact, the closest thing to a modern system of commerce that was established was land speculation.

Within a generation the region's forests and wildlife had been decimated. The shallow coal had been removed, much of the rest had been rendered inaccessible, and the soil had been destroyed. At that corporate systems turned to new sources of raw materials, and the process was repeated in other developing regions. The pioneers who had attempted to settle southern and eastern Oklahoma either dispersed or were forced to remain in a chronically depressed region.

The settling of the state's western plains, however, was a microcosm of the development of the rest of the nation. Its pioneers were dynamic, optimistic, ingenious, and determined. Their land was forbidding, and yet it was potentially very rich. Early Oklahomans endured great hardships, and they adjusted to conditions on the prairie. They developed new technologies: adjusted their social, economic, and political system; and learned both to support themselves and to profit from the land's resources.

Unfortunately, however, this pioneer society was too successful in developing its natural resources. The same qualities—"rugged individualism," aggressiveness, flexibility, and greed—that allowed them to overcome physical barriers also drove them to subjugate nature. Within a generation they had transformed the "Great American Desert" into one of the world's most productive agricultural areas and most important suppliers of energy.

The settling of the western frontier was more than a morality play. The method by which the land was developed was the logical outgrowth of the corporate capitalist system. Its growth was guided by agents of an expansionistic economic system based in the Northeast and in Europe. Their fervent campaign to dominate nature was the legacy of both an ethical system that urged humans to generate profits from the land and by more concrete pressures for inexpensive raw materials and an outlet for excess population. Their dramatic success, then, was a component of a larger process, the development of the capitalist world-market system.

The success of the expansionist system was achieved, however, with a great deal of difficulty. The undue haste with which it transformed virgin land into an economic entity encouraged overproduction, panics, erosion, overpopulation, graft, and exploitation. These social problems prompted frontiersmen to develop a variety of radical ideologies ranging from agrarianism to socialism to reformism. These rebellious pioneers did not always reject the frontier capitalist's ethics. Some protested only when the system threatened their family or community. The cruelty with which the capitalist world-market system guided the settling of the frontier, however, also prompted the development of one of the strongest Socialist movements in America.

One way of viewing the growth of frontier radicalism is to theorize that the frontier ethos—the capitalist's determination to transform nature into an economic resource—produced its antithesis, a cooperative, communal, humanistic ideology, frontier socialism. Capitalist entrepreneurs, especially those in faraway corporate centers, found it easy to take for granted the soil, water, trees, and minerals of the frontier, as well as its inhabitants. The persons who worked the land, however, had to respect nature or they would be destroyed by it. They resented the cavalier manner in which the railroads, bankers, and merchants treated their home. Soon farmers and workers realized that the wastefulness and callousness of the capitalist system was a threat to their livelihood.

It is probable that the last of America's frontiers produced the strongest Socialist movement because the dynamics of frontier capitalism were especially clear in Oklahoma. Perhaps Oklahomans had previously been vaguely familiar with the destructiveness of the process because they had witnessed it in their earlier homes. They came to Oklahoma knowing that it represented their last chance to become self-sufficient by pioneering a new land. They watched in horror as the last frontier was immediately decimated. Since Oklahomans witnessed the entire process, they were especially open to revolutionary alternatives to a competitive system that could destroy a virgin wilderness within a single generation.

The methods of the Great Frontier, however, destroyed its political antithesis as quickly as they dominated the frontier's natural resources. Despite the considerable talents possessed by a coalition of Oklahoma's farmers, renters, miners, and laborers, none of the young state's radical political movements were able to alter the basic dynamics of the Great Frontier. Within a generation three sets of political alliances failed in their challenge to the capitalist's approach to building a new society. The fact that the Populists, the Socialists and the neopopulists were crushed, dispersed, and, for the most part, forgotten should not, however, tarnish the memory of their brief battle. Oklahomans, who are especially nostalgic for the prairie and the hills as they were before their exploitation, should also remember the political cultures that were sacrificed to the Great Frontier.

Notes

PREFACE

1. This book is in the tradition of the scholarship of Frederick Jackson Turner. I have tried to keep historiographical analysis to a minimum, however. The book began as a case study designed to test various theories on the American frontier experience as well as the debate over the failure of socialism in America. A study of Oklahoma seemed promising because the state included two distinctive cultural regions, northern and western Oklahoma and the southern and eastern part of the state. These two regions in many ways illustrated the dynamics of two differing American frontiers, the frontiers of the Midwest and the South. As a result, Oklahoma seemed ideal for a comparative study.

The case study was not entirely successful. The evidence necessary to prove crucial components of my hypothesis remained elusive. On the other hand, research yielded a bounty of insights into Oklahoma's cultural heritage that did not fit easily into a social scientist's methodology. Consequently, this study assumed the form of parallel chapters that illustrate crucial dynamics in the socio-economic development and the political consciousness of Oklahoma's two cultural regions. The chapters are not meant to prove causal connections, even though they provide a plausible and, in my opinion, convincing model.

Two problems of the study were questions about the difference between Oklahoma's cultural regions and about the depth of Oklahomans' political consciousness. These questions were answered convincingly enough to satisfy the requirements of the parallel chapters, but they probably could not have been answered with the precision necessary to prove causal connections in a traditional social-scientific analysis.

The first problematical issue was the question of how different were Oklahoma's two culture regions from each other. I have never come across a scholar who challenges the difference between two regions, but there is disagreement over the precise boundaries, and there remains a great deal of uncertainty about crucial aspects of the regions' social structures, especially

their family structures. Faced with two equally promising fields of study,
quantitative research into the regions' sociology or an analysis of the meaning of the bifurcation to Oklahoma, I chose the interpretative path. The
combination of previously published sources and my research confirms what
Oklahomans already knew, that the two regions were different. The question of how different, though, must still be answered with the less-than-
ideal answer of "different enough" for the purpose of analysis. Whether
such an answer is "good enough" is up to the reader.

The second dilemma is the question about the quality of radical thought
embraced by Oklahomans. The debate among modern historians over
whether Oklahomans were "real" Socialists was prompted by Garin Burbank, who gave a somewhat ambivalent answer to the question. The discussion was further polarized by the interpretation of H. Wayne Morgan,
who dismissed the state's Socialists as by-products of "modernization."
Since then nearly every Oklahoma historian has been obliged to comment
on the depth of Socialist thought. Perhaps the entire exchange was unfortunate. In fact, James Green, who has provided the best analysis of the
subject (except, perhaps, for the musings of Oscar Ameringer), has since
urged me to sidestep the entire question.

I would have accepted Green's advice if this book were just a historical
monograph. I could have described Oklahoma socialism on its own terms as
an ideology spawned by a set of social, political, and intellectual circumstances. This book is also an exercise in soul-searching, however. Many
Oklahomans are preoccupied with questions about the existence and the
fate of an allegedly profound political consciousness. Oklahomans are confused by the contrast between the short-sightedness and corruption of their
county commissioners, legislators, and judges and the idealism of the early
advocates of "industrial democracy." We want to believe that our politics
has been different, but we remain skeptical. For that reason I have decided
to retain the blunt methodological tool of distinguishing between true radicals with a deep appreciation of their social and political conditions and
reformers who are merely belligerent. Such a distinction may be too sim-
plistic for a social scientist, but it forthrightly addresses the concerns and
the fears of contemporary Oklahomans, and consequently it is unavoidable
for a book of this sort.

CHAPTER 1

1. Walter Prescott Webb, *The Great Frontier*, pp. 1–3, 7–11.
2. Ibid., pp. 3–9, 13–36.
3. Ibid., pp. 30, 33, 38–78, 73–82.

4. Fernand Braudel, *The Mediterranean and the Mediterranean World in the Age of Phillip II*, 1:100–105.

5. Frederick Jackson Turner, "Problems in American History," in *Frontier and Section: Selected Essays of Frederick Jackson Turner*, ed. Ray Allen Billington, pp. 31–36; Paul Gates, *The Farmer's Age: Agriculture, 1815–1860*, pp. 2–7; Allan Bogue, *From Prairie to Corn Belt: Farming on the Illinois and Iowa Prairie in the Nineteenth Century*, pp. 15–18.

6. Frederick Jackson Turner, "The Significance of the American Frontier," in *The Early Writings of Frederick Jackson Turner*, ed. Edward Everett, pp. 187–89, 196–215; Frederick Jackson Turner, *The Frontier in American History*, pp. 19–29, 86–94.

7. Fred Shannon, "A Post-Mortem on the Labor-Safety Valve Theory," in George Rogers Taylor, ed., *the Turner Thesis*, pp. 51–61.

8. Walter Prescott Webb, *The Great Plains*, pp. 507–22.

9. David Ellis, "The Homestead Clause in Railroad Grants," in David Ellis, ed., *The Frontier in American Development*, pp. 47–53, 71–73; Leslie Decker, "The Great Speculation: An Interpretation of Mid-Continent Pioneering," in ibid., pp. 357–79.

10. Ray Allen Billington, Introduction, in Ray Allen Billington, ed., *Essays on Walter Prescott Webb*, p. xx; Eugene Hollon, "Walter Prescott Webb's Arid West: Four Decades Later, in Kenneth Phillips and Elliott West, eds., *Walter Prescott Webb Memorial Lectures*, pp. 53–60.

11. Arrell M. Gibson, *Oklahoma: A History of Five Centuries*, pp. 287–309, 317, 334, 348; Oscar Ameringer, *If You Don't Weaken: The Autobiography of Oscar Ameringer*, pp. 259–72.

12. Roy Gittinger, *The Formation of the State of Oklahoma, 1803–1906*, pp. 175–95.

13. Gibson, *Oklahoma*, pp. 296, 308–309; Edward E. Dale and Jesse Lee Rader, eds., *Readings in Oklahoma History*, pp. 599–601.

14. Gittinger, *Formation*, pp. 162–74.

15. Edwin C. McReynolds, *Oklahoma: A History of the Sooner State*, pp. 281–92; Dale and Rader, eds., *Readings*, pp. 581–92; Gittinger, *Formation*, pp. 163–74.

16. Gittinger, *Formation*, pp. 175–78.

17. James Green, *Grass-Roots Socialism: Radical Movements in the Southwest, 1895–1943*, pp. 2–3.

18. Howard Meredith, "Agrarian Socialism in Oklahoma" (Ph.D. diss., University of Oklahoma, 1969), pp. 13–16.

19. Stephen Jones, *Oklahoma Politics in the State and Nation*, 1:101–19.

20. Howard Meredith, "Oscar Ameringer and Agrarian Socialism," *Chronicles of Oklahoma* 42, no. 1 (Spring, 1967):74–80; Danney Goble, *Progressive Oklahoma: The Making of a New Kind of State*, pp. 158–65.

21. Edward Everett Dale, *Frontier Historian: The Life and Work of Edward Everett Dale*, ed. Arrell M. Gibson, pp. 338–39.

CHAPTER 2

1. Michael Doran, "Origin of Culture Areas in Oklahoma, 1830–1900" (Ph.D. diss., University of Oregon, 1974), pp. 3–4; Howard Wayne Morgan, *Oklahoma: A Bicentennial History*, pp. 14–18.

2. Doran, "Origin of Culture Areas," p. 16.

3. Ibid., pp. 29, 32, 90–91, 172–75, 180, 184.

4. Work Projects Administration, *Oklahoma: A Guide to the Sooner State*, pp. 24–29, 37–48; James Dilisio, "Standards of Living and Spatio-Temporal Trends in Regional Inequality in Oklahoma" (Master's thesis, University of Oklahoma, 1975), fig. 55.

5. Douglas Hale, "The People of Oklahoma: Economics and Social Change," in Anne Morgan and Wayne Morgan, eds., *Oklahoma: New Views of the Forty-sixth State*, pp. 33, 39, 41, 48–50.

6. Ibid., p. 40.

7. Sheila Manes, "Pioneers and Survivors: Oklahoma's Landless Farmers," in ibid., p. 107.

8. Ellen Rosen, "Peasant Socialism in America: The Socialist Party in Oklahoma Before the First World War" (Ph.D. diss., City University of New York, 1976), pp. 68–70, 182, 202–203.

9. Angie Debo, transcripts of oral-history interview conducted by Glenna Matthews and Gloria Valencia-Weber, Marshall, Oklahoma, December 11, 1981, p. 7.

10. Ibid., p. 8.

11. Karl Polanyi, *The Great Transformation*, pp. 43–47, 54–55.

12. Ibid., pp. 47–49, 68–70.

13. Ibid., pp. 59–67.

14. *Ardmore Alliance Courier*, February 1, June 1, 1894; April 12, 1895; January 17, 1896; *Indiahoma Union Signal*, August 22, November 21, 1905.

15. *Indiahoma Union Signal*, November 7, 14, 21, December 26, 1905; May 31, June 14, 1906.

16. Craig Miner, *The Corporation and the Indian, 1865 to 1907*, pp. 200–207.

17. Work Projects Administration, *Oklahoma*, pp. 23–24; Angie Debo, *The Road to Disappearance: A History of the Creek Indians*, pp. 331–43.

18. Angie Debo, *The Rise and Fall of the Choctaw Republic*, pp. 58–79, 111; Arrell M. Gibson, *The Chickasaws*, pp. 224–46; Edwin C. McReynolds, *The Seminoles*, pp. 316–17; Work Projects Administration, *Oklahoma*, p. 24.

19. Debo, *Road to Disappearance*, pp. 171–85, 189; Ameringer, *If You Don't Weaken*, pp. 233–36.

20. Debo, *Choctaw Republic*, pp. 102–103, 110–12.

21. Ibid., p. 147.

22. Ibid., pp. 94–95, 132–50, 170–72.

23. Ibid., pp. 110–14, 163, 169–74, 183–93.

24. Gibson, *The Chickasaws*, pp. 250–51, 254–55; Debo, *Road to Disappearance*, pp. 360–77.

25. Debo, *Choctaw Republic*, pp. 134–37, 142–44, 152; Goble, *Progressive Oklahoma*, pp. 46–55, 62–64, 66–68.

26. Debo, *Road to Disappearance*, pp. 259–61; Debo, *Choctaw Republic*, pp. 116–27, 213, 216, 224.

27. Craig Miner, "The Struggle for an East-West Railway," *Chronicles of Oklahoma* 47, no. 1 (Spring, 1969):560–76.

28. Debo, *Choctaw Republic*, pp. 116–25.

29. Miner, "The Struggle for an East-West Railway," p. 576; Debo, *Choctaw Republic*, p. 120.

30. Miner, "The Struggle for an East-West Railway," p. 560.

31. Debo, *Choctaw Republic*, pp. 125–31, 134–36, 139–44. Later similar pattern developed in the extraction of petroleum. Careless efforts to extract the resources frequently ruined entire mines and wells; careless excavation of coal ruined the seams and rendered the shafts unstable. Oil wells were ruined when shortsighted drillers allowed gas to escape so that the oil that remained would not flow.

32. Personal conversation with Clark Morter, Oklahoma City, March, 1979. Debo, *Choctaw Republic*, pp. 223–33; Debo, *Road to Disappearance*, p. 225; Miner, "The Struggle for an East-West Railway," p. 566.

33. Claude Curran, "Forest and Forest Industries in Oklahoma," in John W. Morris, ed., *Geography of Oklahoma*, pp. 83–85, 90–91.

34. Debo, *Choctaw Republic*, , pp. 134–36.

35. Lonnie Underhill and Daniel Littlefield, "Quail Hunting in Early Oklahoma," *Chronicles of Oklahoma* 49, no. 3 (Autumn, 1971):315–21; Lonnie Underhill and Daniel Littlefield, "Wild Turkey in Oklahoma," *Chronicles of Oklahoma* 48, no. 4 (Winter, 1970–71): 376–88.

36. I. G. Gunning, *When Coal Was King: Coal Mining Industry in Eastern Oklahoma*, p 11.

37. Frederick Ryan, *The Rehabilitation of Oklahoma Coal Mining Communities*, pp. 41–44; Debo, *Choctaw Republic*, , pp. 144–51.

38. Frederick Ryan, *A History of Labor Legislation in Oklahoma*, pp. 71–72, 147–48.

39. Ryan, *Rehabilitation of Oklahoma Coal Mining Communities*, pp. 21–29, 70–72; Philip Kalisch, "Ordeal of the Oklahoma Coal Miner," *Chronicles of Oklahoma* 48, no. 3 (Autumn, 1970): 333–40.

40. Gene Aldrich, "A History of the Coal Industry in Oklahoma to 1907" (Ph.D. diss., University of Oklahoma, 1952), pp. 88–89; Ryan, *Rehabilitation of Coal Mining Communities*, pp. 50–58.

41. Debo, *Choctaw Republic*, pp. 145–50.

42. Gunning, *When Coal Was King*, pp. 1–24; Ryan, *Rehabilitation of Coal Mining Communities*, pp. 50–57.

43. Gunning, *When Coal Was King*, pp. 29–34; Ryan, *Rehabilitation of Coal Mining Communities*, pp. 58–60.

44. Ryan, *Rehabilitation of Coal Mining Communities*, pp. 45–49.

45. Goble, *Progressive Oklahoma*, pp. 63–64, 70–71, 78–86.

46. William H. Murray, *Memoirs of Governor Murray and the True History of Oklahoma*, pp. 233–57.

47. Gibson, *The Chickasaws*, pp. 252–56, 261–67, 274–78.

48. Debo, *Choctaw Republic*, p. 127.

49. Ibid., pp. 198–211.

50. Goble, *Progressive Oklahoma*, pp. 76–83; Debo, *Choctaw Republic*, p. 211.

51. *Harlow's Weekly* (Oklahoma City), November 10, 1913, p. 12.

52. Ibid., pp. 12–13.

53. Interview with Henry Everidge, Frogville, Oklahoma, March, 1979.

54. Goble, *Progressive Oklahoma*, pp. 78–86.

55. Debo, *Road to Disappearance*, p. 164.

56. Ibid., pp. 361–77; Debo, *Choctaw Republic*, pp. 260–90: Robert Hoxie, "The End of the Savage Indian Policy in the United States Senate," *Chronicles of Oklahoma* 55, no. 2 (Summer, 1977): 157–79.

57. Murray, *Memoirs*, pp. 238–39.

58. Susan Work, "Rights of the Seminole Nation Related to Railroad Rights of Way."

59. Edward Everett Dale and James Morison, *Pioneer Judge: The Life of Robert Williams*, pp. 381–97; Garin Burbank, *When Farmers Voted Red: The Gospel of Socialism in the Oklahoma Countryside, 1910–1923*, pp. 91–94.

60. Murray, *Memoirs*, pp. 202, 235–48, 2909; Dale and Rader, eds., *Readings*, p. 383.

61. *Harlow's Weekly*, February 13, 1913.

62. Goble, *Progressive Oklahoma*, pp. 156–59; Manes, "Pioneers and Survivors," pp. 103–10; Debo, *Choctaw Republic*, pp. 113, 121–23.

63. *Harlow's Weekly*, March 1, 1913; Burbank, *When Farmers Voted Red*, pp. 5–7.

64. Charles Webb, "Distribution of Cotton Production in Oklahoma, 1907–1962," (Master's thesis, University of Oklahoma, 1963), p. 7.

65. Debo, *Choctaw Republic*, pp. 171–78.

66. Murray, *Memoirs*, p. 135.

67. Ameringer, *If You Don't Weaken*, p. 233.

l, November 7, 1905; Hurst, *The Forty-sixth Sta*

ve Oklahoma, pp. 175–80; Ardmore Alliance Courie
uary 8, February 22, March 29, April 12, 1894; Jul
itical History," p. 83; Harlow's Weekly, February 13

wyn, Democratic Promise: The Populist Movement i

ney, From Populism to Progressivism in Alabama,
5.
8, 324–32.
ocratic Promise, pp. 503, 546–52.
xii, 322–24, 402–404, 563.
of Culture Areas," pp. 3–16.
arian Socialism," pp. 4–17.
and Donovan Hoffsommer, "Square Deal for Eschiti:
Progressive Era," in Donovan Hoffsommer, ed., Rail-
. 88–94; Goble, Progressive Oklahoma, pp. 170–77.
sive Oklahoma, pp. 170–77.
e Enid Railroad War," pp. 164–75.
Roots Socialism, pp. 53–64; Jones, Oklahoma Politics,

sive Oklahoma, pp. 18–23.
t, Alfalfa Bill Murray, pp. 53–54; Green, Grass-Roots
County Populist (Newkirk), February 14, April 1, June
November 4, 1894; Ardmore Alliance Courier, Feb-
May 10, June 1, 1894; February 22, 1906; Howard
arian Reform Press in Oklahoma," Chronicles of Okla-
ing, 1972): 87–88. Unfortunately, it is impossible to
he reformist or the revolutionary agrarian ideologies
region or another. Predictably, fewer newspapers were
aller number of literary sources survived the territorial
e of the later stages of Oklahoma's settlement. Perhaps
uld have indicated a correlation between ideology and
possible, however, that the differences between the
ot yet clear enough to produce distinctive political

ion Signal, June 27, 1905.
, August 11, August 29, September 21, 1905; August

ll, The Emergence of the New South, p. 41.
, Man over Money, pp. 5, 26, 69.

---

68. Ibid., p. 232.
69. Murray, *Memoirs*, pp. 130–31.
70. Ibid., pp. 190–92.
71. Green, *Grass-Roots Socialism*, pp. xviii, 70–71.
72. Robert Dykstra, *The Cattle Towns*, pp. 112–49.
73. Gary McWilliams, *Ill Fares the Land*, pp. 206–27.
74. James R. Scales and Danney Goble, *Oklahoma Politics: A History*, p. 9.
75. Allan Bogue, "Farm Tenants in the Nineteenth-Century Middle West," in Trudy Peterson, ed., *Farmers, Bureaucrats, and Middlemen*, pp. 113–14.

CHAPTER 3

1. Morgan, *Oklahoma*, pp. 2, 12–13, 50–52.
2. Gibson, *Oklahoma*, pp. 260–67, 287–94.
3. Gittinger, *Formation*, pp. 119–24; Dale and Rader, eds., *Readings*, pp. 457–66.
4. Gittinger, *Formation*, pp. 169–70; McReynolds, *Oklahoma*, p. 307.
5. Neil Johnson, *The Chickasaw Rancher*, pp. 192–93.
6. Bobby Johnson, "Pilgrims on the Prairie," in Donald E. Green, ed., *Rural Oklahoma*, p. 14; Green, *Grass-Roots Socialism*, p. 65.
7. Allie B. Wallace, *Frontier Life in Oklahoma*, p. 18.
8. Wallace, *Frontier Life*, pp. 9–10, 23.
9. Morgan, *Oklahoma*, pp. 64–71.
10. Johnson, "Pilgrims," p. 11.
11. Debo, transcripts, January 20, 1982, pp. 1–5.
12. Ibid., p. 5.
13. Donald E. Green, "Beginnings of Wheat Culture in Oklahoma," in Green, ed., *Rural Oklahoma*, pp. 56–57; Morgan, *Oklahoma*, pp. 63, 65–69; Johnson, "Pilgrims," pp. 13–15.
14. *Newkirk Populist*, February 14, 1894, p. 1.
15. Green, "Beginnings of Wheat Culture," pp. 56–59.
16. Ibid., pp. 59–67; Johnson, "Pilgrims," pp. 15–20.
17. Johnson, "Pilgrims," p. 16; Green, "Beginnings of Wheat Culture," pp. 57–58.
18. Green, "Beginnings of Wheat Culture," pp. 57–58, 62–66; Dale and Rader, eds., *Readings*, pp. 561–62.
19. Green, "Beginnings of Wheat Culture," pp. 45–73; Dale and Rader, eds., *Readings*, pp. 771–73.
20. Jesse Harder, "Wheat Production in Northwest Oklahoma, 1893–1932" (Master's thesis, University of Oklahoma, 1932), pp. 11, 13, 23–24, 26–27, 32; Goble, *Progressive Oklahoma*, pp. 28–32.

21. Donald E. Green, *Panhandle Pioneer: Henry Hitch and His Family*, pp. 39–62; Johnson, "Pilgrims," pp. 15–20

22. Work Projects Administration, *Oklahoma*, p. 167; Meredith, "Agrarian Socialism," p. 42; Michael Reggio, "Troubled Times: Homesteading in the Shortgrass Country, 1892–1900," *Chronicles of Oklahoma* 57, no. 2 (Summer, 1979): 199, 204–206, 208–11.

23. John Alley, *City Beginnings in Oklahoma Territory*, pp. 29–30, 42–45; Dale and Rader, eds., *Readings*, pp. 474–76, 527–31; Boo Browning, "The Wizard of Fourth and Broadway," *Oklahoma Monthly*, November, 1978, pp. 61–67.

24. Albert McRill, *And Satan Came Also*, pp. 1–7.

25. Ibid., pp. 7–15; Alley, *City Beginnings in Oklahoma Territory*, pp. 32–37.

26. McRill, *And Satan Came Also*, pp. 11–20, 25–32, 54–59.

27. Goble, *Progressive Oklahoma*, pp. 32–38; Work Projects Administration, *Oklahoma*, pp. 137–38.

28. Berlin Chapman, "The Enid Railroad War: An Archival Study," *Chronicles of Oklahoma* 43, no. 2 (Summer, 1965): 146–49.

29. Chapman, "The Enid Railroad War," pp. 164–71; Goble, *Progressive Oklahoma*, pp. 15–23, 25–32.

30. Chapman, "The Enid Railroad War," pp. 176–85.

31. John W. Morris, *Ghost Towns of Oklahoma*, pp. 6, 51, 91, 110; Irvin Hurst, *Forty-sixth Star: A History of the Oklahoma Constitutional Convention and Early Statehood*, pp. 60–63.

32. Walter M. Harrison, *Out of My Wastebasket*, pp. 77–95.

33. Norman Crockett, "The Opening of Oklahoma, Businessman's Frontier," *Chronicles of Oklahoma* 55, no. 1 (Spring, 1978): 88–89.

34. Ibid., pp. 92–93.

35. Ibid., pp. 85–87, 94–95.

36. J. Stanley Clark, *The Oil Century: From the Drake Well to the Conservation Era*, pp. 111, 128–29.

37. Roy McClintock, "Oil in Oklahoma" (manuscript), pp. 7–8.

38. David Boles, "Prairie Oil and Gas Company," *Chronicles of Oklahoma* 46, no. 2 (Summer, 1968): 195–98.

39. Work Projects Administration, *Oklahoma*, pp. 38–39; Robert Gregory, *Oil in Oklahoma*, pp. 2–10; McClintock, "Oil in Oklahoma," pp. 13–15.

40. Drew Deberry, "The Ethics of the Oklahoma Oil Boom, 1905–1929" (Master's thesis, University of Oklahoma, 1976), pp. 4, 88–89.

41. John Joseph Mathews, *Life and Death of an Oilman: The Career of E. W. Marland*, pp. 76–85.

42. Ibid., pp. 87–94.

43. Ibid., p. 115.

44. Charles
45. Blue Cl
icles of Oklahor
the Oklahoma
1914, October

1. Donald
tion," *Chronicle*
Paul Wilson, "T
of Oklahoma 43,
2. Walter Pre
3. See also W
Tindall, The Persi
Populism and Poli
4. Norman Pe
5. *Oklahoma I*
6. Scales, "Po
pp. 106–107.
7. Robert Mill
Oklahoma Territo
of this writing, M
populism.
8. Jones, *Okla*
pp. 267–73; Scales
9. Meredith, "
10. Ryan, *Histor*
homa, pp. 160–65,
11. Howard Mer
Chronicles of Oklaho
12. Meredith, "A
tics, pp. 41–43; Hur
13. *Indiahoma Un*
14. Ibid., June 21
15. Ibid., June 14
16. Goble, *Progres*
17. Dale and Rade
18. Goble, *Progres*
Oklahoma Politics, pp.
19. Scales and Gob
20. Goble, *Progress*

Indiahoma Union Sign
p. 2.
21. Goble, *Progressi*
May 25, June 25, Febr
26, 1895; Scales, "Pol
1913.
22. Lawrence Good
America, p. 1.
23. Sheldon Hack
pp. 48–56.
24. Ibid., pp. 71–7
25. Ibid., pp. 85–8
26. Goodwyn, *Dem*
27. Ibid., pp. xvi–
28. Doran, "Origin
29. Meredith, "Ag
30. Peter Peterson
A Footnote from the
roads in Oklahoma, p
31. Goble, *Progres*
32. Chapman, "Th
33. Green, *Grass*
pp. 109–14.
34. Goble, *Progres*
35. Keith L. Bryan
Socialism, p. 61; Kay
13, 28, August 29,
ruary 22, April 19,
Meredith, "The Agr
homa 50, no. 3 (Spr
determine whether
were stronger in one
published, and a sm
period than did thos
the lost evidence wo
region. It is equally
two regions were
ideologies.
36. *Indiahoma U*
37. Ibid., June 2
30, 1906.
38. George Tind
39. Bruce Palme

40. Chester McArthur Destler, *American Radicalism, 1865–1901*, pp. 3, 72–77, 197–201.
41. Norman Pollack, *The Populist Response to Industrial America: Midwestern Populist Thought*, pp. 9, 12–16, 68, 143.
42. Miller, "Bases of Partisan Choice," pp. 11–12.
43. Argensinger, *Populism and Politics*, pp. 65, 67, 71, 73; Miller, "Bases of Partisan Choice," pp. 3, 5, 18–22.
44. *Enid Coming Events*, July 4, 1895.
45. Ibid.
46. *Stillwater People's Voice*, April 11, 1906.
47. *Oklahoma Representative* (Guthrie), July 5, 1894, quoted in Miller, "Bases of Partisan Choice," p. 14.
48. *Indiahoma Union Signal*, November 7, 1905.
49. *Ardmore Alliance Courier*, October 11, 1895.
50. Ibid., May 18, 1894.
51. Ibid., October 4, 1895.
52. Ibid., November 30, 1893.
53. Ibid., September 20, 1895.
54. John Simpson, *Militant Voice of Agriculture*.
55. Ibid., p. 82.
56. Ibid., p. 78.
57. *Ardmore Alliance Courier*, May 3, 1894; December 14, 1893.
58. *Indiahoma Union Signal*, June 20, 1907.
59. Ibid., April 4, 1907.
60. Ibid., April 18, 1907.
61. Ibid., May 26, 1905.
62. Ibid., March 29, 1906.
63. Ibid., May 26, 1905; see also November 14, 1905.
64. *Ardmore Alliance Courier*, October 4, 1895; see also Pickens, "Oklahoma Populism," pp. 279–82.
65. *Ardmore Alliance Courier*, April 19, 1894.

CHAPTER 5

1. Green, *Grass-Roots Socialism*, pp. 67–73.
2. U.S. Department of Commerce, *Population of Oklahoma and Indian Territory, 1907*, pp. 3–7; U.S. Department of Commerce, *Thirteenth Census of the United States, 1910: Population of Oklahoma*, p. 7.
3. Daily Oklahoman, *The Oklahoma Almanac*, 1:98–103; Burbank, *When Farmers Voted Red*, pp. 7–10.
4. Personal interview with Henry Everidge, March, 1976; see also Webb, "Distribution of Cotton Production," p. 7.

5. *Farmer-Stockman* (Oklahoma City), November 25, 1915.

6. Ryan, *History of Labor Legislation*, pp. 64–69; Daily Oklahoman, *Oklahoma Almanac*, p. 78.

7. *Harlow's Weekly*, September 4, 1912.

8. *Ardmore Daily Ardmorite*, January 10, 1912.

9. Scales, "Political History of Oklahoma," pp. 90–95.

10. *Farmer-Stockman*, February 10, 1912.

11. Ibid., February 10, 1916.

12. Ibid., May 25, 1916.

13. Ibid., October 25, 1915.

14. Ibid., October 10, 1914.

15. Ibid., February 10, 1916.

16. Ibid., October 10, 1915.

17. Burbank, *When Farmers Voted Red*, pp. 6–10, 91–93; Green, *Grass-Roots Socialism*, pp. 256–58.

18. *Farmer-Stockman*, January 22, 1914.

19. Ibid., April 2, 1914.

20. Ibid., March 5, 1914.

21. Ibid., March 19, 1914.

22. Ibid., March 12, 1914.

23. Ibid., March 12, 1914.

24. Ibid., March 12, 1914.

25. Ibid., March 19, 1914.

26. Ibid., November 25, December 10, 1914.

27. Ibid., April 2, 1914.

28. Ibid., March 12, 1914.

29. Ibid., May 7, 1914.

30. Ibid., September 10, 1914.

31. Ibid., May 7, 1914.

32. Ibid., March 19, 1915.

33. Ibid., November 25, 1915.

34. Ibid., October 25, 1914; November 25, 1915; *Harlow's Weekly*, January 22, 1918.

35. *Farmer-Stockman*, December 15, 1915.

36. Ibid., October 25, December 25, 1914.

37. Ibid., December 12, 1915.

38. *Durant Independent Farmer*, January 10, 1910.

39. Personal interview with Everidge, March, 1976.

40. George Milburn, "Garlic," in *Oklahoma Town*, pp. 163–71.

41. Burbank, *When Farmers Voted Red*, p. 96; Carter Goodrich, *Migration and Economic Opportunity: The Report of the Study of Population Redistribution*, pp. 694–99; Green, *Grass-Roots Socialism*, pp. 320–23.

CHAPTER 6

1. N. James Wilson, "Oklahoma and Midwestern Farmers in Transition, 1880–1910," In Green, ed., *Rural Oklahoma*, pp. 29–36.

2. Green, "Beginnings of Wheat Culture," pp. 59–61.

3. *Harlow's Weekly*, April 22, 1922, June 12, 1918.

4. Green, ed., *Rural Oklahoma*, pp. 64–73; *Harlow's Weekly*, July 11, 1917.

5. Robert Smith, "Dark Morning at Dover," in Donovan Hoffsommer, ed., *Railroads in Oklahoma*, pp. 81–89; Goble, *Progressive Oklahoma*, pp. 170–71.

6. Morgan, *Oklahoma*, pp. 10–14; Work Projects Administration, *Oklahoma*, pp. 39–45.

7. Clark, *The Oil Century*, p. 141; L. D. Glasscock, *Then Came Oil*, pp. 153, 112–24, 162–64, 166–68, 209–44.

8. Dale and Rader, eds., *Readings*, pp. 771–77.

9. McClintock, "Oil in Oklahoma," pp. 18–19; *Harlow's Weekly*, July 24, August 28, 1915.

10. McClintock, "Oil in Oklahoma," p. 18.

11. Ibid., pp. 12, 15–16, 18.

12. Ibid., pp. 8, 12–13, 16.

13. Ibid., pp. 12, 27.

14. Ibid., pp. 11–22, 27.

15. Ibid., pp. 6, 19, 26–27.

16. Ibid., pp. 11–19, 33–36.

17. Ibid., pp. 30–31,

18. James Gilbert, "Three Sands: Oklahoma Oil Field and Community of the 1920s" (Master's thesis, University of Oklahoma, 1967), pp. 14–21; *Harlow's Weekly*, January 3, 1917; McClintock, "Oil in Oklahoma," pp. 13–37.

19. Deberry, "Ethics of the Oklahoma Oil Boom," pp. 11–12, 25.

20. Gilbert, "Three Sands," pp. 13–20.

21. *Harlow's Weekly*, September 15, 1915.

22. Ellsworth Collings and Alma Miller England, *The 101 Ranch*, pp. xiii, 30–41.

23. Ibid., pp. 30–36; *Harlow's Weekly*, September 18, 1915, September 19, 1917.

24. Collings and England, *The 101 Ranch*, pp. 112–20.

25. Ibid., pp. 102–12.

26. A. Botkin, ed., *Folk-Say: A Regional Miscellany*, 2:63–64.

27. Thomas Frederick Saarinen, *Perceptions of the Drouth Hazard on the Great Plains*, pp. 97–102.

CHAPTER 7

1. Meredith, "Agrarian Socialism," pp. 22–25, 32–37.
2. *Oklahoma Socialist* (Oklahoma City), December 11, 1902.
3. Ibid., September 6, 1901.
4. Meredith, "Agrarian Socialism," pp. 37–39, 58–60.
5. Jones, *Oklahoma Politics*, pp. 105–108/
6. *Appeal to Reason* (Girard, Kansas), September 8, 1906.
7. Meredith, "Agrarian Socialism," pp. 62–66.
8. *American Guardian* (Oklahoma City), December 14, 1934.
9. Ibid., pp. 29–30, 56–57, 60–62.
10. Ibid., pp. 129–32; Samuel Kirkpatrick, David Morgan, and Larry Edwards, *Oklahoma Voting Patterns: Congressional Elections*, pp. 39–41.
11. Meredith, "Agrarian Socialism," pp. 154–60; Kirkpatrick, Morgan, and Edwards, *Oklahoma Voting Patterns*, pp. 42–44; Green, *Grass-Roots Socialism*, pp. 286–96.
12. Meredith, "Agrarian Socialism," pp. 186–88; Kirkpatrick, Morgan, and Edwards, *Oklahoma Voting Patterns*, pp. 45–48.
13. Meredith, "Agrarian Socialism," pp. 187–90; Green, *Grass-Roots Socialism*, pp. 352–53.
14. Green, *Grass-Roots Socialism*, pp. 353–54.
15. Ibid., pp. 317–19.
16. Quoted in Scales, "Political History," p. 178.
17. *Harlow's Weekly*, May 20, 1916; Green, *Grass-Roots Socialism*, pp. 320–22.
18. Donald Graham, "Red, White and Black: An Interpretation of Ethnic and Racial Attitudes of Agrarian Radicals in Texas and Oklahoma" (Master's thesis, University of Saskatchewan, 1973), pp. 285–94; Scales and Goble, *Oklahoma Politics*, p. 47.
19. Graham, "Red, White and Black," pp. 285–86.
20. Ibid., pp. 312–14.
21. Ibid., pp. 315–23.
22. Ibid., pp. 86, 330–32.
23. Ibid., pp. 332–34; Scales and Goble, *Oklahoma Politics*, p. 86.
24. Scales and Goble, *Oklahoma Politics*, p. 86.
25. *Oklahoma Socialist*, February 1, 1905.
26. Green, *Grass-Roots Socialism*, pp. 144–51.
27. Manes, "Pioneers and Survivors," in Morgan and Morgan, eds., *Oklahoma*, pp. 117–19.
28. Green, *Grass-Roots Socialism*, pp. xix, 126–43.
29. Ibid., p. 144.
30. Ibid., pp. xii–xx, 126–29.
31. Ibid., pp. 358–61.

32. Burbank, *When Farmers Voted Red*, pp. xiii–xviii, 3–7, 184–89.

33. Green, *Grass-Roots Socialism*, pp. 357–60.

34. *New Century* (Sulphur), September 6, 1912.

35. *Oklahoma Pioneer* (Oklahoma City), August 27, 1912.

36. Ameringer, *If You Don't Weaken*, pp. 253–56.

37. Ibid., pp. 228–29.

38. Ibid., pp. 237–39.

39. Ibid., pp. 245–53.

40. *Sword of Truth* (Sentinel), January 1, 1913.

41. *Johnson County Socialist* (Tishomingo), February 2, 1912.

42. *New Century*, February 4, 1911.

43. Ibid., November 22, 1911.

44. Meredith, "Agrarian Socialism," pp. 87–88, 148–50.

45. *Oklahoma Socialist*, February 1, 1905.

46. *New Century*, September 27, 1912.

47. *Social Economist* (Bonham, Texas), June 6, 1901.

48. *New Century*, September 6, 1912.

49. *Ardmore X-Ray*, October 12, 1914.

50. *New Century*, January 17, 1913.

51. *Okemah Sledgehammer*, April 23, 1914.

52. Ibid., June 19, 26, August 7, 1913.

53. Ibid., June 19, August 14, 21, September 11, December 25, 1913.

54. Ibid., June 19, 26, 1913.

55. Ibid., June 19, 1913.

56. Ibid.

57. Ibid., December 25, 1913.

58. Ibid., February 19, 1914.

59. Ibid., September 25, 1914.

60. Ibid., February 19, 1914.

61. Ibid., October 16, 1913.

62. Green, *Grass-Roots Socialism*, pp. 81, 302; *New Century*, February 7, 1913.

63. Green, *Grass-Roots Socialism*, pp. 81, 83–85.

64. Ibid., pp. 322–29.

65. U.S. Commission on Industrial Relations, *Final Report and Testimony*, 9:9067–68.

66. Ibid., p. 9067.

67. Ibid., pp. 9068–69.

68. *New Century*, February 16, 1913.

69. Ibid.

70. U.S. Commission on Industrial Relations, *Final Report*, pp. 9067–69.

71. Green, *Grass-Roots Socialism*, pp. 65–76.

72. *Stillwater Gazette*, August 21, 1902.

73. Green, *Grass-Roots Socialism*, p. 161.
74. Ameringer, *If You Don't Weaken*, pp. 262–63.
75. Ibid. pp. 263–65.
76. *Ellis County Socialist* (Shattuck), September 28, 1916.
77. *Beckham County Advocate* (Sayre), May 15, 1913.
78. *Sayre Agitator*, April 3, 1914.
79. *Sentinel Sword of Truth*, March 5, 1913.
80. *Otter Valley Socialist* (Snyder), January 13, December 22, 1915.
81. *Otter Valley Socialist*, January 13, 1915.
82. *Ellis County Socialist* (Shattuck), October 14, 1915.
83. *Grant County Socialist* (Medford), December 7, 1912.
84. *Otter Valley Socialist*, January 13, 1915.
85. *Carter Express*, October 16, 1914.
86. *Otter Valley Socialist*, January 13, 1915.
87. *Beckham County Advocate* (Sayre), June 19, 1913.
88. *Woods County Constructive Socialist* (Alva), August 7, 1912.
89. *Ellis County Socialist*, October 21, 1915.
90. *Grant County Socialist* (Medford), December 7, 1912.
91. *Woods County Constructive Socialist*, September 6, 1911.
92. *Otter Valley Socialist*, January 13, 1915.
93. *Common People* (Stillwater), November 9, 1903.
94. Ibid., December 17, 1903; August 4, 1904.
95. Ibid., January 14, 1904.
96. Ibid., December 21, 1903.
97. Ibid., April 7, 1903.
98. *Pawhuska World Wide War*, September 16, 1915.
99. Ibid., December 18, September 23, 1915.
100. Ibid., October 7, 1916.
101. Ibid., October 28, September 16, 1915.
102. Ibid., July 29, 1916.
103. Ibid., October 7, 1915.

CHAPTER 8

1. George Gorton, *A Big-Ass Boy in the Oilfields*, pp. 1–15.
2. William Cunningham, *The Green Corn Rebellion*, pp. 128–31.
3. Ibid., pp. 137–49.
4. Ryan, *History of Labor Legislation*, pp. 18–23.
5. Ibid., pp. 20–24.
6. Gorton, *Big-Ass Boy*, pp. 1–30.
7. Gary Nall, "King Cotton in Oklahoma," in Green, ed., *Rural Oklahoma*, pp. 46–47.
8. Burton Rascoe, *We Were Interrupted* p. 51.

9. Ryan, *History of Labor Legislation*, p. 65.

10. Rascoe, *We Were Interrupted* p. 37.

11. Ibid., p. 51.

12. Rascoe, *We Were Interrupted* p. 49.

13. Ibid., pp. 52–53.

14. Ibid., pp. 49, 63.

15. Charles Bush, "The Green Corn Rebellion" (Master's thesis, University of Oklahoma, 1932), p. 4.

16. Ibid., pp. 3–5.

17. Ibid., p. 5.

18. Ibid., p. 4.

19. Rascoe, *We Were Interrupted* p. 49–50.

20. Meredith, "Agrarian Socialism," pp. 205–10.

21. Harder, "Wheat Production," p. 4.

22. The percentages occasionally exceeded 100 percent because some fields extended across the boundaries, and the farm's entire acreage counted in the home county's total.

23. Ibid., p. 72.

24. Ibid., p. 72.

25. Ibid., p. 173.

26. Paul Bonnefield, *The Dust Bowl: Men, Dirt, and Depression*, pp. 11, 20.

27. Green, ed., *Rural Oklahoma*, p. 67.

28. Ibid., pp. 70–73; Nall, "King Cotton," pp. 38–43.

29. Green, ed., *Rural Oklahoma*, pp. 252–66, 308–15.

30. Webb, "Distribution of Cotton Production," p. 9.

31. Nall, "King Cotton," p. 44.

32. Ibid., pp. 40–46, 49–50.

33. Ben Barr, "Accounting Problems of Cooperative Cotton Gins" (Master's thesis, University of Oklahoma, 1950), p. 6; Clark, *The Oil Century*, p. 129.

34. Gilbert, "Three Sands," pp. 35–40.

35. Ibid., pp. 35–40, 112–13.

36. Ibid., pp. 114–17, 119–20.

37. Ibid., pp. 91–100.

38. Ibid., pp. 57–64.

39. Ibid., pp. 2–3, 12–20, 35–38, 40–53.

CHAPTER 9

1. Danney Goble and James Scales, "Depression Politics: Personality and the Problem of Relief," p. 198; Kenneth Hendrickson, Jr., *Hard Times*

in Oklahoma: The Depression Years, pp. 20–21; see also Marty Hauan, *He Buys Organs for Churches and Pianos for Bawdy Houses*, pp. 190–210.

2. *Harlow's Weekly*, December 25, January 15, 1916, January 29, 1918.

3. Ibid., March 25, 1916.

4. Duane Gage, "Al Jennings: The People's Choice," *Chronicles of Oklahoma* 46, no. 3 (Autumn, 1968): 242–49.

5. Ibid., p. 247.

6. Green, *Grass-Roots Socialism*, pp. 321–23; Burbank, *When Farmers Voted Red*, pp. 136–37.

7. *Johnston County Socialist*, February 2, 1916; *Harlow's Weekly*, May 20, 1916.

8. *Harlow's Weekly*, September 25, 1915.

9. Stanley Clark, "Texas Fever in Oklahoma," *Chronicles of Oklahoma* 29, no. 4 (Fall, 1951): 429–43.

10. Sherry Warwick, "Anti-War Resistance in the Southwest During World War I" (Master's thesis, University of Oklahoma, 1973), pp. 40–41; *Harlow's Weekly*, January 1, February 26, 1916; Meredith, "Agrarian Socialism," pp. 165–71.

11. Bush, "Green Corn Rebellion," pp. 4–13.

12. Ibid., p. 7.

13. Quoted in Warwick, "Anti-War Resistance," p. 36.

14. Ibid., pp. 70–73; Green, *Grass-Roots Socialism*, p. 360.

15. Warwick, "Anti-War Resistance," p. 711; Green, *Grass-Roots Socialism*, p. 360.

16. Anonymous, from Ned DeWitt, "WPA Writers Project on Oil in Oklahoma" (Western History Collections, University of Oklahoma), quoted in Ann Hodges Morgan and Rennard Strickland, eds., *Oklahoma Memories*, pp. 177, 176.

17. Burbank, *When Farmers Voted Red*, pp. 150–53, 213–15.

18. Green, *Grass-Roots Socialism*, p. 366.

19. Ameringer, *If You Don't Weaken*, pp. 350–55. The text of Bush's description appears in ibid., pp. 347–49.

20. Meredith, "Agrarian Socialism," pp. 174–75.

21. Bush, "Green Corn Rebellion," pp. 55–56.

22. *Harlow's Weekly*, August 1, 1917; April 3, 24, 1918; November 14, 1917; Virginia Pope, "the Green Corn Rebellion: A Study in Newspaper Self-Censorship" (Master's thesis, Oklahoma State University, 1940), pp. 8–10, 25.

23. Green, *Grass-Roots Socialism*, p. 374.

24. O. A. Hilton, "The Oklahoma Council of Defense in the First World War," *Chronicles of Oklahoma* 20, no. 1 (1942): 1; Green, *Grass-Roots Socialism*, pp. 354–56, 378–79.

25. Hilton, "Oklahoma Council of Defense," pp. 33–34.

26. Walter M. Harrison, *Me and My Big Mouth*, p. 37.

27. James Morton Smith, "Criminal Syndicalism in Oklahoma: A History of the Law and Its Application" (Master's thesis, University of Oklahoma, 1946) p. 36; Hilton, "Oklahoma Council of Defense," pp. 34–38.

28. Smith, "Criminal Syndicalism," p. 36.

29. William Lamp, *Tulsa County in the World War*, pp. 69, 76.

30. D. C. Rose, *Sooners in the War: Official Report of the Oklahoma State Council of Defense*, p. 61.

31. James Fowler, "Tar and Feather Patriotism," *Chronicles of Oklahoma* 56, no. 4 (Winter, 1978–79): 409–29; National Civil Liberties Bureau, *The Knights of Liberty Mob and the IWW Prisoners at Tulsa, Oklahoma*, pp. 4–6; Gilbert C. Fite and H. C. Peterson, *Opponents of the War, 1917–1918*, pp. 169–75.

32. National Civil Liberties Bureau, *Knights of Liberty Mob*, pp. 9–10.

33. Ibid., pp. 7–8.

34. Ibid., pp. 13–14.

35. Smith, "Criminal Syndicalism," p. 34.

36. Sheldon Neuringer, "Governor Walton's War on the Ku Klux Klan," *Chronicles of Oklahoma* 45, no. 2 (Summer, 1967): 153–60; Blue Clark, "A History of the Ku Klux Klan in Oklahoma" (Master's thesis, University of Oklahoma, 1976) pp. 260–75.

37. George Milburn, *Oklahoma Town*, p. 3.

CHAPTER 10

1. *Harlow's Weekly*, August 1, 8, December 12, 1917.

2. Ibid., January 2, 16, May 22, 1918.

3. Gary Crowder, "Northern Lights: Developing a Regional Cinema," *Cineaste* 10, no. 1 (Winter, 1979–80): 10–20.

4. *Harlow's Weekly*, May 22, 1918.

5. Anonymous, from DeWitt, "WPA Writers Project on Oil in Oklahoma," quoted in Morgan and Strickland, eds., *Oklahoma Memories*, pp. 177–78.

6. Quoted in Smith, "Criminal Syndicalism in Oklahoma," pp. 17, 43.

7. Quoted in ibid., pp. 53–56.

8. Ibid., pp. 58–61.

9. Scott Ellsworth, *Death in a Promised Land: The Tulsa Race Riot of 1921*, pp. 2–3, 11–14, 19.

10. *Daily Oklahoman*, April 27, 1921.

11. *Harlow's Weekly*, February 12, 1916.

12. Ibid., March 25, 1916; January 17, 1917.

13. Ibid., August 14, 28, September 4, 1918.

14. Ibid., January 17, 1918.

15. Ibid., January 1, 1916; June 20, 1917.

16. Scales, "Political History," pp. 201–206. Perhaps the term "Southern Progressive" would serve as well as "neopopulists." Reformers who were active from statehood to World War I have usually been described as progressives. One aspect of the ideology was a moderation prompted by an awareness that radicalism often inspired repression. Perhaps the main difference between these progressives and the reformers of the postwar era that I have called Neopopulists is that the Neopopulists had a much more vivid awareness of the dangers of repression.

17. Mary Hays Marable and Elaine Boylan, A Handbook of Oklahoma Writers, pp. 167–76.

18. Harlow's Weekly, October 30, November 6, 1915; March 11, 1916.

19. Ibid., October 16, 30, December 11, 1915; January 22, March 23, 1916.

20. Ibid., September 25, 1915.

21. Ibid., October 30, 1915.

22. Ibid., December 11, 25, 1915.

23. Ibid., October 2, 1915.

24. Ibid., August 8, 1917.

25. Matthews, Life and Death of an Oilman, pp. 148–51.

26. Ibid., pp. 137–39.

27. Ernest Bynum, Personal Recollections of Ex-Governor Walton: A Record of Personal Observation, preface, pp. 4, 9–10.

28. Ibid., pp. 9–10, 74–79.

29. Ibid., pp. 43–54.

30. Ibid., pp. 19–20, 24–27.

31. Scales, "Political History," p. 202.

32. Harlow's Weekly, October 17, November 7, 1917.

33. Scales, "Political History," pp. 202–206; Harlow's Weekly, May 15, December 25, 1918.

34. Scales, "Political History," p. 202.

35. Ibid., p. 203.

36. Ibid., p. 204.

37. Ibid., pp. 236–38, 220–34; Matthews, Life and Death of an Oilman, pp. 140–41.

38. Gilbert C. Fite, "The Non-Partisan League in Oklahoma," Chronicles of Oklahoma 24, no. 2 (Summer, 1946): 146–57.

39. Ibid., pp. 147–48.

40. Ibid., pp. 148–52.

41. Ibid., pp. 145–52.

42. Ibid., pp. 153–57.

43. Ameringer, *If You Don't Weaken*, pp. 373–74; Scales, "Political History," pp. 198–232.

44. Scales, "Political History," pp. 23–32.

45. *Harlow's Weekly*, March 3, 1922; Ameringer, *If You Don't Weaken*, pp. 374–81.

46. William McBee, *The Oklahoma Revolution*, pp. 2–7.

47. Bynum, *Personal Recollections of Walton*, pp. 9–15.

48. McBee, *The Oklahoma Revolution*, pp. 8–10, 19–20.

49. Jones, *Oklahoma Politics*, pp. 115–18.

50. Hauan, *He Buys Organs*, pp. 190–210. Political commentators were shocked by the success of the coalition. The willingness of Oklahoma laborers and farmers to lay aside their differences has always been underestimated. Even Ameringer was surprised in 1907 when he discovered the extent of class consciousness among the state's farmers. As late as 1964 the state's farmers, especially those in Little Dixie, confused nearly every observer and defeated a right-to-work initiative. Marty Huaun, who led the seemingly hopeless campaign, said that union leaders were reluctant to fight back, and polls showed that Oklahomans favored right-to-work by a two-to-one ratio. Moreover, since 250 of 256 newspapers and all three television stations favored the initiative, the gap seemed insurmountable. The rank-and-file union members, however, joined with the leaders of the Farmers' Union in a successful campaign. The turning point came when Zeb Lawter, president of the Farmers' Union, addressed his constituency in an election-eve television broadcast with the following admonition: "Don't let your sons and daughters come to Oklahoma City and Tulsa looking for a job unless they can expect a living wage. Assure your kids a fair shake in the city by voting against this anti-worker law the big-money interests are trying to fool you into accepting." When he analyzed the election returns, Huaun realized it was the farmers who had turned the tide. The heavily union precincts of Oklahoma City and Tulsa produced a precarious lead of less than 7,000 which was reversed in the Republican northwest. After the farm vote in the southeast was tabulated, however, right-to-work was defeated by 24,288 votes.

51. Ameringer, *If You Don't Weaken*, pp. 378–79.

52. Ibid.

53. Jones, *Oklahoma Politics*, p. 34; Ameringer, *If You Don't Weaken*, pp. 380–81.

54. Bynum, *Personal Recollections of Governor Walton*, pp. 80–91.

55. McBee, *Oklahoma Revolution*, p. 42.

56. Bynum, *Personal Recollections of Governor Walton*, p. 20.

57. Ameringer, *If You Don't Weaken*, pp. 385–86.

58. Bynum, *Personal Recollections of Governor Walton*, pp. 20, 72, 79–87.

59. Ameringer, *Oklahoma Leader* (Oklahoma City), July 7, 1923.
60. Ibid., pp. 380, 385.
61. Ibid., p. 385.
62. Ibid., p. 386.
63. Jones, *Oklahoma Politics*, pp. 34–37; McBee, *The Oklahoma Revolution*, pp. 69–71.
64. Green, *Grass-Roots Socialism*, pp. 408–37.

CHAPTER 11

1. Donald Worster, *Dust Bowl: The Southern Plains in the 1930s*, pp. 4, 106–107.
2. Cary McWilliams, *Ill Fares the Land* pp. 188–94.
3. Ibid., pp. 195–98.
4. Ibid., pp. 199–200.
5. Ibid., p. 199.
6. Ibid., pp. 194–97; Worster, *Dust Bowl*, pp. 48–51.
7. McWilliams, *Ill Fares the Land*, pp. 200–205.
8. Quoted in ibid., p. 200.
9. Ibid., p. 201.
10. Ibid., pp. 196–98.
11. Ibid., p. 205.
12. Ibid., p. 205.
13. Ibid., pp. 205–206.
14. Ibid., pp. 206–207.
15. Green, *Grass-Roots Socialism*, pp. 374–95.
16. Ibid., pp. 382–92; *Harlow's Weekly*, June 20, 1917; James Weinstein, *The Decline of Socialism in America, 1912–1923*, pp. 161–85.

Bibliography

MEMOIRS, MANUSCRIPTS, AND INTERVIEWS

Bynum, Ernest. *Personal Recollections of Ex-Governor Walton: A Record of Personal Observation.* Oklahoma City: E. T. Bynum, 1924.

Colcord, Charles. *The Autobiography of Charles Colcord.* Tulsa: C. C. Helmerich, 1970.

Debo, Angie. Transcript of oral-history interview by Glenna Matthews and Gloria Valencia Weber, Marshall, Oklahoma, December 11, 1981; January 20, 1982.

Everidge, Henry. Personal interview, Frogville, Oklahoma, March 17, 1976.

McClintock, Roy. "Oil in Oklahoma." Manuscript. McClintock Collection, Oklahoma State Library, Oklahoma City.

Morgan, Ann Hodges, and Rennard Strickland, eds. *Oklahoma Memories.* Norman: University of Oklahoma Press, 1981.

Rascoe, Burton. *We Were Interrupted.* Garden City, N.Y.: Doubleday, 1947.

Simpson, John. *Militant Voice of Agriculture.* Oklahoma City: Mrs. John Simpson, 1934.

Wallace, Allie B. *Frontier Life in Oklahoma.* Washington, D.C.: Public Affairs Press, 1964.

BOOKS

Alley, John. *City Beginnings in Oklahoma Territory.* Norman: University of Oklahoma Press, 1939.

Ameringer, Oscar. *If You Don't Weaken.* Norman: University of Oklahoma Press, 1983.

Argensinger, Peter. *Populism and Politics.* Lexington: University of Kentucky Press, 1974.

Billington, Ray Allen. "Introduction." In Ray Allen Billington, ed. *Essays on Walter Prescott Webb*. Austin: University of Texas Press, 1976.

Bogue, Allan. *From Prairie to Farm Belt: Farming on the Illinois and Iowa Prairie in the Nineteenth Century*. Chicago: University of Chicago Press, 1963.

Bonnifield, Paul. *The Dust Bowl: Men, Dirt, and Depression*. Albuquerque: University of New Mexico Press, 1979.

Botkin, Benjamin. *The American Play-Party Song with a Collection of Oklahoma Texts and Tunes*. Lincoln: University of Nebraska Press, 1937.

Braudel, Fernand. *The Mediterranean and the Mediterranean World in the Age of Phillip II*. Vol. 1. New York: Harper, Row, 1972.

Bryant, Keith L., Jr. *Alfalfa Bill Murray*. Norman: University of Oklahoma Press, 1968.

Burbank, Garin. *When Farmers Voted Red: The Gospel of Socialism in the Oklahoma Countryside, 1910–1923*. Westport, Conn.: Greenwood Press, 1976.

Clark, J. Stanley. *The Oil Century: From the Drake Well to the Era of Conservation*. Norman: University of Oklahoma Press, 1958.

Collings, Ellsworth, and Alma Miller England. *The 101 Ranch*. Norman: University of Oklahoma Press, 1957.

Cunningham, William. *The Green Corn Rebellion*. New York: Vanguard Press, 1935.

Dale, Edward Everett. *Frontier Historian: The Life and Work of Edward Everett Dale*. Edited by Arrell M. Gibson. Norman: University of Oklahoma Press, 1976.

———, and James Morrison. *Pioneer Judge: The Life of Robert Williams*. Cedar Rapids, Iowa: Torch Press, 1958.

———, and Jesse Lee Rader, eds. *Readings in Oklahoma History*. Evanston, Ill.: Row, Peterson, 1930.

Debo, Angie. *The Rise and Fall of the Choctaw Republic*. Norman: University of Oklahoma Press, 1941.

———. *The Road to Disappearance: A History of the Creek Indians*. Norman: University of Oklahoma Press, 1941.

Destler, Chester McArthur. *American Radicalism, 1865–1901*. Chicago: University of Chicago Press, 1966.

Dykstra, Robert. *The Cattle Towns*. New York: Knopf, 1968.

Ellis, Robert, ed. *The Frontier in American Development*. Ithaca, N.Y.: Cornell University Press, 1969.

Ellsworth, Scott. *Death in a Promised Land: The Tulsa Race Riot of 1921*. Baton Rouge: Louisiana State University Press, 1975.

Fite, Gilbert C., and H. C. Peterson. *Opponents of the War, 1917–1918*. Madison, Wis.: University of Wisconsin Press, 1957.

Gates, Paul. *The Farmers' Age: Agriculture, 1815–1860*. New York: Holt, Rinehart, 1960.

Gibson, Arrell M. *The Chickasaws*. Norman: University of Oklahoma Press, 1971.

———. *Oklahoma: A History of Five Centuries*. Oklahoma City: Harlow Publishing Corp., 1965.

———. *The West in the Life of the Nation*. Lexington, Mass.: D.C. Heath, 1976.

Gittinger, Roy. *The Formation of the State of Oklahoma, 1830–1906*. Berkeley: University of California Press, 1917.

Glasscock, L. D. *Then Came Oil*. Indianapolis, Ind.: Bobbs, Merrill, 1938.

Goble, Danney. *Progressive Oklahoma: The Making of a New Kind of State*. Norman: University of Oklahoma Press, 1980.

Goodrich, Carter. *Migration and Economic Opportunity: The Report of the Study of Population Redistribution*. Philadelphia: Wharton School of Finance, 1936.

Goodwyn, Lawrence. *Democratic Promise: The Populist Movement in America*. New York: Oxford University Press, 1976.

Gorton, George. *A Big-Ass Boy in the Oilfields*. Berlin, Wis.: Napco Press, 1975.

Green, Donald E. *Panhandle Pioneer: Henry Hitch and His Family*. Norman: University of Oklahoma Press, 1979.

———, ed. *Rural Oklahoma*. Oklahoma City: Oklahoma Historical Society, 1977.

Green, James. *Grass-Roots Socialism: Radical Movements in the Southwest, 1895–1943*. Baton Rouge: Louisiana State University Press, 1978.

Gregory, Robert. *Oil in Oklahoma*. Muskogee, Okla.: Leake Industry, 1979.

Gunning, I. G. *When Coal Was King: The Coal Mining Industry in Eastern Oklahoma*. Poteau, Okla.: Eastern Oklahoma Historical Society, 1975.

Guthrie, Woody. *Seeds of Man: An Experience Lived and Dreamed*. New York: Kangaroo Pocket Books, 1977.

Hackney, Sheldon. *From Populism to Progressivism in Alabama*. Princeton, N.J.: Princeton University Press, 1969.

Hair, William Ivory. *Bourbonism and Agrarian Protest*. Baton Rouge: Louisiana State University Press, 1969.

Harrison, Walter. *Me and My Big Mouth*. Oklahoma City: W. Harrison, 1949.

————. *Out of My Wastebasket*. Oklahoma City: W. Harrison, 1949.

Hauan, Marty. *He Buys Organs for Churches and Pianos for Bawdy Houses*. Oklahoma City: Midwest Political Publications, 1976.

Hurst, Irwin. *The Forty-sixth Star: A History of Oklahoma's Constitutional Convention and Early Statehood*. Oklahoma City: Semco Color Press, 1957.

Johnson, Neil. *The Chickasaw Rancher*. Stillwater, Okla.: Redlands Press, 1967.

Jones, Stephen. *Oklahoma Politics in the State and Nation*. Vol. 1. Enid, Okla.: Haymaker Press, 1974.

Kirkpatrick, Samuel, David Morgan, and Larry Edwards. *Oklahoma Voting Patterns: Congressional Elections*. Norman: Bureau of Government Research, University of Oklahoma, 1976.

Lamp, William. *Tulsa County in the World War*. Tulsa, Okla.: Tulsa Council of Defense, 1919.

McBee, William. *The Oklahoma Revolution*. Oklahoma City: Modern Publishers, 1956.

McReynolds, Edwin C. *Oklahoma: A History of the Sooner State*. Rev. ed. Norman: University of Oklahoma Press, 1954.

————. *The Seminoles*. Norman: University of Oklahoma Press, 1954.

McRill, Albert. *And Satan Came Also*. Oklahoma City: Britton Press, 1955.

McWilliams, Cary. *Ill Fares the Land*. Boston: Little, Brown, 1942.

Marable, Mary Hays, and Elaine Boylan. *A Handbook of Oklahoma Writers*. Norman: University of Oklahoma Press, 1938.

Mathews, John Joseph. *Life and Death of an Oilman: The Career of E. W. Marland*. Norman: University of Oklahoma Press, 1951.

Milburn, George. *Oklahoma Town*. New York: Harcourt, Brace, 1931.

Miner, Craig. *The Corporation and the Indian, 1865 to 1907*. Columbia: University of Missouri Press, 1976.

Morgan, Howard Wayne. *Oklahoma: A Bicentennial History*. New York: Norton, 1977.

Morris, John W. *Ghost Towns of Oklahoma*. Norman: University of Oklahoma Press, 1977.

————, and Edwin McReynolds. *Oklahoma Geography*. Oklahoma City: Harlow Publishing Corp., 1965.

Murray, William H. *Memoirs of Governor Murray and the True History of Oklahoma*. Boston: Meador Press, 1945.

National Civil Liberties Bureau. *The Knights of Liberty Mob and the IWW Prisoners at Tulsa, Oklahoma*. New York, 1918.

Palmer, Bruce. *Man over Money*. Chapel Hill: University of North Carolina Press, 1980.

Peterson, Trudy. *Farmers, Bureaucrats, and Middlemen*. Washington, D.C.: Howard University Press, 1980.

Polanyi, Karl. *The Great Transformation*. New York: Farrar and Rinehart, 1944.

Pollack, Norman. *The Populist Response to Industrial America: Midwestern Populist Thought*. Cambridge, Mass.: Harvard University Press, 1962.

Poole, Richard, and James Tarver. *Oklahoma Population Trends*. Stillwater, Okla.: Oklahoma State University Press, 1968.

Rhyne, Jennings. *Social and Community Problems of Oklahoma*. Guthrie, Okla.: Cooperative Publishing, 1929.

Rose, D. C. *Sooners in the War: Official Report of the Oklahoma State Council of Defense*. Oklahoma City: Oklahoma Council of Defense, 1919.

Ryan, Frederick. *A History of Labor Legislation in Oklahoma*. Norman: University of Oklahoma Press, 1932.

———. *The Rehabilitation of Oklahoma Coal Mining Communities*. Norman: University of Oklahoma Press, 1934.

Saarinen, Thomas Frederick. *Perceptions of the Drouth Hazard on the Great Plains*. Chicago: University of Chicago Press, 1966.

Scales, James Ralph, and Danney Goble. *Oklahoma Politics: A History*. Norman: University of Oklahoma Press, 1982.

Tindall, George. *The Persistent Tradition in New South Politics*. Baton Rouge: Louisiana State University Press, 1975.

Tobin, Gregory, ed. *Walter Prescott Webb Memorial Lectures*. Austin: University of Texas Press, 1970.

Turner, Frederick Jackson. *Frontier and Section: Selected Essays of Frederick Jackson Turner*. Edited by Ray Allen Billington. Englewood Cliffs, N.J.: Prentice-Hall, 1961.

Wallerstein, Immanuel. *The Modern World System: Capitalist Agriculture and the Origins of the European World Market System*. New York: Academic Press, 1977.

Webb, Walter Prescott. *The Great Frontier*. Boston: Houghton Mifflin, 1952.

———. *The Great Plains*. Boston: Houghton Mifflin, 1936.

Weinstein, James. *The Decline of Socialism in America, 1912–1923*. New York: Monthly Review, 1967.

Work Projects Administration. *Oklahoma: A Guide to the Sooner State*. Norman: University of Oklahoma Press, 1941.

Worster, Donald. *Dustbowl: The Southern Plains in the 1930's*. New York: Oxford University Press, 1979.

ARTICLES

Bogue, Allan. "Farm Tenants in the Nineteenth-Century Middle West."
Farmers, Bureaucrats and Middlemen. Edited by Trudy Peterson. Washington, D.C., 1980.

Boles, David. "Effect of the Ku Klux Klan on the Gubernatorial Election of 1926." *Chronicles of Oklahoma* 55, no. 4 (Winter, 1977–78).

———. "Prairie Oil and Gas Company." *Chronicles of Oklahoma* 46,
no. 2 (Summer, 1968).

Braswell, Vernon. "The Oklahoma Free Homes Bill." *Chronicles of
Oklahoma* 44, no. 4 (Winter, 1966–67).

Browning, Boo. "The Wizard of Fourth and Broadway." *Oklahoma
Monthly,* November, 1978.

Chapman, Berlin. "The Enid Railroad War: An Archival Study."
Chronicles of Oklahoma 43, no. 2 (Summer, 1965).

Clark, Blue. "The Beginnings of Oil and Gas Conservation in Oklahoma." *Chronicles of Oklahoma* 55, no. 4 (Winter, 1978).

Clark, Stanley. "Texas Fever in Oklahoma." *Chronicles of Oklahoma* 29,
no. 4 (Fall, 1952).

Crockett, Norman. "The Opening of Oklahoma: A Businessman's Frontier." *Chronicles of Oklahoma* 55, no. 1 (Spring, 1978).

Curran, Claude. "Forest and Forest Industries in Oklahoma." In John
W. Morris, ed. *Geography of Oklahoma.* Oklahoma City: Oklahoma
Historical Society, 1977.

Decker, Leslie. "The Great Speculation: An Interpretation of Mid-
Continent Pioneering." In David Ellis, ed. *The Frontier in American
Development.* Ithaca, N.Y.: Cornell University Press, 1969.

Ellis, David. "The Homestead Clause in Railroad Grants." In David
Ellis, ed. *The Frontier in American Development.* Ithaca, N.Y.: Cornell
University Press, 1969.

Fisher, LeRoy. "Oklahoma Territory, 1890–1907." *Chronicles of Oklahoma* 53, no. 1 (Spring, 1975).

Fite, Gilbert. "The Non-Partisan League in Oklahoma." *Chronicles of
Oklahoma* 24, no. 3 (Autumn, 1946).

Fowler, James. "Tar and Feather Patriotism." *Chronicles of Oklahoma* 56,
no. 4 (Winter, 1979).

Gage, Duane. "Al Jennings: The People's Choice." *Chronicles of Oklahoma* 42, no. 3 (Autumn, 1968).

Gibson, Arrell. "Indian Pioneer Legacy: A Guide to Oklahoma Litera-
ture." *Chronicles of Oklahoma* 56, no. 1 (Spring, 1978).

Goble, Danney, and James Scales. "Depression Politics: Personality and the Problem of Relief." In Kenneth Hendrickson, ed. *Hard Times in Oklahoma: The Depression Years*. Oklahoma City: Oklahoma Historical Society, 1983.

Green, Donald. "Beginnings of Wheat Culture in Oklahoma." In Donald Green, ed. *Rural Oklahoma*. Oklahoma City: Oklahoma Historical Society, 1977.

Hale, Douglas. "The People of Oklahoma: Economics and Social Change." In Anne Hodges Morgan and H. Wayne Morgan, eds. *Oklahoma: New Views of the Forty-sixth State*. Norman: University of Oklahoma Press, 1982.

Hilton, O. A. "The Oklahoma Council of Defense in the First World War." *Chronicles of Oklahoma* 20, no. 1 (Spring, 1942).

Hollon, Eugene Walter. "Prescott Webb's Arid West: Four Decades Later." In Kenneth Phillips and Elliott West, eds. *Walter Prescott Webb Memorial Lectures*. Austin: University of Texas Press, 1976.

Hoxie, Robert. "The End of the Savage Indian Policy in the United States Senate: 1880–1900." *Chronicles of Oklahoma* 55, no. 2 (Summer, 1977).

Johnson, Bobbie. "Pilgrims on the Prairie." In Donald Green, ed. *Rural Oklahoma*. Oklahoma City: Oklahoma Historical Society, 1977.

Kalisch, Philip. "Ordeal of the Oklahoma Coal Miner." *Chronicles of Oklahoma* 48, no. 3 (Autumn, 1970).

Manes, Sheila. "Pioneers and Survivors: Oklahoma's Landless Farmers." In Anne Hodges Morgan and H. Wayne Morgan, eds. *Oklahoma: New Views of the Forty-sixth State*. Norman: University of Oklahoma Press, 1982.

Meredith, Howard. "Agrarian Reform Press in Oklahoma." *Chronicles of Oklahoma* 50, no. 1 (Spring, 1972).

———. "Oscar Ameringer and the Concept of Agrarian Socialism." *Chronicles of Oklahoma* 45, no. 1 (Spring, 1967).

Miller, Robert. "Bases of Partisan Choice in the Politics of the Oklahoma Territory, 1890–1904." Unpublished.

Miner, Craig. "The Struggle for the East-West Railway." *Chronicles of Oklahoma* 47, no. 1 (Spring, 1969).

Nall, Gary. "King Cotton in Rural Oklahoma." In Donald Green, ed. *Rural Oklahoma*. Oklahoma City: Oklahoma Historical Society, 1977.

Neuringer, Sheldon. "Governor Walton's War on the Ku Klux Klan." *Chronicles of Oklahoma* 45, no. 2 (Summer, 1967).

Pickens, Donald. "Oklahoma Populism and Historical Interpretation." *Chronicles of Oklahoma* 43, no. 3 (Autumn, 1965).

Reggio, Michael. "Troubled Times Homesteading in the Shortgrass Country, 1892–1900." *Chronicles of Oklahoma* 55, no. 2 (Summer, 1979).

Shannon, Fred. "A Post-Mortem on the Labor-Safety Valve Theory." In George Rogers Taylor, ed. *The Turner Thesis*. Boston: D. C. Heath, 1949.

Smith, Robert. "Dark Morning at Dover." *Railroads in Oklahoma*. Oklahoma City: Oklahoma Historical Society, 1977.

Turner, Frederick Jackson. "The Significance of the American Frontier." In Frederick Jackson Turner, *The Early Writings of Frederick Jackson Turner*. Edited by Edward Everett. Madison: University of Wisconsin Press, 1938.

Underhill, Lonnie, and Daniel Littlefield. "Quail Hunting in Early Oklahoma." *Chronicles of Oklahoma* 49, no. 3 (Autumn, 1971).

―――, and ―――. "Wild Turkey in Oklahoma." *Chronicles of Oklahoma* 48, no. 4 (Winter, 1970).

Wilson, N. James. "Oklahoma and Midwestern Farmers in Transition, 1880–1910." In Donald Green, ed. *Rural Oklahoma*. Oklahoma City: Oklahoma Historical Society, 1977.

Wilson, Terry Paul. "The Demise of Populism in Oklahoma Territory." *Chronicles of Oklahoma* 43, no. 3 (Autumn, 1965).

Work, Susan. "Rights of the Seminole Nation Related to Railroad Rights of Way." Oklahoma City: Native American Service Association, n.d.

DISSERTATIONS AND THESES

Aldrich, Gene. "A History of the Coal Industry in Oklahoma to 1907." Ph.D. dissertation, University of Oklahoma, 1952.

Barr, Ben. "Accounting Problems of Cooperative Cotton Gins." Master's thesis, University of Oklahoma, 1950.

Bush, Charles. "The Green Corn Rebellion." Master's thesis, University of Oklahoma, 1932.

Clark, Carter Blue. "A History of the Ku Klux Klan in Oklahoma." Master's thesis, University of Oklahoma, 1976.

Deberry, Drew. "The Ethics of the Oklahoma Oil Boom, 1905–1929." Master's thesis, University of Oklahoma, 1976.

Dilisio, James. "Standards of Living and Spatial-Temporal Trends in Regional Inequality in Oklahoma." Master's thesis, University of Oklahoma, 1975.

Doran, Michael. "Origins of Culture Areas in Oklahoma, 1830–1900." Master's thesis, University of Oregon, 1974.

Gilbert, James. "Three Sands: Oklahoma Oil Fields and Community of the 1920's." Master's thesis, University of Oklahoma, 1967.

Graham, Donald. "Red, White, and Black: An Interpretation of Ethnic and Racial Attitudes of Agrarian Radicals in Texas and Oklahoma." Master's thesis, University of Saskatchewan, 1973.

Harder, Jesse. "Wheat Production in Northwest Oklahoma, 1893–1932." Master's thesis, University of Oklahoma, 1932.

Meredith, Howard. "Agrarian Socialism in Oklahoma." Ph.D. dissertation, University of Oklahoma, 1970.

Pope, Virginia. "The Green Corn Rebellion: A Study in Newspaper Self-Censorship." Master's thesis, University of Oklahoma, 1940.

Rosen, Ellen. "Peasant Socialism in Oklahoma: The Socialist Party in Oklahoma Before the First World War." Ph.D. dissertation, City University of New York, 1976.

Scales, James. "Political History of Oklahoma, 1907–1949." Ph.D. dissertation, University of Oklahoma, 1949.

Smith, James Morton. "Criminal Syndicalism in Oklahoma: A History of the Law and Its Application." Master's thesis, University of Oklahoma, 1946.

Warwick, Sherry. "Anti-War Resistance in the Southwest During World War I." Master's thesis, University of Oklahoma, 1973.

Webb, Charles. "Distribution of Cotton Production in Oklahoma, 1907–1962." Master's thesis, University of Oklahoma, 1963.

Womack, John. "Oklahoma's Green Corn Rebellion: The Importance of Fools." Undergraduate thesis, Yale University, 1961.

NEWSPAPERS

American Guardian (Oklahoma City)

Appeal to Reason (Girard, Kansas)

Ardmore Alliance Courier

Ardmore Daily Ardmorite

Ardmore X-Ray

Beckham County Advocate (Sayre)

Capital-Democrat (Wewoka)

Carter Express (Carter)

Common People (Stillwater)

Daily Oklahoman (Oklahoma City)

Durant Independent Farmer

Ellis County Socialist (Shattuck)

Enid Coming Events

Farmer-Stockman (Oklahoma City)
Grant County Socialist (Medford)
Harlow's Weekly (Oklahoma City)
Indiahoma Union Signal (Oklahoma City)
Johnston County Socialist (Tishomingo)
Kay County Socialist (Newkirk)
New Century (Sulphur)
Newkirk Populist
Norman People's Voice
Okemah Sledgehammer
Oklahoma Leader (Oklahoma City)
Oklahoma Monthly (Oklahoma City)
Oklahoma Pioneer (Oklahoma City)
Oklahoma Representative (Guthrie)
Otter Valley Socialist (Snyder)
Reconstructionist (Oklahoma City)
Sayre Agitator
Sentinel Sword of Truth
Social Democrat (Oklahoma City)
Social Economist (Bonham, Texas)
Stillwater People's Voice
Tishomingo Capital-Democrat
Woods County Constructive Socialist (Alva)

Index

Alfalfa County, Okla.: 174
Alliance Courier: 91–96
Ameringer, Oscar: 44, 129, 141–43, 150, 153–55, 182, 185–86, 199–207, 211–13
Appeal to Reason: 76–77, 136, 156
Ardmore X-Ray: 146
Atchison, Topeka and Santa Fe Railroad: 46
Atlantic Pacific Railroad: 31

Bartlesville, Okla.: 117
Beard, Charles A.: 79
Beaver County Socialist: 161
Berg, Victor: 195
Billington, Ray Allen: 4
Bogue, Allan: 4, 47
Boley, Okla.: 134
Boudinot, Elias: 49
Braudel, Fernand: 3
Bryan, William Jennings: 82–83
Burbank, Garin: 136, 138–40, 144, 182, 185
Bush, Charles: 169–72, 183, 186
Bynum, Ernest: 202–203, 208

Candee, Helen: 51
Capitol Democrat: 187
Checotah, Oklahoma: 61

Cherokee Nation: 28–29, 38
Chicago, Rock Island and Pacific Railroad: 35
Chickasaw Nation: 28, 34, 36, 38, 100
Choctaw County, Okla.: 112
Choctaw Nation: 28, 31, 33–36, 38–40, 72
Clark, Stanley: 140–41, 200
Coalgate, Okla.: 61
Creek Nation: 28–29, 40
Criminal Syndicalism Act: 195
Crockett, Norman: 62–63
Cumby, Tad: 129–30, 141–42
Cunningham, William: 166–67
Cushing, Okla.: 117, 120

Dale, Edward Everett: 14
Daniels, Arthur: 73
Dawes Commission: 38, 40
Debo, Angie: 52
Debs, Eugene V.: 76, 130, 140, 153, 209
Destler, Chester: 88
Doran, Michael: 19
Dykstra, Robert: 46

Ellis County Socialist: 157–58
Enid, Okla.: 55, 60
Enid Coming Events: 89

Erick, Okla.: 61
Eufala, Okla.: 61, 134
Everidge, Henry: 39, 106, 112

Farmers' Alliance: 8, 153, 219
Farmer-Labor Reconstruction
  League: 205–208, 210
Flynn, Dennis: 73–74, 83–84
Frogville, Okla.: 39

Gardenhire, George: 73
Garfield County, Okla.: 173–74
Gates, Paul: 4
Gibson, Arrel: 49
Goble, Danney: 179
Gompers, Samuel: 79
Goodwyn, Lawrence: 80–82, 136
Gore, Thomas: 197
Gould, Jay: 35, 63
Grandfather Clause: 133
Grant County, Okla.: 173
Grant County Socialist: 157, 159
Great Frontier: 3, 6–8, 25, 48,
  65, 67, 68, 114, 116, 124, 164
Green, James: 136, 138–40, 182,
  185
Green Corn Rebellion: 182–86,
  194, 201
Guthrie, Okla.: 55

Hackney, Sheldon: 80–82
Hale, Douglas: 20–21
Harlow, Victor: 197–201,
  204–205
Harrison, Luther, 195
Harrison, Walter: 189
Hayward, William: 155
Healdton, Okla.: 117–18, 168
Hogan, Dan: 207

Hogg, James: 73, 82
Hughes County, Okla.: 109

Indiahoma Union Signal: 90,
  92–94
Indian Nations: 6–7, 29, 31–32,
  34, 36, 42, 99
Indian Territory: 6, 19–23, 31,
  33, 41, 43, 54, 71–72, 99; see
  also Indian Nations
Industrial Democracy: 135, 161
International Workers of the
  World: 115, 140, 156, 189,
  192, 194–96

Jennings, Al: 156, 180
Johnson County Socialist: 144
"Jones Family": 146

Kay County, Okla.: 53
Kickapoo Indians: 58–59
Kingfisher County, Okla.: 53, 55,
  107–108
Knights of Labor: 36
Ku Klux Klan: 190–92, 212–13,
  219, 221

McAlester, J. H.: 33–34
McClintok, R. W.: 118–19
McCurtain Gazette: 187
McWilliams, Carey: 46, 215–16,
  218
Madill, Okla.: 101
Major County, Okla.: 174
Manes, Sheila: 21, 136
Marland, E. W.: 66–67, 200–
  202, 205
Marshall County, Okla.: 105, 180

Meredith, James: 75, 182–83
Mid-Continent Oil Field: 177
Milburn, George: 112, 192
Miller, George: 122
Miller, Joe: 122
Miller, Robert: 88
Miller, Zack: 122
Morgan, J. P.: 116
Murray, William: 36–37, 40–45,
    89, 187, 221

Nagle, Pat: 131, 137, 141, 200
Neopopulism: 219, 225
New Century: 145–46
Non-Partisan League: 205–10

Ofuskee County, Okla.: 107
O'Hare, Kate: 185
Oklahoma City, Okla.: 8, 19, 55,
    58–61, 104
Oklahoma Farmer Stockman: 102,
    106
Oklahoma Farmers' Union: 74–
    77, 86–87, 89–90, 92–96,
    127, 129, 206
Oklahoma Legal Research
    Project: 40
Oklahoma Renters' Union: 150–
    52, 193
Oklahoma Socialist: 128
Oklahoma Territory: 15, 21–22,
    48–49, 54–55, 62–63, 70–72
Otter Valley Socialist: 157–59
Owen, Robert: 38, 41, 197

Palmer, Bruce: 82
Parker, "Hanging Judge": 6
Payne, David: 48, 59
Pew, Edgar: 190–91

Polanyi, Karl: 22–23
Pollack, Norman: 88
Populism and Populist party: 8,
    10, 14, 71–74, 76–78, 82–96,
    198
Ponca City, Okla.: 117
Prairie Oil and Gas Co.: 64,
    119–21

Rascoe, Burton: 169–72
Rentiesville, Okla.: 134
Robertson, James: 204–205
Rosen, Ellen: 21
Ross, John: 38
Ryan, Frederick: 167

Saarinen, Thomas Frederick: 125
Sayre, Okla.: 61, 156
Sayre Agitator: 156
Scales, James: 179
Seminole County, Okla.: 109,
    134, 185
Seminole Land Co.: 58–59
Seminole Nation: 28
Sentinel Sword of Truth: 156
Shawnee, Okla.: 61, 104
    206
Simpson, John: 92–93, 188,
Sinclair, Harry: 66, 117, 121
Sledgehammer: 146–49
Social Economist: 145
Socialism and Socialist party: 8,
    10, 14, 24, 25, 127–65, 198,
    217, 219–21, 224–26
Slick, Tom: 66, 117
Standard Oil Co.: 64–65, 116,
    119–21
Stillwater Common People: 160
Stillwater Gazette: 153
Stillwater Peoples Voice: 90

Tecumseh, Okla.: 61
Tillman County, Okla.: 176
Tindall, George: 87
Tonkawa Oil Field: 177–78
Tulsa, Okla.: 8, 19, 61, 105, 117, 190–91
Turner, Frederick Jackson: 4, 14

Wallace, Allie B.: 51
Wallerstein, Immanuel: 3
Walton, Jack: 11, 202–203, 210–11
Warwick, Sherry: 182–83
Wayland, Julius: 129
Wear, Homer: 195–96

Weaver, James B.: 59
Webb, Walter Prescott: 3, 71, 156
West, Charles: 118
Williams, Carl: 102–106, 109, 111
Williams, Robert: 41, 131–34, 180, 207
Wills, Bob: 196
Wilson, George: 207, 211–12
Womack, John, Jr.: 182–83
Woods County Constructive Socialist: 159
Woodward County, Okla.: 173
Working Class Union: 140, 193
World Wide War: 161–62

Closing the Frontier,
designed by Bill Cason and Ed Shaw, was set in various sizes of
Goudy Old Style by G & S Typesetters and printed offset on 60-
pound Glatfelter Smooth Antique, B-31, a permanized sheet, by
Cushing-Malloy, Inc., with case binding by John H. Dekker &
Sons.